WORTH A DETOUR

SOUTH ISLAND

WORTH A DETOUR

SOUTH ISLAND

Hidden places and unusual destinations off the beaten track

PETER JANSSEN

Contents

Dedication	9
Acknowledgements	9
Introduction	10

MARLBOROUGH — 12

1. Marlborough Sounds — 13
2. Karaka Pa, Picton — 14
3. Picton Village Bakkerij — 14
4. *Edwin Fox* Maritime Heritage Project — 15
5. Queen Charlotte Drive — 16
6. Queen Charlotte Track — 16
7. Green-lipped Mussels, Havelock — 17
8. Rai Valley Cottage — 17
9. Whites Bay — 18
10. Monkey Bay — 19
11. Rarangi Beach — 19
12. Wairau Lagoons/Te Pokohiwi — 20
13. Makana Confections — 21
14. Wither Hills Farm Park — 22
15. Burleigh Gourmet Pies — 22
16. Riverlands Cob Cottage — 23
17. Dominion Salt Works, Lake Grassmere — 23
18. Marlborough Vineyards — 24

NELSON — 29

1. Cape Farewell and Farewell Spit — 30
2. The River Inn — 31
3. Grove Scenic Reserve, Takaka — 32
4. Abel Tasman Memorial — 32
5. Wainui Falls, Takaka — 33
6. Paynes Ford — 33
7. Harwoods Hole, Takaka Hill — 34
8. Tokongawha/Split Apple Rock — 35
9. Riwaka Resurgence — 35
10. Motueka Saltwater Baths — 36
11. Moutere Inn — 37
12. St Paul's Lutheran Church, Upper Moutere — 37
13. Mapua Wharf — 38
14. Jester House Café — 39
15. Broadgreen House — 39
16. McCashins (Mac's) Brewery — 40
17. Pic's Peanut Butter — 41
18. MacMillans Hand Thrown Ceramics — 41
19. Theatre Royal — 42
20. South, Elliott and Seymour Heritage Streets — 42
21. Montgomery Square Markets — 43
22. Botanic Reserve — 44
23. Centre of New Zealand — 44
24. The Boulder Bank/Te Taero o Kereopa — 44
25. Glenduan Topdressing Airstrip — 46
26. Tophouse Hotel, Nelson Lakes — 47
27. Kawatiri Railway Walkway — 47
28. Lake Rotoroa — 48
29. Nelson Vineyards — 49

BULLER — 51

1. Owen River Tavern — 52
2. Maruia Falls — 52
3. Murchison — 53
4. Six Mile Hydro Station, Murchison — 54
5. Lyell — 54
6. Inangahua Hall — 55
7. The Oparara Basin, Karamea — 56
8. Charming Creek Walkway — 57
9. Denniston and the Incline — 58
10. Westport Municipal Chambers — 59
11. Buller River at Westport — 59
12. Carters Beach — 60
13. Mitchell's Gully Gold Mine, Charleston — 60

14. Fox River Caves	61	19. Quartzopolis, Town of Light	64
15. Truman Track	62	20. Bearded Mining Company	65
16. Blacks Point Museum and Stamper Battery	62	21. Reefton Distillery	66
		22. Waiuta	67
17. Reefton School of Mines	63		
18. The Future Dough Company, Reefton	64		

WESTLAND 68

1. Nelson Creek	69	stone	81
2. Lake Brunner	69	20. Luminaries Walk	82
3. Barrytown Knifemaking	70	21. IaNZart	82
4. Formerly The Blackball Hilton Hotel	71	22. Lake Kaniere	83
		23. Woodstock /Royal Mail Hotel	83
5. Blackball Salami Company	72	24. Lake Mahinapua	85
6. Brunner Mine Industrial Site	72	25. Jones Creek, Ross	86
7. Point Elizabeth Walkway	73	26. Guy Menzies Park, Harihari	86
8. On Yer Bike	74	27. Okarito	87
9. Grey River Bar and Breakwaters	75	28. Shhhh Shed	89
10. High Street Barber Shop	75	29. Franz Josef Glacier Hot Pools	89
11. West Coast Washing Lines	76	30. Gillespies Beach	90
12. Kumara Races	76	31. Munro Beach	90
13. Theatre Royal Hotel	77	32. Hunt Beach	91
14. Otira Gorge and Township	78	33. Whitebait on the West Coast	91
15. Hokitika Glow-worm Dell	79	34. West Coast Sandflies	92
16. Hokitika Sock World	79	35. Hapuka Estuary	92
17. Bonz 'n' Stonz	80	36. Jackson Bay	93
18. Driftwood Beach Sculptures Hokitika	80	37. Haast Pass Road from Haast to Wanaka	94
19. Fossicking for Pounamu/Green-			

KAIKOURA AND CANTERBURY INCLUDING ARTHUR'S PASS 96

Kaikoura 97

1. Crayfish	98	15. Oxford Butchery	109
2. Fyffe House	98	16. Springfield Donut	110
3. Earthquake Reconstruction	99	17. Arthurs Pass	110
4. Molesworth Station	99	18. The Mt Cook Lily - Super-sized Buttercup	111
5. Hanmer Springs Forests	101		
6. Lewis Pass	102	19. Cave Stream	112
7. Maruia Springs	102	20. Glentunnel Library and Post Office	112
8. Weka Pass Railway	103		
9. Historic Hurunui Hotel and the Star and Garter Hotel, Waikari	103	21. The Rakaia Gorge	113
		22. Broadfield Garden	113
10. North Canterbury Wineries	105	23. Ellesmere A&P Grounds, Leeston	114
11. Inland Scenic Route 72	106	24. Salmon Fishing in the Rakaia	115
12. Kaiapoi Pa	106	25. Trotts Garden Ashburton	116
13. The Kaiapoi Letterbox Sculpture	108	26. Ashburton Domain	117
14. Blackwells Department Store, Kaiapoi	108	27. Mt Somers	118
		28. Lake Clearwater	118

CHRISTCHURCH CITY AND THE BANKS PENINSULA 120

1. The Arts Centre of Christchurch 121
2. Ice Cream Charlie, the Home of the Vanilla Ice 123
3. New Regent Street 124
4. Margaret Mahy Playground 124
5. Kate Sheppard Memorial 125
6. 185 Empty White Chairs 127
7. A Tale of Three Cathedrals 127
8. Quake City 129
9. Velocity Karts 129
10. Riccarton Market 130
11. Show Week 130
12. Cabbage Trees, Burnside High School 131
13. Three Boys Brewery 131
14. Dame Ngaio Marsh's House 132
15. Taylors Mistake 133
16. Orana Park 134
17. Steam Scene – Canterbury Steam Preservation Society 135
18. The Whare, Halswell Quarry Gardens 136
19. Kaituna Valley Scenic Reserve 136
20. Birdlings Flat and Kaikorete Spit 137
21. Bridal Path Walkway 138
22. Port Hills Rest Houses 138
23. Lyttelton Harbour 139
24. Quail Island/Otamahua, Lyttelton Harbour 139
25. The Thornycroft Torpedo Boat Museum 141
26. Ohinetahi Garden 142
27. Allandale Gaol 143
28. Two-thousand-year-old Totara Tree 143
29. French Peak Winery 144
30. Barrys Bay Cheese Factory 145
31. Onawe Peninsula, Akaroa Harbour 145
32. Okains Bay Museum 146
33. German and Portuguese Akaroa 148

SOUTH CANTERBURY/MACKENZIE COUNTRY 150

1. Peel Forest Park 151
2. The Giant Jersey 151
3. Geraldine Vintage Car and Machinery Museum 152
4. Barker's Preserves and Talbot Forest Cheese Geraldine 153
5. South Canterbury Blackcurrants 154
6. Temuka Pottery 154
7. Caroline Bay 155
8. Aigantighe Art Museum 156
9. Richard Pearse Aeroplane Replica 157
10. York Street Gallery of Fine Art 158
11. Timaru Botanic Gardens 158
12. Kakahu Escarpment and Lime Kilns 159
13. McKenzie and his Dog Statue Fairlie 160
14. Mackenzie and Hakataramea Passes 160
15. Aoraki Mackenzie International Dark Sky Reserve 161
16. Tasman Glacier, Aoraki/Mt Cook National Park 162
17. Black Stilt Country 163
18. Upper Waitaki Power Project 163
19. The Rock Piles of Omarama 164
20. The White Horse Monument, the Hunters Hills, Waimate 165
21. Waimate Parks 165
22. Dr Margaret Cruickshank Statue 166
23. St Augustine's Church 166
24. St Patrick's Church 167
25. Waimate Silo Murals and the Empress Flour Mill 167
26. Kapua Moa Swamp 168
27. Ted's Bottle, Waihao Forks Hotel 168
28. Paterson Cob Cottage 170

NORTH OTAGO

1. Benmore Dam — 172
2. Waitaki Valley Wineries — 173
3. Nicol's Forge, Duntroon — 174
4. Waitaki Valley Limestone and Fossil Country — 175
5. Maori Rock Drawings, Duntroon — 176
6. Danseys Pass — 177
7. Historic Oamaru — 177
8. Criterion Hotel — 179
9. Janet Frame House — 180
10. Whitestone Cheese — 180
11. Yellow-eyed Penguin/Hoiho Colony — 181
12. Totara Estate and Clarks Mill — 182
13. Oamaru Dog Trial Grounds, Waianakura (North Otago) — 183
14. Katiki Point — 184
15. Shag Point — 185
16. Puketapu Summit – Palmerston — 185
17. Macraes Gold Mine — 186
18. Matanaka — 187
19. Evansdale Cheese Factory — 188
20. Huriawa Pa, Karitane Beach — 188
21. Mapoutahi Pa — 190

CENTRAL OTAGO

1. Naseby — 193
2. Maniototo Curling International, Naseby — 193
3. Ranfurly Art Deco — 194
4. Bonspiel at Oturehua — 195
5. Hayes Engineering Works — 196
6. Ophir — 197
7. Chatto Creek, New Zealand's Smallest Post Office — 198
8. Earnscleugh Historic Tailings, Alexandra — 199
9. Flat Top Hill and Butchers Dam — 199
10. Mitchell's Cottage — 200
11. Jimmy's Pies — 201
12. Lake Onslow — 202
13. Somebody's Darling — 203
14. Bendigo Goldfields — 203
15. Cromwell Chafer Beetle Reserve — 204
16. The Sluicings and Stewart Town — 205
17. Highlands Motorsport Park and Museum — 206
18. Jackson's Orchard — 207
19. Shrek Museum — 207
20. Lindis Pass Road — 208
21. Lake Wanaka Islands — 208
22. That Wanaka Tree — 209
23. Glendhu Bay Motor Camp Ground — 210
24. The Paddock, Lake Hawea — 210
25. AJ Hackett Bungy — 211
26. Edith Cavell Bridge — 212
27. Oxenbridge Tunnel — 212
28. The Road to Skippers — 213
29. Queenstown Hill/Te Tapunui — 214
30. Moke Lake — 215
31. Little Paradise Lodge, Mt Creighton, Glenorchy — 215
32. Glenorchy, the Dart Valley and a Lost Railway Shed — 216
33. Central Otago Vineyards — 217

DUNEDIN AND THE OTAGO PENINSULA

1. New Zealand's Tallest Tree — 222
2. Mt Cargill/Kapukataumahaka — 222
3. Aramoana Beach and Breakwater — 223
4. Port Chalmers — 224
5. Careys Bay Hotel — 225
6. Lady Thorn Dell — 226
7. Signal Hill — 226
8. Ross Creek Reservoir — 227
9. Dunedin Botanic Gardens — 227
10. University of Otago — 228
11. Dunedin Museum of Natural Mystery — 229
12. Olveston — 229
13. Trees of Knox Church — 230
14. The Savoy Tearooms/Etrusco — 231
15. Dunedin Public Art Gallery and Dunedin Street Art — 232

16. New Zealand Sports Hall of Fame	233
17. Otago Settlers Museum	233
18. Historic Dunedin	234
19. Cheese Rolls	235
20. Dunedin Gasworks Museum	235
21. St Clair Hot Salt Water Pool	236
22. Tunnel Beach	237
23. Glenfalloch Woodland Garden	238
24. Sandymount Walks	239
25. The Pyramids and Victory Beach – Okia Reserve	239
26. Otakau Marae	240

SOUTH OTAGO AND THE CATLINS 242

1. Sinclair Wetlands/Te Nohoaka o Tukiauaka 243
2. Benhar Pottery 243
3. Bull Creek 244
4. Clutha Punt - Tuapeka Mouth 245
5. Lawrence and Gabriel's Gully 245
6. Whale Fossil Lookout 246
7. Nugget Point 247
8. Tunnel Hill 248
9. Jacks Blowhole 248
10. Cannibal Bay 249
11. The Dolphin at Pounawea 250
12. Traills Tractor 250
13. Niagara Falls and Waikawa 251
14. Curious Curio Bay 251
15. Slope Point 252
16. Waipapa Point 253

SOUTHLAND 254

1. Waikaia Bottle House and Switzers Museum 255
2. Croydon Aviation Heritage Centre 256
3. Eastern Southland Gallery 257
4. Fleming's Creamoata Mill 257
5. Hokonui Moonshine Museum 258
6. Gore Gardens and Aviaries 259
7. Minnie Dean's Grave, Old Winton Cemetery 260
8. Sweetbreads, Top End Takeaways, Winton 261
9. Forest Hill and Tussock Creek Reserves, Central Southland 261
10. The Stumpery, Queen's Garden, Invercargill 262
11. The Queen's Chair, Grand Hotel, Invercargill 263
12. E Hayes and Sons Ltd 263
13. The White House and The Greenroofs 264
14. Two Churches and Temple 265
15. Bluff 265
16. Riverton 267
17. Cosy Nook/Mullet Bay 268
18. Otautau War Memorial 268
19. Monkey Island/ Te Puka o Takitimu 269
20. Clifden Suspension Bridge 270
21. Lake Hauroko and the 1000-year-old Totara 270
22. Lake Monowai 271
23. Mossburn 272
24. Gunn's Camp 274
25. Lake Marian and the Marian Falls 274
26. Hollyford Airstrip 275
27. Humboldt Falls 276
28. Cook's Globe, Rakiura Museum 276
29. Kiwi Watching 277

Glossary 278

Dedication

To all the dedicated volunteers without whom New Zealand's human and natural history would be much diminished.

Acknowledgements

Without all your helpful suggestions this book would have been much shorter. Thank you.

Helen Adams, Winton Bebbington, Kevin Brewer, Rose Carson, Melissa Carson, Tito Costa, Grant Hadfield, John Haig, Susan Holmes, Lloyd Houghton, Harry Janssen, Lyn Janssen, Teresa Janssen, Dora Moffit, Jonathan Pierce, Sarah Raman, Peter Rickard, Nick Seaman, Katrina Smith, Wilma Smith, Alison Southby.

Introduction

Over the past few years while researching a number of guide books I have travelled just about every road and visited every town and hamlet in New Zealand. I have enjoyed finding the more offbeat attractions, the quirky places bypassed by most travellers and the eccentric characters that have great stories to tell. Many of the places are well known locally, but often ignored by visitors short on time. Even our bigger cities have corners and places that remain unexplored by most. This book is a varied collection of the places throughout the country that I think are worth a small detour. There is something for everyone (I hope), from the collection of antique sock machines and homemade baking; backcountry pubs and old-time wineries through to empty beaches and fascinating back country roads.

By its very nature a book of this type comes down to personal choice, but I trust through experience that the choices are good ones, though I'm more than ready to hear about other places I might have missed.

New Zealand South Island

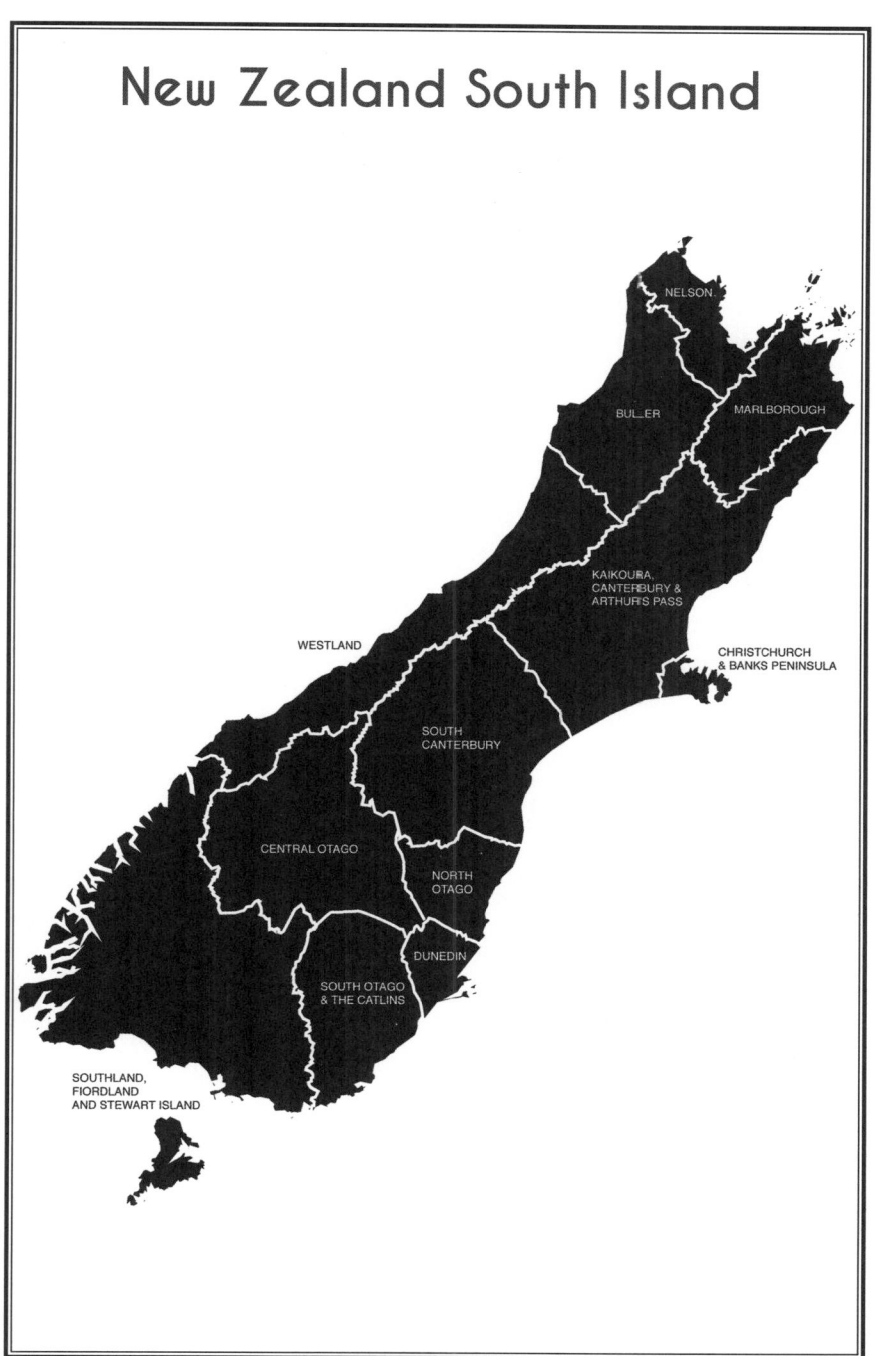

MARLBOROUGH

1. Marlborough Sounds
2. Karaka Pa, Picton
3. Picton Village Bakkerij
4. *Edwin Fox* Maritime Heritage Project
5. Queen Charlotte Drive
6. Queen Charlotte Track
7. Green-lipped Mussels, Havelock
8. Rai Valley Cottage
9. Whites Bay
10. Monkey Bay
11. Rarangi Beach
12. Wairau Lagoons/Te Pokohiwi
13. Makana Confections
14. Wither Hills Farm Park
15. Burleigh Gourmet Pies
16. Riverlands Cob Cottage
17. Dominion Salt Works, Lake Grassmere
18. Marlborough Vineyards

1. Marlborough Sounds

When waterborne transport was common, the bays and inlets of the Marlborough Sounds formed a natural highway and were readily accessible. The sheltered waters were ideal for Maori waka, while Captain James Cook and French explorer Dumont d'Urville used the sounds as a base during their voyages of discovery. Early whalers were also attracted to the area for easy and safe access to Cook Strait. Much of the land was cleared for farming, but this steep and rugged terrain is not easy land to tame. Once road transport became the norm, the area became a backwater, and for most people the experience of the Sounds is limited to the ferry trip from Picton to Wellington or motoring along Queen Charlotte Drive.

The Sounds are an intricate and complex system of drowned valleys with fingers of bush-clad land and islands reaching well out into Cook Strait. With over 1500 km of coastline, many of the myriad bays, beaches and coves are only accessible by water. It is the perfect place for boating, kayaking, tramping, fishing (blue cod is the prized fish in this area), and just getting away from it all.

For the casual visitor, the Sounds are not the easiest place to explore. Picton in Queen Charlotte Sound and Havelock on Pelorus/Kenepuru Sounds both have boat operators offering everything from boat hire to day trips for pleasure, fishing, or access to accommodation. The Queen Charlotte Track winds 71 km through marvellous landscapes, and while the full track will take four days, the proximity to the water means that short options are readily available.

Even driving in the Sounds is not so straightforward. Hilly and steep with endless bays and channels, roads in the area are almost without exception narrow, winding and slow, and often gravel. But take your time and discover the hidden beauty of this wonderful corner of New Zealand, from the tree-lined coves of Tennyson Inlet through to the wild waters of French Pass and the old whaling station at Port Underwood.

2. Karaka Pa, Picton

Te Pae o Te Karaka pa was named after the Ngati Mamoe Chief Te Karaka, who settled here around 1700. Te Karaka was killed when Ngai Tahu led by Tu Ahuriri captured the pa in 1720, and the pa in turn became a Ngai Tahu stronghold.

In the 1820s musket-wielding Te Atiawa invaded the Sounds and, after capturing several pa nearby, made their move on Te Karaka. The defenders had been warned by others fleeing from the invaders to escape, but they decided to make a stand, believing that they were safe in their strongly fortified pa. Approaching from the sea in waka, Te Atiawa launched an assault with heavy musket fire. Now realising that escape was the only option, the occupants fled through the land gates, but ran straight into a trap. Te Atiawa warriors had hidden in the bush and few escaped the deadly ambush. The pa was burnt, subsequently abandoned and never reoccupied.

In addition to great views over Queen Charlotte Sound, this pa is particularly well preserved with the clear outline of defensive ditches, house sites and kumara pits. Tracks from the pa lead down to two shingle beaches. The visit to the pa site is an easy twenty-minute return walk.

 From Picton take the Waikawa Road to Waikawa Bay and then continue along the narrow road towards Port Underwood.
The walk is well marked on the left-hand side of the road.

3. Picton Village Bakkerij

Once a dowdy port town with little to hold the thousands of travellers using the Cook Strait Ferry, Picton is the ugly duckling that is fast evolving into a beautiful swan. Whether you are passing through or staying a while make sure you visit the Picton Village Bakkerij.

Established by Peter and Rachel Van Beek, they created one of the best small bakeries in New Zealand by combining the best of Dutch and Kiwi baking styles. Spoiled for choice, you won't quite know where to start. Will it be a fresh filled roll or sandwich described by a reviewer as the best in the country? Or one of the varieties of pies and savouries including Moroccan lamb or steak, mushroom and bacon?

Whatever you choose make sure you leave room for the award-winning cherry and almond tart. A cherry filling is poured onto a base of almond paste, topped with almonds and pastry and then baked. Luscious and rich, the result is a very satisfying dessert.

Marlborough, like Central Otago, has the ideal climate for growing cherries, but the rise of sauvignon blanc has seen the old cherry orchards swept aside by the relentless march of the grapevines, and today only a handful of cherry orchards remain.

 46 Auckland Street, Picton.
 03 573 7082

4. *Edwin Fox* Maritime Heritage Project

Built in Calcutta in 1853 of hard Burmese teak, the *Edwin Fox* is of typical East Indiaman design and construction, and just one of two surviving New Zealand immigrant ships (the other is the *Star of India* in San Diego). The ship's first voyage to New Zealand was twenty years later in 1873, arriving in Lyttelton carrying 140 passengers. In the intervening years the ship carried cargo and passengers, including transporting convicts to Australia.

Through the early part of the twentieth century the ship was gradually stripped down and used as a coal hulk and today is only partially restored. Billed as the ninth-oldest ship in the world, one is left wondering where (and what) the other eight older ships are. Not exactly riveting viewing, the *Edwin Fox* will mainly appeal to those with a keen interest in maritime history.

Dunbar Wharf, Picton.
 03 573 6868
 www.edwinfoxsociety.com

5. Queen Charlotte Drive

Linking Picton with Havelock (en route to Nelson), the winding 40-km road may be slow, but it is certainly picturesque. There are great views out over Queen Charlotte and Mapua sounds and the short walkway at Cullen's Lookout, 3 km from Havelock, is well worth the stop.

 At Picton Queen Charlotte Drive climbs up the hill immediately to the right of the ferry. At Havelock, the Drive is well signposted, 1km to the east of the town.

6. Queen Charlotte Track

This 71-km track essentially follows the ridge between Queen Charlotte and Kenepuru sounds and includes numerous bays and coastal bush. The track is not particularly steep (the highest point is around 400 m) and is well formed, and most sections can be undertaken by anyone who is well prepared and moderately fit. While the entire track can be completed in three to five days (the most preferred route is north to south, from Ship Cove to Anakiwa), easy water access allows walkers to do shorter stretches depending on their timetable, using Picton as a base. Parts of the track are also available to mountain bikes.

 www.qctrack.co.nz

7. Green-lipped Mussels, Havelock

The green-lipped mussel *Perna canaliculus* is found only in New Zealand and takes its name from the distinctly green-coloured edge to the shell. Not only are they one of the largest mussel species in the world and taste good, but they also have important health benefits as they contain a natural anti-inflammatory and the consumption of mussels or mussel powder has a significant impact on easing arthritic pain, repairing damaged joint tissue and increasing joint mobility.

Mussels are one of New Zealand's greatest taste treats, but the world is fast catching on and now the green-lipped mussel has become one of our most important exports. In 2018 New Zealand mussel exports exceeded $348 million and 645 mussel farms produce more than 100,000 tonnes per year (in 1983 just six tonnes of mussels were harvested).

Marlborough is one of the largest mussel-producing regions in New Zealand and the industry is centred on Havelock with mussel barges constantly streaming in and out of the small town, bringing huge sacks of mussels to be processed on the town's waterfront. Havelock celebrates our most famous shellfish with the annual Mussel Festival in April and if you can't make the festival, The Slip Inn at the Havelock Marina and the Mussel Pot in the town's main street both offer a wide variety of fresh mussel dishes.

8. Rai Valley Cottage

Once a very common type of house construction, few totara slab cottages have survived beyond the nineteenth century. The cottage was built in 1881, with the totara slabs cut on site and fixed with hand-forged nails; the fireplace is constructed of local river stones and the roof of wooden shingles. It is not a big house by any standard, and with a low-pitched roof it feels even smaller, so it is difficult to imagine how such a small and basic cottage housed the Turner family of six until 1909 in addition to providing food and accommodation for passing travellers. The small main room is both the living area and kitchen all rolled into one and must have been a real squeeze on a cold winter's evening. Maybe everyone just went to bed early. Open at all times the interior is visible through glass panels.

📍 1.5 km north of Rai Valley village (SH 6) on the road to Tennyson Inlet.

9. Whites Bay

This small, sandy, bush-clad bay on the northern side of Cloudy Bay is in direct contrast to the dry open country south of the Wairau River. Sheltered from the worst of the weather, the bay is popular and safe for swimming, and in certain conditions even has good surf.

Whites Bay was known to Maori as Te Pukeatea; and this was also the name of a pa overlooking the bay. The pa stood in the area where the road to the bay meets the Port Underwood Road though now not a trace remains. This was not the main pa of the area – that was Wairau pa, located on the banks of the Wairau River. The Treaty of Waitangi, on its journey around the South Island, was signed just north east of Whites Bay on Horahora Kakahu Island.

The origin of the name greatly adds to its appeal. In 1828 an African-American slave with the intriguing and rather colourful name of Black Jack White jumped ship just to the north at Port Underwood making the bay, which was eventually renamed after him, his new home.

The first Cook Strait telegraph cable was hauled ashore here in 1886, linking the South Island to Lyall Bay in Wellington. The telegraphers' building, prefabricated in Australia and housing staff from 1867 to 1873, is still on site today.

From the bay are several short walks – Pukatea Walk (ten minutes), Black Jack/Loop Track (one and a half hours) and the Rarangi Bay Track (one hour one way) – as well as the all-day tramp to Mt Robertson (1036 m).

📍 Port Underwood Road, 5 km from Rarangi Beach, east of Blenheim.

10. Monkey Bay

Local legend tells that in the late nineteenth century a visiting sailor saw a monkey scampering around the bay. While no one else saw the monkey and whether or not the sailor had been drinking is not recorded, however pet monkeys were common on sailing ships so it is possibly true. True or not the name has stuck, and a local vineyard has even branded its wine Monkey Bay.

A short flight of beautifully built stone steps lead over a small bluff to a little shingle cove open to the southerly swells and giving excellent views south over Cloudy Bay and Cape Campbell. A sea arch pierces the rock behind the bay, which booms in heavy weather as the waves crash into the small opening. You can walk to Whites Bay from here, but you will need to return the same way unless you have arranged transport to pick you up. By the car park are a number of shallow sea caves containing glow-worms visible at night.

> From Blenheim, take the road to Rarangi Beach and Port Underwood. At the north end of Rarangi Beach, just before the road starts to climb the hill, turn right to the beginning of the track.

11. Rarangi Beach

Perfectly named (place where the sun rises), Rarangi catches the early morning sun as it first rises over Cook Strait. Wild and windswept, the beach — a mix of sand and shingle — has its own special beauty, but care must be taken when swimming here. The small settlement huddles away from the worst of the wind behind low dunes and this place has held a special attraction for artists. At the northern end of the beach is a simple DOC camping site.

Long stretches of the dunes are conservation land and are home to a number of rare native insects. The stone moth inhabits lichen-covered stones, while the golden tussock moth is confined to sand tussock; both are endemic to Marlborough and endangered. The rare Kapito spider – shy, elusive and poisonous – is also found along the dunes. Especially appealing is the mat daisy jumper, a tiny insect that inhabits raoulia mats, a tough plant that grows over gravel. Unable to fly, the jumper, like a flea, can spring up to 10 cm high.

> From Tuamarina on SH 1 just north of Blenheim, turn east into Hunters Road which in turn becomes Pembers Road and then Rarangi Road.

12. Wairau Lagoons/Te Pokohiwi

The Wairau Bar is one of New Zealand's most important archaeological sites, accidentally discovered in March 1942 when Jim Eyles, then sixteen years old, was digging an air-raid shelter near the family home. Among the shingle Jim was sharp-eyed enough to notice that the bones, shells and blackened stones were unusual – and he kept on digging.

What Jim unearthed proved to be one of the oldest occupied sites in New Zealand, dating back to at least the thirteenth century and, as subsequent excavations discovered, closely linked to the initial settlement by settlers from Eastern Polynesia.

The middens along the bar have yielded evidence that the early Maori had a wide diet that included fish, seals, kiore, tuatara, porpoise, shellfish, kuri and birds – some of which are now extinct. Of the extinct birds, bones have been found of at least six species of moa, the flightless New Zealand swan, the New Zealand crow and the gigantic Haast eagle. Evidence suggests that over 8000 moa were slaughtered and over 2000 moa eggs consumed.

Along with the evidence of food, there were also distinctly Eastern Polynesian-style fishhooks, chisels, adzes and harpoon points. More important were necklaces consisting of cotton-reel-shaped pieces held together by cord in a style common in the Marquesas Islands, east of Tahiti. This has led archaeologists to surmise that the origins of the legendary homeland of Hawaiki was somewhere in Eastern Polynesia. In all fifty burial sites have been excavated and almost 2000 personal items have been recovered from this area.

This track through the Wairau lagoons to a point overlooking the Wairau Bar unfortunately begins through the middle of Blenheim's sewerage treatment plant, but it quickly emerges onto a vast saltmarsh of interlacing lagoons and languid tidal creeks that are home to some unique salt-tolerant plants and alive with aquatic bird life. Open and windswept, the track meanders across the saltmarsh. While generally it is well maintained and flat, it is boggy and very wet in places, so you will need waterproof footwear – or even gumboots.

 The track begins at the end of Hardings Road, 5.5 km south of Blenheim off SH 1.

13. Makana Confections

Located in the heart of wine country, this chocolatier makes a welcome diversion from wine tasting. Many of the chocolates feature macadamia nuts, the most popular of which is the macadamia butter toffee crunch, a rich and superb combination of nuts and smooth toffee.

All chocolates are made on the premises, are preservative free and use natural ingredients where possible.

What makes Makana especially appealing is that the only sell direct to the public from their stores so you can be guarantee that the chocolate is fresh and has not been sitting on a shop shelf for a year. Large windows in the shop open on to the chocolate-making area where the visitor can see all the production stages of these delicious handmade chocolates. Of course, tasting samples adds to the appeal. Makana also has stores in Kerikeri and Newmarket in Auckland.

 Corner Rapaura and O'Dwyer Roads.
 Open daily 9 am to 5.30 pm.
 www.makana.co.nz

14. Wither Hills Farm Park

Overlooking Blenheim to the south, the Wither Hills form an essential part of the Marlborough landscape. Folded grass-covered hills largely devoid of trees are especially attractive in the evening light. It is difficult to believe this terrain was once covered in dense native forest. Maori destroyed much of the initial forest by fire, either deliberately or accidentally, and what little was left was cleared by early European settlers. Once gone, the bush never recovered, and a fire in 2000 raged over 6000 ha, demonstrating the fragile nature of this landscape in a climate of dry summers with strong warm winds.

Easily accessible from several points near Blenheim, Wither Hills Farm Park offers a wide range of walking and mountain bike tracks. The open, tawny, tussock country has great views over the town, Wairau Plain and Cloudy Bay.

 The park entrance on Taylors Pass Road gives access to the shorter Forest Hills, Rotary Lookout, Lower Farm, Short Loop and Stockyard tracks and the mountain bike park.

15. Burleigh Gourmet Pies

Rattled by the Canterbury earthquakes and unsettled by changing personal circumstances, Jane Dickenson and Rod Burdis decided it was time for a complete change. Moving to Blenheim in 2012, they bought a small food business on the outskirts of town, building on Jane's hospitality experience and her talent for making excellent coffee. Rod decided to try his hand at pie making and rolled out three varieties, pork belly, jerk chicken and steak with blue cheese.

Word of mouth did the rest and today Burleigh Gourmet Pies is a badly kept local secret. Keeping focused on providing a tasty, chunky filling and the thinnest pastry, today Burleigh produces thirteen varieties of pie, along with a wide range of fresh, good quality food. And now there is a Burleigh

Gourmet food truck roaming the streets of Blenheim. This place gets busy but there is plenty of parking so no need to rush.

📍 72 New Renwick Rd, Burleigh, Blenheim.
🕐 Open 7 am to 3 pm Tuesday to Saturday.
📞 03 579 2531

16. Riverlands Cob Cottage

This cottage was built prior to 1860 of a mud and tussock mix with wooden shingles – the use of cob reflects the lack of accessible timber on the Wairau Plain and cob construction was more likely to last in drier climates. The cottage was restored in the early 1960s, and the tiny rooms, complete with colonial furniture, can be viewed through glass panels.

📍 On SH 1 just south of Blenheim.

17. Dominion Salt Works, Lake Grassmere

New Zealand's only solar salt works, the system at Lake Grassmere is pretty simple. Salt water is pumped from the sea into huge shallow ponds on the northern side of the naturally shallow lake and is gradually evaporated by the action of wind and sun until the salt is sufficiently concentrated to be cleansed of impurity and dried as natural salt. Covering almost 700 ha, Lake Grassmere is ideal for the operation and is in fact more a sea lagoon than a lake. Located in Marlborough, a region with a naturally dry, sunny and often windy climate, the lake has no natural inflow other than rainwater, is shallow and exposed to wind and sun. However, Grassmere was not used for salt production until the 1940s when George Skellerup needed a solution to salt shortages during the Second World War – though in the end construction delays meant that salt was not produced until long after the war had ended.

Today, Grassmere produces 60,000–70,000 tonnes, though it is significantly supplemented by imported salt. Towering structures supporting the large conveyor belts (and looking very much like a roller coaster) pile the salt up to 20 metres high before it is bagged and freighted by train around the country. Beyond the works, hectare after hectare of shallow ponds with salt water at various stages of evaporation stretch across the lake. These ponds on occasions turn vivid pink, coloured by both algae and tiny pink-coloured shrimp that thrive in the briny water. Unfortunately, daily tours have been discontinued and the company only takes group tours by arrangement, but it is worth the short detour as the ponds and salt piles are right by the road and all the operations are clearly visible.

The salt works are just off SH 1 between Ward and Seddon, south of Blenheim.

18. Marlborough Vineyards

New Zealand wines now need little introduction. With over twenty years of continual growth, wine exports reach over $1.7 billion dollars in 2018. Over 2000 vineyards grew 38,000 ha of grapes with Marlborough accounting for 26,000 ha, followed by Hawkes Bay with 4700 ha. Of the 38,000 ha, 30,000 ha are in white grapes and 8,000 ha in red. Sauvignon blanc grapes alone cover 23,100 ha.

Of the red grapes grown, pinot noir make up 72 percent, followed by merlot at 15 percent while sauvignon blanc accounted for 77 percent of white grapes, with chardonnay at just 11 percent.

Without a doubt Marlborough is the most extensive wine-growing region in New Zealand and, for wine lovers, it has the most vineyards open to visitors all year round. It was sauvignon blanc wines from Marlborough that catapulted New Zealand wines onto the world stage, and it is still the wine that is distinctly New Zealand in flavour, and for which New Zealand is best known. Sauvignon blanc wine accounts for over 77 per cent of the wine produced in this area, though most vineyards produce several other varietals.

The wine-growing area is compact, easy to access, and bike tours are popular. The handsome open landscape, with the Wither Hills to the south and the Richmond Range to the north, complements the hot dry summers for which the region is famous. If you go to no other wine area in New Zealand, make time for this one.

The famous Marlborough Wine and Food Festival, held in February each year, combines wine, food and entertainment, and showcases wines from over forty vineyards (www.wine-marlborough-festival.co.nz).

Brancott Estate

Grapes were grown in the Marlborough area in the nineteenth century but by 1970 vineyards had completely disappeared from the region.

In the early 70s Montana wines were looking to substantially expand their operations, but found that the land in the established North Island wine growing areas was both limited and expensive. Looking to the South Island, Montana recognised Marlborough as having both the potential and space to greatly increase their vineyards. With incredibly secrecy, they purchased over 110 ha and began planting in 1973. However, the area was quite different from Hawkes Bay and Gisborne and the first plantings were a disaster. Perseverance paid off and in 1979 the first sauvignon blanc vines were planted. The rest, they say, is history.

Now known as the Brancott Estate, this was the first vineyard to be planted in 1973, but now grapes cover the flat Wairau plains with a carpet of green as far as the eye can see (and beyond). A smart modern restaurant and tasting room is perched on a narrow ridge high above the plain and sauvignon blanc is still grown on the land below.

📍 180 Brancott Road, Brancott Vineyard, Fairhall.
🕐 Cellar door open daily from 10:00 am to 4.30 pm.
   Restaurant open daily from 11:30 am to 3:00 pm.
📞 03 5206975

Cloudy Bay Vineyards

Cloudy Bay is one of the most internationally recognised New Zealand wine labels and probably the one label that established sauvignon blanc as a leading New World wine on the global wine stage. The vineyard is open for tastings and often has limited-release wines available.

  Jacksons Road.
  Cellar door open daily 10 am to 4.30 pm.
  www.cloudybay.co.nz

Forrest Estate

Modern sculptures set in a large expansive garden line the drive into Forrest Estate, which produces a wide range of both red and white wines from their vineyards in Marlborough and Hawke's Bay. A great spot for combining wine tasting and a picnic lunch.

The estate also hosts the popular Grape Ride, a 102-km cycle tour held annually in April.

  Blicks Road, Renwick.
  Cellar door open daily 10 am to 4 pm.
  www.forrest.co.nz

Framingham Wine Company

Well known for their rieslings and aromatics, the entrance to this long-established vineyard is through a formal rose-laden courtyard garden. A visit to Framingham's atmospheric underground cellar is a must.

  Conders Bend Road.
  Cellar door open daily 11 am to 4 pm.
  www.framingham.co.nz

Wither Hills Vineyard

Without a doubt, Wither Hills is one of the country's most stylish vineyards and is worth visiting for its architecture as well as its wines. Winemaker Brent Marris had a strong influence on the building design, which combines the functionality of a working vineyard with a form that blends into the distinct Marlborough environment. The winery offers wine tasting of vintages as well as varieties, a restaurant, and a splendid view over the Wairau Valley from the top of the building.

  11 New Renwick Road.
  Cellar door open daily 10 am to 4.30 pm.
  www.witherhills.co.nz

Spy Valley Wines

Taking its name from the nearby satellite monitoring site, this family-owned vineyard is known for it cool-climate grape varieties, and in addition to its respected sauvignon blanc, it also produces riesling, pinot gris, merlot and pinot noir. Opened in 2003, this smart modern winery features an award-winning tasting room designed by New Zealand architects Wraight and Associates, contemporary New Zealand art by Tom Sladden, wine antiques and a dramatic outdoor sculpture that picks up on the spy theme.

  Lake Timara Road, off Waihopai Valley Road, Renwick.
  Cellar door open 10 am to 4 pm.
  www.spyvalleywine.co.nz

Bladen Wines

This vineyard of only 8 ha may be small but it has a long list of awards for its aromatics. Planted in 1989 and with its first vintage in 1997, the vineyard's grapes are mainly hand-harvested and are all single vineyard wines with the exception of sauvignon blanc. The tiny tasting room is little more than a hole in the wall, but there is every chance that you will meet the owners and winemaker.

📍 Conders Bend Road, Renwick.
🕐 Cellar door open daily 11 am to 4.30 pm mid October to end April.
🌐 www.bladen.co.nz

NELSON

1. Cape Farewell and Farewell Spit
2. The River Inn
3. Grove Scenic Reserve, Takaka
4. Abel Tasman Memorial
5. Wainui Falls, Takaka
6. Paynes Ford
7. Harwoods Hole, Takaka Hill
8. Tokongawha/Split Apple Rock
9. Riwaka Resurgence
10. Motueka Saltwater Baths
11. Moutere Inn
12. St Paul's Lutheran Church, Upper Moutere
13. Mapua Wharf
14. Jester House Café
15. Broadgreen House
16. McCashins (Mac's) Brewery
17. Pic's Peanut Butter
18. MacMillans Hand Thrown Ceramics
19. Theatre Royal
20. South, Ellictt and Seymour Heritage Streets
21. Montgomery Square Markets
22. Botanic Reserve
23. Centre of New Zealand
24. The Boulder Bank/Te Taero o Kereopa
25. Glenduan Topdressing Airstrip
26. Tophouse Hotel, Nelson Lakes
27. Kawatiri Railway Walkway
28. Lake Rotorca
29. Nelson Vineyards

1. Cape Farewell and Farewell Spit

Just a few kilometres apart, the sheltered waters of Golden Bay are in direct contrast to the wild seascape of the Tasman Sea, and in between these two bodies of water is the unique sandbank that is Farewell Spit. Over 30 km in length, Farewell Spit is one of the longest recurved sand spits in the world and protects a delicate ecosystem, the shallow tidal flats of Golden Bay. Home to a rich variety of bird life, over ninety species have been recorded here, including migratory birds such as godwits and red knots that arrive in their tens of thousands in the spring to feed.

At the end of the Spit are an old lighthouse and a gannet colony. In order to preserve the environment only a small area at the spit's base near Puponga is accessible to the public, although Farewell Spit Eco Tours (www.farewellspit.com) have a licence to take visitors out on to the spit itself. There is an excellent information centre at Puponga (closed June to August) for up-to-date walk information and from which tours out on the Spit can be booked. Nearby Puponga Point is an ancient pa site.

Puponga Farm Park is a working farm at the base of the Spit that acts both as a buffer to preserve its delicate ecosystem and as an area of outstanding beauty. A loop walk follows the 'inside' beach (Golden Bay) and the 'outside' beach (Tasman Sea). From the car park, walk north along the inside beach keeping an eye out for many wading birds feeding in the shallow waters. At the end of the row of pine trees turn left and cut across the Spit through farmland and swamp to the outside beach. In contrast to Golden Bay, the outside beach is a huge stretch of white sand pummelled by relentless surf. The track back to the start is through a narrow gully of nikau palms and across farmland. If you have time, continue further down the outside beach to the rocky cliffs at the end known as Fossil Point where fossils are clearly visible in the mudstone. Little blue penguins and fur seals are also a common sight.

As well as the Spit itself there are several excellent short walks to the Pillar Point Lighthouse that has the best views over the Spit (and on a clear day as far north as Taranaki); Cape Farewell with its dramatic cliffs and sea arches; and to the windswept sands of Wharanaki Beach. This surf-pounded beach of fine golden sand directly faces the wild Tasman Sea, has magnificent wind-sculpted rock formations and is a popular resting place for fur seals.

Confused by the very shallow water, the bay is also a death trap for whales and is the site of regular strandings, mainly by pilot whales. A lively Maori legend has quite a different take on these why so many whales strand here.

The story begins with a fight at Onetahua between kuku (mussels) and pipi for supremacy of the sandy beach. The battle was won by the pipi, who drove the mussels in retreat to the rocks where they cling to this day.

The noisy fight drew the attention of Takaako (a shark) and Te Pu (a whale), who quickly decided that while the fight held no interest for them, the victorious pipi with their large tasty tongues would make good food for their hungry families. Gathering their children about them, Te Pu and Takaako rushed the pipi, which turned out to be far too quick for the great fish and pulled their heads back into the sand. Finding the pipi gone, the whales ended up with only a mouthful of sand and stranded in the shallow water. This David and Goliath defeat by the pipi over the whales and the sharks became known as the battle of Waimapihi.

2. The River Inn

A classic nineteenth century hotel, little has changed at the River Inn since it opened as the Globe Hotel in May 1898. Prior to the Takaka Hill road opening in 1900 this was a busy port settlement and, while the sea trade has long gone, the Waitapu Wharf is still home to a small fishing fleet. Now much quieter, The River Inn has a huge main bar decorated with hunting trophies of deer and pig heads, and the pub hosts an annual pig hunt for charity. However, worth a visit in their own right are the two impressive totem pole type carvings in the bar, created by local artist Neil Baker. A lovely open fireplace attracts the locals in winter and a rustic garden bar is equally appealing in summer. The hotel has rooms available upstairs and camping behind the pub.

Set in a peaceful rural river setting the inn is at the gateway to the world famous Waipupu Springs and has bus connections at the door to Abel Tasman and Heaphy Tracks and wet suits and mountain bikes for hire.

20 Waitapu Wharf Road, Takaka.
03 525 9425

3. Grove Scenic Reserve, Takaka

Easily overlooked, this tiny bush reserve just outside Takaka is the place to let your imagination run wild. This is the forest of every child's storybook, with paths that weave through a fantastical forest of twisted and gnarled old rata trees whose roots entwine weathered limestone rocks and hide secret caves. Between the boulders nikau palms flourish, adding a tropical air to the minuscule forest. This place just makes you want to stop and start building a hut! Best, however, is the narrow path that leads through a cleft in the rock to a wonderful lookout point high above the plain over Golden Bay from where you can survey your entire kingdom. If you are there in mid-December when the rata is a blaze of crimson, then the reserve takes on an even more magical glow. Every child should have their own Grove Reserve to play in!

> Grove Reserve is on the road from Takaka township to Pohara Beach, signposted from Clifton.

4. Abel Tasman Memorial

In December 1640, Dutch explorer Abel Janszoon Tasman arrived off the coast near Wainui in two ships, the *Heemskerck* and the *Zeehaen*. Unfortunately, the stay was both short and unpleasant when his sailors clashed with local Maori, resulting in the death of four of his sailors and several Maori. There is some conjecture that Tasman may have entered either a tapu site or an area that had a rahui placed on it. It is also likely that the very strange ship and oddly dressed white people who suddenly appeared were not surprisingly perceived as harmful spirits.

Naming the area Moordenaars (Murderers) Bay and the country Staten Landt (later changed by a Dutch cartographer to New Zealand), Tasman never set foot on land and departed from the country in early January. Today only two places named by Tasman remain, Cape Maria Van Dieman and Three Kings Islands.

There is a short walk up to the memorial set high on a bluff overlooking Golden Bay.

📍 On the seaward side of Abel Tasman Drive, between Pohara Beach and Ligar Bay.

5. Wainui Falls, Takaka

While most visitors join the mad rush to Totaranui, not so many people bother stopping to visit these falls that are actually inside the Abel Tasman National Park. While the 20-metre falls and the deep shady pool below are an attraction in their own right, the easy bush walk has an appeal all of its own, and you are quite likely to have this walk to yourself. The mature bush is a fine mix of beech, rata and nikau, and the boulder-strewn stream is impressive with huge water-worn rocks the size of small trucks littering its course. The walk takes around one hour return and the track is in good condition, though the wire suspension bridge might be a little challenging for those a bit unsteady on their feet.

📍 From Takaka, take the road to Totaranui. At the Wainui Inlet, a clearly marked road sign to the right leads to the falls.

6. Paynes Ford

An old tramline used between 1880 and 1905 for timber provides an easy track leading to spectacular limestone bluffs that are a rock climber's heaven. Mainly used for sport climbing, the area can only be described as challenging, with route names that say it all, such as *Goodbye Cream Poofters, Stairway of the Gods, Bored on the Rings, Body Nazis, Rat up a Drainpipe* and *You're either Dead or You're Not*. Rough tracks created by rock climbers are also worth exploring as the tracks lead to sheer cliff faces, rocky overhangs and clefts in the limestone bluffs, though none are well formed and it can be a bit of a scramble at times. A rare native forget-me-not grows on the cliff face.

Along the track is a swampy piece of ground that is home to the Rene Orchidston Collection of flax. There is no official 'end' to this track but once you reach the bend in the river the walk becomes a lot less interesting, so it's best to return at this point. In summer the river is a very popular swimming hole on hot days.

 3 km south of Takaka near Paynes Ford Bridge.

7. Harwoods Hole, Takaka Hill

The entire Takaka Hill area is a great place to explore, but the highlight must be the amazing Harwoods Hole, a dramatic tomo dropping down over 170 metres – the deepest vertical cave shaft in the country. Located in the limestone country of the Takaka Hill, the hole wasn't properly explored until December 1958 and the following month the Starlight Cave, which leads from the bottom of the hole, was also discovered.

Harwoods Hole is one of the most visible formations in a vast area that is laced with tomos and caves including the deepest and longest cave systems in New Zealand.

Below Mt Arthur, south of the Takaka Hill, is the deepest cave so far discovered in New Zealand. The Ellis Basin System winds underground for over 33 km (the second longest) and goes down to a depth of 1026 metres. The top five deepest caves in New Zealand are all in the area and in order are; Ellis Basin System, Mt Arthur (1026 m); Nettlebed Cave, Mt Arthur (889 m); Bulmer Cavern, Mt Owen (755 m); HH Cave, Mt Arthur (721 m); and Stormy Pot, Mt Arthur (720 m). The longest cave system is at Mt Owen, a bit further south, which is twice as long as the Ellis Basin System at 67 km.

It is actually hard to see into the hole, but soaring cliffs on all sides give a very good idea of the extent of the drop. A short side track up to the Gorge Creek lookout not only gives you an incredible prospect from the top of the escarpment over Gorge Creek, but also has a view back toward

Harwood Hole giving a much better idea of the tomo's sheer size. While the walk to the hole is easy and takes around one-and-a-half hours return, the last section involves a bit of a scramble over rocks – and as there are no barriers, one slip and it's curtains. Cavers regularly use the hole, so don't go biffing rocks into the shaft.

> From SH 60 (Takaka Hill road), turn into Canaan Road and follow this unsealed narrow road for 10 km to the car park at the end. From the car park, the walk to the hole is around ninety minutes return.

8. Tokongawha/Split Apple Rock

This curious split rock sits just off a narrow beach in Towers Bay just north of Kateriteri. In Maori the name Tokongawha means 'burst open rock' and refers to a legend where either two brothers or two chiefs (depending on the story) fought over this particular rock and, rather than continue the argument, decided to cut the rock in half. Quite why they were fighting over this rock was never mentioned. The rock sits off a long beach of golden sand and is just a short walk from the road.

> From Kaiteriteri Beach take the Sandy Bay Road north for 4 km and then turn into Tokongawha Drive. After 2 km turn right into Moonraker Way, where the parking area is located.

9. Riwaka Resurgence

'Resurgence' conjures up a vision of dramatic rushing water, and while the Riwaka Resurgence is nowhere so dramatic it is a very picturesque spot nonetheless. A short walk meanders through mature beech to the base of a cliff from where the crystal-clear waters of the Riwaka Stream emerge from beneath Takaka Hill, after flowing underground for 4 km.

The cave is popular with divers, who can penetrate the stream system for up to 800 metres, reaching a giant chamber with limestone formations. There is a pleasant picnic spot by the car park.

📍 At the very base of the Takaka Hill Road (SH 60) turn on to Riwaka Valley Road and the Resurgence is 6 km down this road.

10. Motueka Saltwater Baths

Saltwater pools were once very common in New Zealand and a convenient and inexpensive way to provide a public swimming pool. Additionally, salt water and sunshine were also promoted for their health benefits and there was even a Sunshine League established in the 1930s solely dedicated to encourage children to enjoy the outdoors.

Filled at high tide, the pools then remained full at low tide thereby providing all day swimming in the summer months (and in winter for the very hardy). Pools such as Judges Bay in Auckland and St Clair in Dunedin have subsequently become more developed and Motueka, along with a pool on Rangitoto Island, are the only two remaining pools of this type in New Zealand.

Originally built in 1938, the pool was further developed in the 1940s and 1950s, and Beach Domain was a popular picnic and recreation spot for locals. Over time the pools became rundown but when the local council proposed demolishing the pool in the early 90s, locals banded together and revived the pool. Ten years later the pools again faced closure, but huge public pressure again saved the pool and today the saltwater pools are an integral part of Motueka life.

📍 Beach Domain. North Street and Everett Street, Motueka.

11. Moutere Inn

Not so easy to find, the lovely old Motuere Inn sits on a low north-facing rise and large windows and a pleasure terrace make the best of the views and sunshine. Inside an open spacious bar is lined with historical photos, letters and documents dating over 100 years. The wine list only features wines grown within a radius of 10 km of the pub and has offered over 400 different beers on tap since 2008.

Built in 1850 by German settler Cordt Benseman as a family home, it was extended in 1857 and at the same time obtained a hotel licence. There is considerable debate regarding the Moutere Inn as New Zealand's oldest hotel and framed document hanging the wall details their claim against other old New Zealand hotels. It can claim to have never been destroyed by fire, never moved and been continuously licensed since 1857.

  1406 Upper Moutere Highway, Upper Moutere.
  03 543 2759
  www.moutereinn.co.nz

12. St Paul's Lutheran Church, Upper Moutere

On June 14, 1843, The *St Pauli* sailed into Nelson carrying on board 123 German settlers mainly from North Germany and the Rhineland. While some stayed in Nelson, others headed to the Moutere Valley, but life was tough with poor soil and floods and by 1844 over half the immigrants had left the district. A further immigrant ship the *Skiold* arrived in September 1844 with 144 Germans, and they established a prosperous settlement called Ranzau on the Waimea plain (later renamed Hope).

Eventually settlers moved back to the Moutere Valley forming a new settlement, Sarau, at Upper Moutere and with more Germans arriving by the 1850s, the township was flourishing.

Although a foundation stone for a Lutheran Church was laid in 1844 at Moutere the church was never built, and the first St Paul's church was finally opened in 1864 with Johann Heine as the Pastor. Fifty years later the church had badly deteriorated and was finally pulled down to be replaced in 1905 with the church standing today.

Few tangible legacies of the German settlement remain; even the town names changed when everything German fell out of favour during World War One. The St Paul's Lutheran Church is an exception with the small cemetery surrounding the church full of gravestones with German names and inscriptions in German. The church bell was made in Germany and named Anna after Pastor Heine's wife.

The church offers guided church and cemetery tours.

 Moutere Hwy, Upper Moutere.
 03 543 2839

13. Mapua Wharf

Appropriately Mapua means 'abundance' in Maori and European settlement began in the middle of the nineteenth century when fisherman James Heatly set up camp at the western entrance of the tidal Waimea Inlet to hunt rabbits for sale in nearby Nelson.

Poor roading in the early twentieth century led to the construction of a substantial wharf in 1915 to accommodate large ships to transport apples from the flourishing orchards in the area. The wharf quickly became the centre of the small township with the first shop opening in 1921 followed by storage sheds, fish freezers and shipping offices. A ferry operated between Mapua Wharf and Rabbit Island and still runs transporting pedestrians and cyclists across the swift flowing inlet.

Today rabbits are no longer the attraction, and the old packing houses and fish freezers have been converted into a range of craft and designer stores, cafés, bars and restaurants including the Golden Bear Brewing Company and The Smokehouse, famous for its superb fish. A small museum is located on the wharf itself and Mapua Wharf is the perfect base to explore the myriad cycle tracks and quiet beaches on Rabbit Island.

At the very end of Aranui Road, Mapua.

14. Jester House Café

Established in 1991 by Judy and Steve Richards, Jester House is a local institution in the best possible sense. The couple purchased a modest time-worn house on a small block of land in Tasman and set about a transformation that included a garden café as well as a family home. This is no ordinary café and garden but a magical place that is carefully built and environmentally thoughtful. If this sounds just a bit earnest, then its time for a visit. The café building is electric and full of eye-catching details, while the garden is full of intricate stonework, hidden surprises and whimsical delights.

Add to this the legendary baking and winner of the New Zealand's Café of the Year and you can't possibly drive past.

Then there are the eels and your children will never forgive you for not stopping. A small stream runs between the road and the café and over the years the native longfin eels have become café aficionados too and lurk quietly in the shallow water waiting to be fed by hand. It's scary and exciting all at the same time.

 320 Aporo Road, Tasman.
 03 526 6742
 www.jesterhouse.co.nz

15. Broadgreen House

What's another old historic house, you say? Well, two things makes this house exceptional. Firstly, the original condition of the building is amazing, having been owned by only two families prior to being purchased by the city in 1965. Built in 1855 of cob construction, Broadgreen House is typical of a comfortable home of the mid-Victorian period, and some rooms still retain Victorian wallpaper. The second reason this house is special is the fantastic kitchen. Packed with every conceivable Victorian gadget available at the time for cooking and baking, there is both an open hearth and a coal range, a special oven for bread baking, and a separate dairy for the cool storage of butter, cheese and milk. The floors are the original smart red-and-black tiles and the feel of the whole place is so inviting that you just want to fire up the range, open up Mrs Beeton's cookbook and get going. In short, this is a kitchen even a modern chef would die for. The cellar under the house is the hole from which the mud for the cob walls was extracted; and if you feel the urge to dress up, then the upstairs costume room has a collection of original nineteenth-century dress.

276 Nayland Road, Stoke.
Open daily 10.30 am to 4.30 pm, closed Good Friday and Christmas Day.
03 547 0403
Entrance fee.

16. McCashins (Mac's) Brewery

Opened in 1981, Mac's Brewery, established by Terry and Bev McCashin, led the revolution in introducing New Zealanders to naturally brewed beer, spawning a whole generation of locally brewed beer and making Mac's beers a household name — which is appropriate considering that Nelson is the only hop-growing region in New Zealand.

No longer producing the Mac's brand, the brewery at Stoke (originally an old cider brewery) now produces beer under the Stoke label and cider under the Rochdale brand and offers tours during weekdays.

660 Main Road, Stoke.
03 547 5357
  www.mccashins.co.nz

17. Pic's Peanut Butter

In some ways this is an extraordinary story and in other ways it is a very ordinary story. It starts simply enough with Pic Picot finding that his favourite snack food, peanut butter, had within a short period of time a disgusting amount of sugar added. So Pic starts making his own, simply roasting and careful preparing a mix made with 100 percent peanuts. Very quickly demand for his perfect peanut butter kept outstripping his supply. Selling out at the local Nelson markets he progressed to a concrete mixer to make larger batches sold through retail outlets and yet demand kept outstripping supply.

Now Pic's Peanut Butter is the top selling brand in New Zealand and is now rapidly expanding in export markets. Within one decade he has moved from his laundry to a purpose-built factory producing peanut, almond and cashew butters.

Tours are available daily at the new factory and take around forty minutes with kids able to try their hand at making their own peanut butter. Bookings essential.

   18 Elms Street, Wakatu Estate, Nelson.
   03 544 8402
         www.picspeanutbutter.com

18. MacMillans Hand Thrown Ceramics

Nelson has long been famous for its pottery, and is still home to numerous potters including many internationally recognised for their craft (the Nelson information centre has a special brochure on local potters' studios).

MacMillans specialises in durable, highly coloured tableware, but also offers visitors an opportunity to create something of their own using their own clay and glazes. They provide bisque ware (undecorated pottery) that can then be individually decorated by hand, and which is then fired, packed and posted to the creator. Beginners can also try their hand at creating their own pottery and very few leave without successfully producing something.

- 92 Bateup Road, Richmond.
- Open daily Wednesday to Sunday 10 am to 4 pm.
- 03 5445853
- www.alchemyarts.co.nz

19. Theatre Royal

New Zealand's oldest wooden theatre (and very likely the oldest in Australasia) the Theatre Royal opened in on July 18, 1878 to a capacity audience of 1000 when Nelson was a town of just 6000. Despite its grand façade, the theatre had mud floors and, along with theatrical and musical productions, doubled as a boxing ring. Renovated in 1905 the Theatre Royal was Nelson's first moving picture house from 1908 to 1936 when the Majestic Theatre opened.

Sliding into a slow decline the theatre was sold in 1944 to the Nelson Repertory Club and it was not until 2005 that the Theatre Royal was sold to the Nelson Historic Theatre Trust for just $10. After years of painstaking and costly restoration, the theatre reopened on 31 May 2010, this time as 342 seat theatre hosting smaller productions.

- 78 Rutherford St, Nelson.
- 03 548 3840
- www.theatreroyalnelson.co.nz

20. South, Elliott and Seymour Heritage Streets

Nelson is a city that values its heritage and has preserved three streets that reflect three very different periods of the city's heritage, all within an easy walk of the city centre.

Best known is South Street, a short cul-de-sac in the central city which is highly unusual in that the whole street is virtually unaltered since the workers' cottages were built in the 1860s. Several of the cottages are available as accommodation.

Elliot Street, just north of the city centre, is a similarly preserved street, though in this case the houses are mainly from the period 1910 to the 1930s.

The third street, Seymour Street, is south of the city and different in that it represents fifty years of domestic architecture from the late Victorian villa, through the California bungalow and Art Deco, to the post-War 1950s architecture.

21. Montgomery Square Markets

Nelson has always been well famous for it markets both for craft and art as well as fresh produce and homemade goodies.

In order to accommodate both the customers and vendors, the markets have been split over two days. The focus of the Saturday market is fresh locally grown produce, much of it organic, along with artisan bread, cheese, plants, and meat and fish product. As well as food stalls there are also stalls which specialise in art, handicrafts, jewellery, clothing and pottery. Sunday is very different with collectables, recycled goods, antiques, books, retro homewares and CDs.

As to be expected both markets have plenty of food stalls providing tasty snacks and excellent coffee.

If you are only in Nelson mid-week, don't despair, the yummy Nelson Farmers Market is held on Wednesday mornings in Kirby Lane, 105 Bridge Street.

> 📍 Montgomery Square is a large car park, bounded by Rutherford, Hardy, Trafalgar and Bridge Streets.

22. Botanic Reserve

While William Webb Ellis is credited as the first person to pick up a soccer ball and run with it, the rules of rugby were not formalised in Britain until 1862. Gradually, the game was imported to this country, and the first officially recognised match in New Zealand was played on this field, known as the Botanic Reserve, on 14 May 1870 between Nelson Football Club (Town) and Nelson College. The Nelson Football Club originally played an odd mix of soccer and Victorian (Australian) Rules football, but in 1870 changed its name to the Nelson Rugby Club, thereby becoming the first rugby club in the country. At that stage rugby was played by large teams of twenty, and points could only be scored by kicking goals. However, to be able to kick a goal the ball had to be touched down first, which then gave that team the right to 'try' for a goal. For the record, Town beat College two goals to nil and rugby is still played on this field today.

 From the centre of Nelson, the Botanic Reserve is over the footbridge at the end of Hardy Street.

23. Centre of New Zealand

This popular walk begins from the Botanic Reserve and leads up a short but steep hill to a great viewpoint over the city and beyond (around thirty minutes return). Contrary to local belief it is not the geographical centre of New Zealand, but a convenient hill used by an early surveyor, John Browning, who was charged by the government to link up previous surveys.

24. The Boulder Bank/Te Taero o Kereopa

The Boulder Bank is a fascinating natural phenomenon, though at first glance it is hard to believe that such a prominent and clearly defined breakwater is not human construction. Over 13 km in length, the bank is formed by large granodiorite boulders which have moved southwest from MacKay Bluff during northerly storms. That these large stones have been moved by wind, water and tide to form a precise line for such an extent is extraordinary, and it is not surprising that this boulder bank in Nelson is one of the very few examples of its type in the world.

The bank originally extended to Haulashore Island near Tahunanui Beach, but in 1906 a substantial gap was cut near its western end to provide better access to the harbour. The lighthouse at the end of the bank was originally cast in Bath, England, shipped to New Zealand in sections, and reassembled in 1861 to begin working in August 1862.

Like many of the placenames around Aotearoa, Te Taero o Kereopa has a close connection with the exploration of Kupe. When two of Kupe's men, Kereopa and Pani, decided to settle rather than continue voyaging, they deserted in two waka and headed towards Waimea (Tasman Bay). Setting off in hot pursuit in his waka *Matahourua*, Kupe started gaining on the fugitives. In their panic to slow down Kupe, they threw Kupe's daughter overboard. Plucking her from the water, Kupe now redoubled his efforts to catch Pani and Kereopa and eventually started to gain on them as they entered the wide bay.

Kereopa now called on the gods with a powerful karakia to create a barrier between his waka and the *Matahourua*. The gods answered with boulders from Horoirangi (Mackay Bluff) collapsing into the sea and forming a long line, with Kereopa on the inside and Kupe out to sea. Kereopa won the day, keeping ahead of Kupe and finally making it to shore where he disappeared into the deep bush. Today several tribes descend from Kereopa, most notably Ngati Kuia.

Kupe's attention then turned to Pani in his waka *Takaporewa*, who likewise called on the gods and pleaded with local taniwha to delay Kupe, but had much less success. In his haste, Pani's waka overturned in the very rips he had created near Rangitoto Island and all aboard were drowned.

At first glance the Boulder Bank looks so tempting for a good long walk, but in reality it is made of loose stones and boulders and walking along the bank is surprisingly hard work. A short section at the beginning is, however, a smooth level path and an easy short stroll. How far you want to go after that is up to you.

📍 Boulder Bank Drive off SH 6, 7 km north of Nelson.

25. Glenduan Topdressing Airstrip

Usually tucked away at the back of farms, top dressing airstrips are a common feature of rural life in New Zealand. Not only is the Glenduan strip right on the Cable Bay Walkway, but the views from this hilltop are well worth the uphill climb to get there. Stop reading here if flying makes you nervous.

Contrary to the expectations of aviation novices, this airfield is far from flat and is surprisingly steep at the top. The slope assists the plane to gain momentum on take off, but also helps quickly slow down the plane on landing. Taking off the pilot speeds downhill and just flies off into thin air. With a full of a full load of fertiliser there is just no room for error.

It will take about 45 minutes' walk to get to airstrip from the end of Airlie Street and it is all uphill. High above Tasman Bay the views are specular with a semi-circle of seats to enjoy the view and eat your lunch. And no, the small building is not a tiny passenger terminal, but toilets built by DoC for trampers, complete with little low gates to keep out the sheep.

From SH 6 north of Nelson, turn into Glen Road and after 2km park on the left. From this point it is another 10 minute walk to the start via Airlie Street to the right (There is very little parking at end of Airlie Street). You have two options to reach the top, the track to the left through paddocks is steeper, but shorter, while the track to the right is on an access road and longer and easier.

📍 Corner of Glen Road and Airlie Street.

26. Tophouse Hotel, Nelson Lakes

Tophouse is the only survivor of a string of similar guesthouses through the mountains that were built to provide basic food and lodgings for travellers between Nelson, Marlborough and Canterbury. A licence for a hotel was granted in 1844 and the original Tophouse was built in 1846 on the road from Nelson to the lakes, taking its name from its position at the top of the Wairau, Motueka and Buller rivers. The building standing today, and now a Category 1 historic building, was built in 1881, and both internal and external walls are entirely of cob construction. Cob is an ancient building material and is a combination of straw, soil, sand and water – or whatever variations of this mixture were to hand. More suitable for drier climates, cob was often used in areas of New Zealand where wood was scarce. An exposed section in the hallway of the Tophouse Hotel demonstrates how cob was used in its construction.

Even today the hotel has a cosy and welcoming feel, but it wasn't always the case. Tophouse was supposedly haunted by a resident ghost called Sidney (and never, ever Sid!) who disturbed the guests by shaking them awake during the night. Sidney was a tinker who, after being thrown from his horse-drawn cart, died in the hotel. But apparently even ghosts have their price – after a stern talking to and the promise (a promise so far kept) of a slice of Red Leicester cheese for Christmas, Sidney has left the guests to slumber on in peace. Accommodation is still available in the original hotel as well as in adjacent cottages.

 Tophouse is 9 km from St Arnaud, Nelson Lakes.
 03 548 9299
www.tophouse.co.nz

27. Kawatiri Railway Walkway

In 1929 the Nelson/Inangahua railway reached Gowan Bridge, but despite public pressure to complete the project, the line was never extended further south. The eventual closure of the line in 1955 was accompanied by vigorous protest by local women who staged a sit-in on the line, including Sonja Davies who went on to become a well-known trade union activist and Labour Member of Parliament. The Kawatiri walk (thirty minutes return) through beech forest begins at the old Junction railway station (the platform is still there), and includes the Pikomanu railway tunnel and bridge over the Hope River.

  Junction SH 6 and SH 63.

28. Lake Rotoroa

Formed during the last ice age, both Lake Rotoiti and Lake Rotoroa are the result of glacier action in the mountains of the upper Buller River. Reaching into the heart of the most northern section of the Southern Alps, the lakes give access to both lower forest, mainly consisting of silver and red beech, and true alpine terrain, which is snow-covered in winter. The birdlife in the 102,000 ha forest is prolific and includes bellbirds, robins and kaka.

The DOC information centre at St Arnaud at Lake Rotoiti has excellent displays on the natural environment, and up-to-date information on walks and tramping in the area.

Most visitors only visit Rotoiti, which is more accessible and has a wider range of facilities. Rotoroa, a much larger lake, is much quieter and there is excellent fishing for brown trout and hunting in the surrounding area for red deer, chamois and pig.

The lake is 145 m deep and unlike Rotoiti is completely surrounded in beech forest with only a small settlement near the Gowan River outlet. Water taxis are a convenient way to access more remote parts of the lake.

From the picnic area the Rotoroa Nature Walk is an easy loop track that takes about twenty-five minutes return and passes through a diverse variety of native trees, ferns, mosses, vines and shrubs. The longer Braeburn Walk (two hours return) is notable for its profusion of native fuchsia trees. This walk starts on Braeburn Road near the Gowan River bridge.

Drive 5 km from the junction of SH 6 and SH 63 and turn into Gowan Valley Road and drive 12 km to the end.

29. Nelson Vineyards

In 1902 Romeo Braggato was employed by the New Zealand Government to the position of Government Viticulturist and part of that job was to identify areas suitable for growing grapes and producing wine. Braggato identified Nelson as one such region but despite its local German population few grapes were grown and even less wine produced. It wasn't until the 1970s that Nelson became a serious wine producing area and today is recognised for its superb cool climate aromatic wines such as riesling, sauvignon blanc, chardonnay and gewürztraminer.

Seifried Estate

Established in 1973 by Austrian born Herman Seifried and his New Zealand wife Agnes, this is one of the earliest vineyards in the region. Covering over 250 ha, Seifried produces a surprisingly wide range of wine that reflects the regions preference for aromatic and Herman's European influence. Today all three children are involved in the business and along with the more usual wines such as sauvignon blanc, pinot gris, merlot and pinot noir, Seifried also produce the unusual zweigelt and the international famous, Sweet Agnes riesling.

184 Redwood Road, Appleby.
www.seifried.co.nz

Neudorf Vineyards

Reflecting the area's German heritage Neudorf produces elegant fine wines that age well, in particular chardonnay along with sauvignon blanc, pinot noir, rosé and the unusual albarino. The garden setting of the cellar focuses on a 150-year-old barn with a broad veranda overlooking the vines.

Neudorf Road, Upper Moutere.
www.neudorf.co.nz

Fossil Ridge

This family-owned boutique vineyard is one of the closest to Nelson City and at just 3 ha is also one of the smallest. All its wines are produced from this single vineyard. The winery takes it name from the rare marine fossils *Monotis richmondiana* (the winery has fossils on display) which are unique to just two places in the world, one of which is this vineyard. Along with wine (chardonnay, pinot noir and rosé), Fossil Ridge also produces its own olive oil, lime marmalade and macadamia nuts.

Hart Road, Richmond.
www.fossilridge.co.nz

BULLER

1. Owen River Tavern
2. Maruia Falls
3. Murchison
4. Six Mile Hydro Station, Murchison
5. Lyell
6. Inangahua Hall
7. The Oparara Basin, Karamea
8. Charming Creek Walkway
9. Denniston and the Incline
10. Westport Municipal Chambers
11. Buller River at Westport
12. Carters Beach
13. Mitchell's Gully Gold Mine, Charleston
14. Fox River Caves
15. Truman Track
16. Blacks Point Museum and Stamper Battery
17. Reefton School of Mines
18. The Future Dough Company, Reefton
19. Quartzopolis, Town of Light
20. Bearded Mining Company
21. Reefton Distillery
22. Waiuta

1. Owen River Tavern

In the 1880s gold was discovered in the Owen River valley and today the pub is all that remains of the flourishing town that spread out along the river. A small hotel was built in 1888 on a site just a short distance away from the existing pub, but that was burnt to the ground in 1927. Virtually unchanged from when it opened in 1928, the pub has endured, while the rest of the town completely vanished.

Today it is trout that brings visitors to the valley and the Owen River Tavern is more than just a pub – it is the community centre, post office, and even doubles as the local War memorial with a roll of honour to those who fought in the WWII proudly displayed on the wall.

And it was the prospect of trout fishing that lured the current owners Kim and John Sui from Hong Kong in 1997. It is hard to imagine a greater contrast than between Hong Kong and Owen River. Typical of a New Zealand country pub, the walls are lined with historic photos, and in the centre a toasty log burner, overhung with a huge stag head, keeps the pub warm and cosy. Reflecting the owner's origins, the pub also has elements of Chinese style, and serves food that blends kiwi classics with traditional Chinese cuisine, making the Owen River Tavern a unique stop on any South Island tour. Alongside the pub are three motel units and behind the pub a camping ground down by the river.

 1569 Kawatiri-Murchison Highway/SH 6.
 03 523 9273

2. Maruia Falls

On 17 June 1929 at 10.17 am an earthquake measuring 7.8 on the Richter scale struck the northwest of the South Island. Centred on the Lyell Range west of the township of Murchison, the quake killed seventeen people and caused damage as far away as Nelson and Greymouth, much of the destruction coming from slips or the floods from rivers blocked by landslides. Very little evidence of the earthquake remains, but the most dramatic of these transformations to the landscape is the Maruia Falls.

The falls were created in mere seconds by the power of the quake causing a sharp 1-metre drop directly across the Maruia River. The rushing water has since eroded the riverbed further, so the falls are now much higher than in 1929, and today are a popular drop for the more adventurous kayakers.

 On SH 65, 11 km from the junction with SH 6 west of Murchison.

3. Murchison

Once a decaying goldmine town, in recent years Murchison has cleverly reinvented itself as 'Kayak Central'. The nearby rivers – Buller, Matakitaki, Maruia, Matiri and Mangles – offer something for every kayaker from novice to champion. Located in the main street, the New Zealand Kayak School run a range of courses from October to March for beginners through to rodeo experts, including courses on river safety and one just for women. In addition, the school can create a course for individual or group needs and hires out gear and provides accommodation.

If you don't fancy kayaking then Ultimate Descents offers rafting trips from mild to wild (www.rivers.co.nz).

In March, the three-day Buller festival runs rafting and kayaking competitions at all levels of the sport.

There is also good fishing (mainly brown trout, but rainbow trout in the Maruia), hunting, and walking in the area. Murchison is the ideal place from which to access the very rugged bush-clad Upper Buller Gorge. The friendly people at the information centre can help with any queries.

4. Six Mile Hydro Station, Murchison

Commissioned in 1922, Six Mile is one of the first New Zealand hydro power stations and operated right up until 1975 supplying power to the Murchison district. While early power stations such as Six Mile are not so unique, what makes this place special is that most of the infrastructure is still in place. Especially well preserved and protected from the elements is the tiny powerhouse, where the equipment appears in such good working order that it looks as if it would start today with the mere push of a button.

An easy walk from the power station follows the intake pipe up a short hill to the holding pond and beyond that the water race. Still in working order, the water race winds through mature beech forest thick with moss to the intake by a small weir on the Matakitaki River.

Even if you are not an old hydro station aficionado, this easy walk of around one hour will be a very pleasant outing.

 Turn off SH 60 into Fairfax Street (where the museum is) and continue down the Matakitaki Valley for 10 km to the powerhouse.

5. Lyell

If it wasn't for the information boards with photographs showing a flourishing town it would be very difficult to believe this area was once home to thousands of people and the valley alive with feverish activity. Gold was discovered in Lyell Creek in 1862 and, like so many other gold mining settlements, a township mushroomed virtually overnight. By 1873 the busy town of Lyell boasted a school, post office, church, six hotels and even its own newspaper. While other gold towns succumbed to gorse and blackberry, at Lyell the town has not only disappeared but also the bush has returned and today looks virgin and untouched.

On closer inspection faint traces of the past do remain. Here and there in the deep bush stands a crumbling fireplace or the remains of concrete steps. Of special interest is the cemetery where old decaying headstones enclosed by rusting wrought-iron railings are laid out on a hillside looking like a quintessential horror-movie-set graveyard. Further up the creek are the substantial remains of the old stamper battery, rusting and abandoned in the beech forest. Just south of Lyell is the historic Iron Bridge (built 1890), towering over 30 metres above the Buller River on massive stone pylons. If nothing else, Lyell perfectly sums up the old biblical saying, 'Men come and go, but the earth abides'.

> Lyell is north of Inangahua on SH 6.

6. Inangahua Hall

Now doubling as the Inangahua Museum, this simple wooden building is typical of local halls that for so long formed the very centre of life for small communities. Many have been pulled down or substantially altered and what makes this hall unique is that it is largely in original condition. Built in the early 1930s the plain timber building has a varnished wooden interior, a small stage accommodated in a corrugated-iron extension, and a kitchen annex for preparing suppers. Like all such halls, every local event would have taken place here, from meetings and concerts through to dances and weddings.

On 24 May 1968, at 5.24 am, an earthquake measuring 7.1 on the Richter scale hit Inangahua. While only three people died in the quake, damage to the area was compounded by continual strong aftershocks for the next four weeks, fifteen of which registered over 5 on the Richter scale. This small museum has an extensive display of newspaper clippings and photographs of the quake as well as historical information of the surrounding district.

> Inangahua Landing (SH 69).
> September to May. Open daily 10 am to 3 pm except Saturdays.
> Koha/donation.

7. The Oparara Basin, Karamea

Lying just north of Karamea, the access to the Oparara Basin is down 15 km of narrow, winding gravel road, but it is well worth the effort as this area has some of the most stunning limestone landscapes in the country. In addition to these dramatic 35-million-year-old limestone formations, the magnificent virgin bush is prolific with bird life. Cheeky weka are so common you need to keep a good eye on your belongings if you don't want to find them whisked off to a weka nest. Highlights of the basin are the three short walks to the Oparara Arch, Moria Gate, and Box Canyon and Crazy Paving caves.

Oparara Arch: An easy forty-minute walk leads to what is believed to be the largest natural arch in New Zealand. In fact, there are two arches over the Oparara River and huge limestone cliffs enclose both. The main arch is over 200 metres long and has the river flowing through it, while a second gigantic arch towers far above the river and is so huge and yet appears so fragile that it's uncomfortable standing below it.

Moria Gate: Moria Gate is lower and far more delicate compared to the massive Oparara Arch, and is accessible through a small side cave that takes you directly into the arch itself. The rocks within the cave have a dimpled pattern from the action of the water over the years, and if the water is low you can wade upstream for a view of the arch from outside. The walk through beautiful mature beech forest is an easy loop walk that takes around one hour and includes the tranquil Mirror Tarn Lake.

Crazy Paving and Box Canyon Caves: These two caves lie right next to each other and are situated 2 km beyond the Oparara Arch and Moria Gate car park. The 'crazy paving' on the floor of this particular cave comes from the patterns formed by mud that over time has dried and shrunk into geometrical patterns. This cave is also home to New Zealand's only cave spider, and while the elusive creature is not visible, the delicate egg sacs hanging from the roof are plain to see. A little further along and accessed by steps is Box Canyon Cave, a large roomy cave deep in the limestone hill. The short walk to these caves is through beautiful beech forest and a torch is necessary for both. The walk is easy and takes around twenty minutes.

The road into the basin is narrow, winding and unsealed, with stretches where it is difficult to pass so take it easy and take your time. It is not suitable for larger caravans.

📍 From Karamea, drive north for 10 km, then turn right into McCallums Mill Road and follow the unsealed, narrow road for a further 15 km.

8. Charming Creek Walkway

One of the best short walks in the country, this walkway is a great combination of superb natural scenery – such as the Mangatini Falls and the Ngakawau Gorge – and appealing man-made features such as old railway tunnels and a swing bridge.

The private Charming Creek railway was opened in 1914 to bring coal down from the Charming Creek coal mine but was also used to extract timber as well. When the railway closed in 1958, the line was abandoned, and today much of the infrastructure is largely intact. Considerable stretches of the track are still in place; the old bridge foundations still remain as well as the concrete foundations of the 'bins' (an area used for sorting coal). The three tunnels are still useable and are short enough that torches are not needed.

Recent slips and rock falls demonstrate what a daunting task it must have been to both build and maintain this railway line in such steep and rugged country with a very high rainfall. The bush along the way is thick and luxurious and glow-worms can be found in the tunnels and some of the railway cuttings. At the base of the Mangatini Falls is the rare daisy *Celmisia morganii*, found only in the Ngakawau Gorge (most Celmisia are alpine plants). Beyond the falls the track goes through a tunnel to Watson's Mill, a pleasant picnic spot at the confluence of the Ngakawau River and Charming Creek, and the old site of a timber mill. As the walkway follows the railway line, it is for the most part flat; and if you intend to do the whole walk it will take three hours one way.

> The Charming Creek Walkway begins at Tylers Road, Ngakawau, on the southern side of the bridge over the Ngakawau River.

9. Denniston and the Incline

On a bleak plateau high above the sea, only a handful of houses now remain of the once bustling coal-mining village of Denniston, famous for its spectacular incline, and in more recent years for historical novel *The Denniston Rose* by Jenny Patrick, New Zealand's answer to Catherine Cookson.

Opened in 1879 to carry coal from the Rochfort Plateau down to Conn's Creek, the Incline rail system dropped 518 metres in just over 1610 metres. The Incline was a simple arrangement, with the down wagons counterbalancing the up load. Until the road was built in 1900, the Incline was the only way in and out of Denniston, and it carried people, furniture and all manner of goods as well as coal. In 1887 the population of Denniston was 500, and supported three hotels, and eventually peaked at 1500 people in 1911. However, the isolation, improved road transport, and the bleak soil-less landscape slowly led to a decline in the town, and finally the Incline itself closed in August 1967.

At the time it was constructed, locals called it the 'eighth wonder of the world', and today the Institute of Professional Engineers recognises the Incline as one of New Zealand's outstanding engineering feats. Substantial sections of the track, working gear and buildings still remain, and a walking track following the old bridle track weaves its way from Conn's Creek to the top of the Incline. Information panels at the summit feature many historical photos showing the Incline and Denniston in its glory years. The huge brake drum, as well as an original wagon displayed at the actual angle (45 degrees) of the Incline, can be seen in the Coaltown Museum in Westport.

> Denniston is 25 km north of Westport.

10. Westport Municipal Chambers

Dominating the main street of Westport is one of the finest Art Deco buildings in New Zealand. Westport was badly damaged during the Murchison earthquake in 1929 and over the next ten years a number of new buildings in the fashionable Art Deco style were constructed in the town.

A new municipal building and town hall were proposed in 1936 and the council engaged architect Archibald Macdonald to design the buildings. Little is known about Macdonald, but his name is also associated with the Spanish Mission style Midlands Hotel in Wellington (now demolished). Designed in the contemporary Art Moderne Style (a more streamlined offshoot of Art Deco), it is only single storey, but the building – and especially the striking clock tower – stand out in a town of low rise buildings. The building was completed in 1940, but the new town hall behind the municipal chambers was never built. Its striking colour comes from the use Motueka sand in the exterior coating.

Macdonald also designed the Buller County Chambers. This too is in the Art Deco style and in the same street as the Westport Municipal Chambers.

📍 Westport Municipal Chambers: 113 Palmerston Street, Westport.
Buller County Chambers: 161 Palmerston Street, Westport.

11. Buller River at Westport

Beginning as the outlet for Lake Rotoiti, the Buller River passes through some of New Zealand's grandest scenery on its 169-km journey to the sea. Draining a substantial and very wet catchment area on its final stretch to the coast at Westport the river is narrowly confined between two long breakwaters. With a heavy swell running, the river mouth is a place of great drama, especially if a fishing boat or coal barge is navigating the bar. There is easy access out to the end of the breakwater on the north side and the views along the coast are superb – and besides, there's not a lot to do in Westport so this is a great spot to while away a bit of time, especially in the evening with the sun setting over the Tasman Sea. The rare Hector's dolphins are often seen in the area, and if you're lucky to strike stormy weather there's no better place to be.

> From the west end of Palmerston Street, turn right into Gladstone Street and then left into Derby Street, and finally left into Coates Street, which leads to the beach and breakwater.

12. Carters Beach

The only safe swimming beach on the entire West Coast, Carters Beach is a broad north-facing stretch of white sand. In addition to accommodation, there is a golf course and it is very close to the airport. Tauranga Bay, just to the south, is considered a better surfing beach. The car park for the seal colony and the popular Cape Foulwind walk is at the northern end of Tauranga Bay.

> 5 km west of Westport.

13. Mitchell's Gully Gold Mine, Charleston

The real thing is always far more appealing than a replica, and Mitchell's Gully Gold Mine is no tourist mock-up. An actual working mine from 1866 to 1914 and again from 1977 to 1998, the mine today is a maze of old gold workings tucked away among regenerating bush. A trail follows a tramline through short tunnels, past the old workings, and if you bring a torch you can explore some of the mineshafts. There is a water-driven stamper battery, and you can try your hand at panning for gold as well. Glow-worms inhabit the old mines and an evening tour is an option. This isn't a slick tourist trap and the feel is definitely rustic, but what the mine workings lack in sophistication is more than made up by the knowledge of the friendly owner whose family have owned the mine for six generations.

Mitchell's Gully was just one of the many gold mines in the Charleston area, extracting gold washed down from the Alps over thousands of years and mixed in with beach sand. When gold was discovered in August 1866, the area boomed and by October of that year the population had risen to 1200, and by 1869 to almost 20,000. The town supported eighty hotels, three breweries and even a casino, 'Casino De Venice'. Robert Hannah opened his first shoe shop in Charleston (now the Hannah's chain of shoe stores), and when the postmaster was moved from Wellington to Charleston it was considered a promotion. Today just one pub and a handful of houses remain.

 SH 6, 22 km south of Westport.
 Open daily 9 am to 4 pm.
 03 789 6257
 www.mitchellsgullygoldmine.co.nz
$ Entrance fee.

Punakaiki

A stunning combination of sea, beautiful bush and dramatic rock formations, Punakaiki is more than just the Pancake Rocks and Blowhole. There are a number of excellent short walks, good accommodation and cafés, and the road along the coast is spectacular in its own right.

Two special tracks are the Fox River Caves and the Truman Track.

14. Fox River Caves

Attracting visitors since 1908, the caves were discovered by a local farmer looking for stray cattle. The track, an old gold trail, follows the bush-lined northern bank of the Fox River to a limestone cave complete with stalactites and stalagmites. The walk takes two hours return plus whatever time you spend in the caves (allow at least half an hour). You will cross the Fox River several times: you will get your feet wet, the rocks are slippery and the last section before the cave is very greasy. You will need really sturdy footwear with good tread and a torch to explore the caves.

📍 SH 6, 12 km north of Punakaiki.

15. Truman Track

Not to be missed, this short thirty-minute-return track leads through mature forest of matai, rimu and rata to a short coastal strip of flax and then down to a small sandy cove (which is not safe for swimming). There are dramatic views along the coast and at low tide it is possible to explore the sea caves and the rocky shore. Blue penguins nest here from August to February and the best times to see them are around dawn and dusk.

📍 SH 6, 2 km north of Pancake Rocks.

Reefton

16. Blacks Point Museum and Stamper Battery

Blacks Point, just east of Reefton, was once a flourishing gold-mining town and home to large numbers of immigrant miners from Cornwall. Today the old Wellesley Methodist Church (built in 1876) has been turned into a wonderful local museum. No fancy lighting or designer displays here, the Blacks Point Museum is just packed with fascinating historical items relating to gold mining and the hardy people who once lived here. Bearded patriarchs and stoic women gaze out of old photos high on the wall, and a special display is given over to Blacks Point's greatest son, Olympic gold medal winner, runner Jack Lovelock.

The highlight of this gold-mining museum is the working stamper. The water-driven machine crushed the quartz in order to extract the gold and is unique in that so few working stampers have survived. Stampers often worked 24 hours a day, and in some areas where a number of stampers were operating the noise was constant and overwhelming. The sound was relieved at midnight on Saturday through to midnight on Sunday, as Sunday was the only day on which they didn't operate. Today the stamper only works Wednesday and Sunday afternoons.

- Franklin Street, Blacks Point (SH 7).
- Open Labour Weekend to Easter Wednesday, Thursday, Friday and Sunday 9 am to 12 noon and 1 pm to 4 pm; Saturday 1 pm to 4 pm.

17. Reefton School of Mines

Opened in 1886 and not closed until 1970, the School of Mines has altered little from the nineteenth century. Partially constructed of timber and partly corrugated iron, the school still retains original mining equipment and has a great mineral collection, sourced both locally and from around the world and spaciously laid out in wonderful old glass cases. Adjoining the building is a single classroom that has an extensive collection of old technical books on every aspect of mining. Directly to the right of the School of Mines is the old State Coal Offices and behind them the State Coal work shops.

- Shiel Street, Reefton.
  Entry by arrangement with the Reefton Information Centre.
- www.reefton.co.nz
- Koha/donation.

18. The Future Dough Company, Reefton

Housed in two of Reefton's oldest buildings dating back to 1873-74, these premises have always had an association with food. Now combined into a single premises, originally there were two shops – one a tearoom and the other a cake shop. Over 145 years later The Future Dough Company is still serving refreshments to locals and visitors alike.

All the food is made from scratch including the bread, with a focus on fresh ingredients and abhorrence of premixes. It is almost impossible to pick a standout but the traditional Scottish shortbread has to be near the top.

  31 Broadway, Reefton.
  Open seven days.
  03 732 8497
  www.thefuturedoughco.co.nz

19. Quartzopolis, Town of Light

Rich veins of gold in quartz reefs were first discovered at Blacks Point in 1870 with the first gold extracted in 1872, with further discoveries made later in the 1870s. With gold the town boomed and was affectionately known as Quartzopolis. In keeping with its innovative boomtown image, in 1887 the Reefton Electrical Transmission of Power and Lighting Company Ltd was formed to build a power station and provide the town with electricity.

This wasn't New Zealand's first hydroelectric plant – the first had been built two years earlier at Bullendale in Central Otago to supply electricity to a stamper battery. However, the Reefton enterprise was much more ambitious and right from the beginning it was planned to supply electricity to not only local homes, hotels and businesses, but also remarkably for street lighting. After trials at the powerhouse on 1 August 1888, the town was lit by electricity on 4 August – the first town to have electricity, not

Rai Valley Cottage, Rai Valley. (Marlborough # 8)

Whites Bay, Marlborough Region. (Marlborough #9)

Dominion Salt Works, Lake Grassmere. (Marlborough #17)

Wither Hills Winery, Marlborough Region. (Marlborough #18)

Brancott Estate, Marlborough Vineyards. (Marlborough #18)

Motueka salt water baths, Motueka. (Nelson #10)

Left: St Paul's Lutheran Church, Upper Moutere. (Nelson #12)

Mapua Wharf, Mapua. (Nelson #13)

Feeding eels at Jester House Café, Tasman. (Nelson #14)

Broadgreen House (Nelson #15)

Tophouse Hotel, Nelson Lakes. (Nelson #26)

The Punakaiki Coast, Westland. (Buller 14/15)

Truman Track, Punakaiki. (Buller #15)

Bearded Mining Company, Reefton. (Buller #20)

The Blackball Salami Company, Blackball. (Westland #5)
Photo credit Blackball Salami Company

Brunner Mine Industrial Site, Greymouth. (Westland #6)

West Coast Washing Lines. (Westland #11)

The Otira Hotel, Otira Township. (Westland #14)

Left: Hokitika Sock World, Hokitika. (Westland #16)

Driftwood beach sculptures, Hokitika. (Westland #18)

Ian Phillips, IaNZart, Hokitika.
(Westland #21)

The Okarito Lagoon, Okarito.
(Westland #27)

The Shhhh Shed, South Westland (Westland #28)

Hunt Beach, Westland. (Westland #32)

Whitebait stands on the West Coast. (Westland #33)

Above: The Cray Pot, Jackson Bay. (Westland #36)

Left: The Saw in the Log. Haast Pass road from Haast to Wanaka. (Westland #37)

Fyffe House, Kaikoura. (Kaikoura and Canterbury #2)

Broadfield Garden, Rolleston.
(Kaikoura and Canterbury #22)

Salmon fishing in the Rakaia.
(Kaikoura and Canterbury #24)

Trotts Garden, Ashburton. (Kaikoura and Canterbury #25)

Left: The Arts Centre Great Hall, Christchurch.
(Christchurch City and the Banks Peninsula #1

Velocity Karts Blokarts, Christchurch. (Christchurch City and the Banks Peninsula #9)

The Whare, Halswell Quarry Gardens. (Christchurch City and the Banks Peninsula #18)

only in New Zealand, but in the southern hemisphere. Reefton was also was among the very few places in the world to have a public supply of electricity and street lighting.

A report in the *Inangahua Herald* on 6 August was glowing: 'The night was fortunately very favourable for the display, and an immense crowd of people gathered in the street to witness the exhibition, and when, shortly before 8 pm, the powerful light of the arc-lamp burst forth, like a flash of a mighty meteor, a murmur of admiration rose from the spectators ... the illumination reached far up the mountains round the town and gave a very sepulchral appearance to the hill-sides, the trees and stumps standing out in the strange pallid light, like so many tombstones. But if the arc-light was an attraction outside, the interior of the Oddfellow's Hall was infinitely more so. Rows of lamps were suspended down the building, encased in a variety of fantastically shaped shades of different colours, and the whole scene was one of striking splendour. It was indeed a "Hall of dazzling light".'

Several of the original lights in the main street still survive as does the exterior light over the entrance to the Oddfellow's Hall (Bridge Street), still glowing more than 130 years later.

Currently underway is a huge project to rebuild the old power station including all the water races, which will open in stages.

20. Bearded Mining Company

Not so long ago a service group in Reefton built a replica of an 1860s miner's hut in Broadway, the town's main street. Constructed of kaiwaka, or mountain cedar, several local men decided that this was a much more interesting place to spend their day than sitting at home, and duly set up camp and added their own touches to the wooden hut. Today the members of the 'Bearded Mining Company' can be found every day at the hut dressed as old-time miners, playing old songs on the guitar and accordion, or brewing a cup of tea, and ever ready for a chat with passers-by about life on the old goldfields. With all sorts of old equipment they have built an eccentric collection of contraptions, ranging from a stove and blacksmith's forge through to innovative 'central heating'. So, if you're passing through Reefton, stop in and sit a while and maybe there will be a cup of tea going or a song to be sung.

 Broadway, Reefton – you won't be able to miss these guys; and while there is no charge, a donation is appreciated.

21. Reefton Distilling Company

Over 130 years ago the cry in Reefton was, 'Let there be light'. Today the call is, 'Let there be gin'. No doubt local eyebrows were raised when Pasty Bass, originally from Reefton, decided to move back to the town to set up a distillery producing gin, rum and whiskey. No one, including Pasty, would have foreseen the success of her Reefton Distilling Company. Determination, great planning and a superb recipe has seen Little Biddy Gin storm the taste buds of New Zealand's fussiest gin drinkers.

Water is the key ingredient to good gin and Reefton has an excellent supply of both river and spring water. The heart of this gin is the botanical ingredients, most of which are supplied locally including blueberries and tayberries, and limes from nearby Westport. However, it is the New Zealand bush that lifts this gin above the ordinary. On distilling day, two older bushmen get up early and go foraging in the local bush, selecting only the tastiest and freshest shoots and leaves from a range of plants. Producing small quantities of gin, each batch is subtly different, aromatic and full of flavour.

Little Biddy Gin takes its name from an Irish woman miner, a little of over four feet tall, tough and strong and famous for living with two men, neither of whom she was married to. Originally from Lyell, Little Biddy moved to Reefton in her later years where she become known as Old Biddy, and she died in Reefton in 1899, aged eighty-six.

Reefton Distilling Company plans to produce rum and whiskey, but for now, all they can do is try and keep up with the demand for their distinctive gin.

10 Smith Street, Reefton.
 Open 7 days 10 am to 4 pm, Wed 12 pm to 4 pm.
 03 732 7083
 www.reeftondistillingco.com

22. Waiuta

Though very little remains, Waiuta has a special place in the hearts of West Coasters. The site of the Coast's last great gold rush in 1905, it was also the richest and most productive of the area's gold mines, with around half of all the gold mined on the West Coast coming from this one mine. In 1939 the mine had a workforce of 250 and the town a population of over 600, but in 1951 the shaft suddenly collapsed and as it wasn't economical to reopen the shaft, and the mine closed down. Overnight the town was abandoned and within three months only twenty people remained. By 1952 the town virtually disappeared as houses, buildings and anything else worthwhile was scavenged to be used elsewhere. Today only six original buildings remain, though the rugby field complete with goalposts still survives intact.

It is a rather peculiar place to visit, with the odd building still surviving here and there and the remains of others poking out from the scrub and blackberry. Excellent information boards with photos and maps bring the old township alive and there is also a good camping area. The road to Waiuta is only partly sealed and is narrow and winding in places, but the compensation is the lovely beech forest along part of the way.

 Take SH 7 north towards Reefton, and 3 km north of Ikamatua, turn right to Waiuta and follow this road for 17 km (only partly sealed).

WESTLAND

1. Nelson Creek
2. Lake Brunner
3. Barrytown Knifemaking
4. Formerly The Blackball Hilton Hotel
5. Blackball Salami Company
6. Brunner Mine Industrial Site
7. Point Elizabeth Walkway
8. On Yer Bike
9. Grey River Bar and Breakwaters
10. High Street Barber Shop
11. West Coast Washing Lines
12. Kumara Races
13. Theatre Royal Hotel
14. Otira Gorge and Township
15. Hokitika Glow-worm Dell
16. Hokitika Sock World
17. Bonz 'n' Stonz
18. Driftwood Beach Sculptures Hokitika
19. Fossicking for Pounamu/Greenstone
20. Luminaries Walk
21. IaNZart
22. Lake Kaniere
23. Woodstock /Royal Mail Hotel
24. Lake Mahinapua
25. Jones Creek, Ross
26. Guy Menzies Park, Harihari
27. Okarito
28. Shhhh Shed
29. Franz Josef Glacier Hot Pools
30. Gillespies Beach
31. Munro Beach
32. Hunt Beach
33. Whitebait on the West Coast
34. West Coast Sandflies
35. Hapuka Estuary
36. Jackson Bay
37. Haast Pass Road from Haast to Wanaka

1. Nelson Creek

Gold fever swept this area east of Greymouth in 1865 and within days 1200 prospectors descended on the area above the small Nelson Creek stream. The gold was extracted by sluicing and the whole hillside became a maze of channels with all the vegetation stripped bare. Later in the nineteenth century up to eight gold dredges operated along the creek and had considerably more luck extracting gold than the early miners. Finds, however, were meagre and by 1901 only thirty-six people lived in the tiny settlement and although to some extent timber replaced gold, gradually both the dredges and the timber mills were shut down.

Today visitors are attracted by several easy DOC walkways through the old workings now covered by thick bush and the small tunnel and the swing bridge over Nelson Creek will appeal to young and old alike.

From SH 7 north of Greymouth turn off at Ngahere – Nelson Creek is 7 km from the turnoff.

2. Lake Brunner

Inland from Greymouth, this large tree-fringed lake is popular for boating, fishing (brown trout) and swimming and has a number of attractive short walks. From Moana (the Maori name for the lake), on the northern side of the lake, it is possible to hire boats and canoes. The TranzAlpine stops here, and a few hours at Lake Brunner on a good day has a good deal more appeal than Greymouth, the terminal of the TranzAlpine. Two attractive walks are at Iveagh Bay and The Rakaitane Walk.

Iveagh Bay, 10 km south of Moana has majestic kahikatea forest growing right down to the water's edge. If time is an issue, there is a pleasant walk of less than half an hour which involves taking the main Ara O Te Iringa track for a little way, then turn down to the lake and return along the shore. A longer walk (three hours return) leads to a lookout point partway up Mt Te Kinga, while a return trip to the summit (1204 m), with magnificent views over Lake Brunner, the Arnold River Valley and the mountains will take eight hours return.

At Moana, the thirty minute Rakaitane Walk starts at the car park at the end of Ahau Street where the track crosses over the Arnold River via a substantial swingbridge and leads through mixed podocarp forest with great views of the mountains across the lake.

Lake Brunner is accessible via Lake Brunner Road and the Arnold Valley Road which run between Jacksons on SH 73 and Stillwater on SH 7.

3. Barrytown Knifemaking

With no previous experience, you can turn a piece of metal into a professionally made knife in just one day. From forging through to grinding and polishing, Steven Martin's expert guidance takes absolute beginners through the process of making a knife to your own design. In addition to making a knife, there is the opportunity to learn axe throwing, gold panning and, at the end of the day, taste Steven's very special brew, 'White Lightning'. Since 2005 Steve has used 8 km of steel and nursed novices through the process of making 25,000 knives. It is essential to book ahead.

SH 6, Barrytown, 1 km south of the All Nations Hotel.

0800 256433

www.barrytownknifemaking.com

4. Formerly The Blackball Hilton Hotel

Blackball is one of those unique places in New Zealand where fact has blended with fiction, but there is no doubt that the township has had a special role to play in New Zealand's industrial relations history, and this hotel has been at the heart of it all. The town itself evolved around coal mining and rocketed to fame in 1908 when miners struck for three months to extend 'crib time' (lunch) from fifteen to thirty minutes. The miners were taken to court and, as they were breaking the law, fined for their actions — though in a supreme instance of irony the judge hearing the case adjourned for a lunch break of eighty minutes.

It was from the actions of this strike that New Zealand's Labour Party arose, and it is said that the political party was actually formed in the hotel. Without a doubt, the town was a stronghold of militant unionism, and in 1925 the New Zealand Communist Party moved its headquarters from Wellington to Blackball. Today the town is rather run-down, with dilapidated houses huddling amongst the scrub, but the famous Blackball Salami Company and the 'Formerly The Blackball Hilton Hotel' make this detour worthwhile.

Built in 1910 as 'The Dominion', the hotel's current name has a story all of its own. In the late seventies its owners changed the name to 'The Blackball Hilton' — a rather tongue-in-cheek name but with strong local connections as the main street is called Hilton after one of the early mine managers. However, after fierce objection and threat of legal action in 1992 by a well-known hotel chain, the name was altered by adding 'Formerly' to the title. Today the large two-storey wooden hotel is a great place to visit and offers simple accommodation, food and good company. Crammed with memorabilia, old photos and newspaper clippings, the pub exudes old-world charm and offers old-fashioned good hospitality.

  26 Hart Street, Blackball.
  03 732 4705
  www.blackballhilton.co.nz

5. Blackball Salami Company

Equally famous in this small town is the Blackball Salami Company. Initially established just outside of town in 1992, the original premises burnt down in 1999 but was quickly rebuilt in a brand-new building in the main street. Right from the beginning the emphasis was, and still is, on quality.

Their famous salamis are made from a variation of beef & pork and venison & pork. Using very lean meat, the excess fat, silverskin & gristle are trimmed off before the meat is minced, to which special spices are added. Unlike many commercial salamis, these salamis are air dried in an aging room. Processed into the familiar log shape, the salami is then smoked over manuka – an oily and aromatic wood that imparts a delicate flavour all of its own. Finally the salamis are hung until they reach the recommended weight. The result is a wonderfully rich salami, full of taste and low in fat.

While most of the salamis are lean, making them a very healthy option, the Italian has pork fat added (which is how these salamis are traditionally made). In addition to salami, the company also makes excellent sausages, including a great black pudding, all made from top quality lean meat. All their products are gluten free except for the black and white pudding.

11 Hilton Street, Blackball.
03 732 4111
www.blackballsalami.co.nz

6. Brunner Mine Industrial Site

Today the Grey River swifts runs through the picturesque Brunner Gorge just north of Dobson, yet 150 years ago this was a scene of feverish activity at one of New Zealand's earliest and most important industrial sites, and the site of the Brunner Mine disaster.

Coal was discovered in the area in the 1840s by Thomas Brunner, but it wasn't until 1864 that the first mining began in the area, eventually leading to eight mines working in the immediate area. In 1896 a deadly methane gas explosion deep underground in the Brunner Mine killed sixty-five miners in what is still New Zealand's worst mine disaster. It was uncertain if most of the miners died in the explosion itself or by suffocation afterwards. Miners came from all over the West Coast to assist in the rescue and many of these were overcome by the methane gas and had to be carried unconscious from the mine. Particularly tragic were the deaths of the Roberts family, where John and his three sons all lost their lives. A memorial with the names of the dead stands on the north side of the river.

The mines eventually closed in 1942 and the Brunner walk (fifty minutes) leads through the substantial remains on both sides of the river, linked by the suspension bridge built in 1876 and including the impressive Tyneside Chimney.

10 km from Greymouth via either SH 7 or the Taylorville Blackball Road.

7. Point Elizabeth Walkway

Greymouth isn't exactly New Zealand's most attractive town, but just to the north the Point Elizabeth Walkway is a real treat. The track is part of an old gold-mining trail as, originally, wandering gold miners used the beach as a highway to travel north and south along the coast. However, the high cliffs of Point Elizabeth were a major obstacle in the coastal journey and in 1865 this track was constructed to make access much easier. Following the coastline, the track is never far from the roar of the sea just below, and at the point itself a vantage point has views both north and south along this wild coast.

For the most part, the native flora has regenerated from early clearances and today dense groves of kiekie and nikau palm give the track the feel of a tropical jungle. Nikau at Point Elizabeth is at its most southerly growing limit on the West Coast (a clump of nikau on the Banks Peninsula is the only example further south). Apart from a modest uphill section at the beginning, the track is fairly level all the way and takes around three hours one way at a modest pace or two hours return to the lookout.

 From Greymouth, take the road north to Westport over the Grey River Bridge. Immediately over the bridge, turn left and follow the road along the coast 6 km to the very end.

8. On Yer Bike

Do you like mud and plenty of it? The West Coast is famous for its rain, and with rain comes mud. So if you are a messy child at heart, then 'On Yer Bike' is just perfect, rightfully claiming to be 'New Zealand's muddiest off-road adventure'. The tracks are a mixture of mud, water, narrow bush trails and puddles the size of small lakes. With a high water table, even in the driest weather there will still be mud. Protective clothing is available, but dig out some old gear, as it is guaranteed you will get very dirty and wet!

Here you can hire a range of quad bikes for adults and kids, along with buggies that accommodate singles, doubles and four people. A further option is a ride on the amazing 4x4 Hagglund which takes up to fifteen people.

 Coal Creek on SH 6, 5 km north of Greymouth.
 Open daily 8.30 am to 5 pm.
 03 762 7438
 www.onyerbike.co.nz

9. Grey River Bar and Breakwaters

One of the world's most difficult ports, the Grey River mouth is exposed to sudden floods, a constantly shifting sandbar and ocean swells generated by thousands of kilometres of exposed Southern Ocean weather. Two breakwaters, one each side of the river, were constructed to harness the flow of the river to scour the channel, and today the southern breakwater is a great spot to watch fishing boats navigate the wild waters of the bar as they enter the river port. At the beginning of the breakwater is a WWII pill box as part of the town's defence system. The History House, Greymouth's museum, has a video presentation of boats crossing the dramatic Grey River bar which is particularly popular (the museum is currently closed owing to seismic concerns).

 At the end of Packers Quay, Blaketown, Greymouth.

10. High Street Barber Shop

Proudly proclaiming its establishment in 1952, this small barbershop is hard to miss on the main road just south of the central shopping area. The barbershop has only had three owners since Claude Fleury originally opened the business which he later sold to his apprentice Murray Glen. When Murray retired the business was taken over by Yvonne Thompson who still runs the business today. Many of Murray's male customers had never had their hair cut by a woman, but Yvonne was local so the men quickly learnt to adjust. Traditional in the best possible way, the High Street Barber Shop flourishes on a solid base of very loyal and mainly male customers.

This is not the only barber in town. Greymouth is also famous for a wind that whistles down the Grey River valley in winter. Icy cold, the wind is known as The Barber as it cuts into skin like a razor.

There is no need to make an appointment so if you are in Greymouth and your hair is getting out of control, come on in for a friendly welcome and a sharp haircut at this Greymouth institution.

📍 112 High Street, Greymouth.

11. West Coast Washing Lines

New Zealand has very little in the way of regional architecture, with the exception of the half brick, half stucco houses common in the southern part of the South Island. However, here on the West Coast there seems to be a peculiarly local version of the washing line. The line itself is simple – two posts are set a small distance apart and attached to the top of each is a movable arm, with two wires strung from the end. This means the line can be lowered on one side to make pegging out the washing easy, and then lifted to clear the ground and catch the breeze. Once you notice these lines, you can't help seeing them everywhere behind older homes on the West Coast, but not elsewhere in New Zealand. It is possible that these washing lines were once common throughout the country and have only survived into the twenty-first century here on the Coast.

12. Kumara Races

One of New Zealand's most popular country race meetings, the festive Kumara Races, attract around 15,000 people to this normally quiet West Coast town. Races were first held at Kumara in December 1887 but moved to a January meeting in the 1940s. The major race, the Kumara Golden Nugget, still has as its winning prize actual gold nuggets.

Though now upgraded, in the past the track was notorious in that the back straight was obscured by tall manuka growing inside the track, and punters had to wait for the horses to emerge before they could tell whose nag was leading.

To compliment the races, the day also features live bands, 'fashion in the field' and food stalls which include local favourites such as whitebait fritters and venison patties.

www.kumarawestcoast.org

13. Theatre Royal Hotel

Gold was discovered here in 1876 and it was one of New Zealand's last gold rushes. Catering for the thousands of miners pouring into the area, Annie and Otto Anderson (she was from Germany and he was from Scandinavia) set up the Theatre Royal Hotel at the end of 1876. Flush with gold, their customers wanted more than just a bed and food. They wanted entertainment and women and that's exactly what the Andersons provided. International acts travelling the goldfields of the world performed at the hotel, along with local personalities including local Member of Parliament Richard Seddon who sang in the hotel's purpose-built theatre. Dancing girls who worked through the night (the law stated that they should not work later than 6 am) danced with the miners for a fee and, of course, also provided more personal services.

Like all gold rush towns, the good times in Kumara came to an end and gradually the town's forty hotels closed down. When Mark and Kerri Fitzgibbon bought the old hotel in 2010 it was abandoned and close to ruin. A short time later reborn and renovated, the Theatre Royal went on win the HANZ award for Best Country Hotel two years in row, in 2014 and 2015.

The hotel reflects all the elegance of the Victoria era yet is contemporary and comfortable. Today Kumara is no longer a town to rush through and whether it is good coffee, high tea or something more substantial, the Theatre Royal is an essential stop on any visit to the West Coast.

 81 Seddon Street, Kumara.
 03 736 9277
 theatreroyalhotel.co.nz

14. Otira Gorge and Township

Originally a Maori trail through the mountains, the steep descent through the Otira Gorge below Arthur's Pass has been a great feat of road engineering. Work began in April 1865, but the road was not opened until 1886. At one stage during the construction, six men drowned in one week. The road continues to provide a challenge, especially around Candy's Bend and Starvation Point, where even now the road is covered by an open tunnel to protect it from water and loose rock in the very unstable terrain. On the 13-km stretch between Arthur's Pass and Otira township alone, there are eleven bridges. The Otira Viaduct, over 440 m long and opened in 1999, bypasses the worst of the road, and there is an excellent lookout point over the viaduct at Death's Corner, part of the old road.

Underground, the railway faced an equally big challenge. While the railway line didn't reach Otira until 1900, work had begun as early as 1887 and at one point 600 workers and their families lived at Otira. Begun in 1908, the tunnel wasn't opened until 1923, and at 8.55 km was, at the time, the longest railway tunnel outside of Europe.

At the foot of the gorge, Otira township became an important rail centre, both during the tunnel construction and later as a service centre. Gradually the town went into decline until in the 1990s just a few rundown houses, a shabby pub and a handful of large railway sheds remained.

Aucklanders Chris and Bill Hennah bought the lease of the land at Otira in 1998 for $80,000 which included seventeen houses, the community hall, fire station, the hotel and local swimming pool, and a little later they purchased the school. The price is a good indication of the state of the buildings and while the settlement had a certain charm, it was dilapidated and run down.

In 2010 most of the town including the rundown hotel was again up for sale and finally purchased in 2014 by Lester Rountree, a retired deer farmer who began an outstanding transformation of the old hotel which he renamed the Otira Stagecoach Hotel.

Still a work in progress, the hotel has been largely restored and repainted. Lester, with a great fondness for everything old, has turned the hotel into an Aladdin's cave with every wall, shelf and floor space packed with period furniture, antiques, collectables and the just plain quirky. Outside are old horse drawn vehicles and, yes, a stage coach. Sure, it's a little chaotic, but always intriguing and unexpected and today the Otira Hotel is a good place to break your journey. But beware: it will be much more than a five-minute stop.

 12 km north of Arthurs Pass on SH 73.

Hokitika

15. Hokitika Glow-worm Dell

Glow worms are common in New Zealand and favour any cool, damp shady spot, but it is less common to see them in large numbers. On the northern edge of Hokitika is a small abandoned quarry shaded by large trees. Densely covered in mosses and ferns, the old rock walls drip with water and create the perfect environment for a host of glow worms. Come here at night and you are in for a treat. However, for the best effect keep torchlight to a minimum and be as quiet as possible, as glow worms are sensitive to noise and will 'turn off' their glowing bottoms. The Dell is just a two minute walk from the road or a twenty minute walk from the town, and is free.

 On SH 6, 1.5 km north of the town centre.

16. Hokitika Sock World

There is no two ways about it, you are guaranteed never to find another place like this. It is a safe bet that very few people have given socks much thought, but everyone wears them, and millions are produced each year to protect our delicate feet.

Established in 2004 by local personality Jacqui Grant, Sock World houses an extraordinary collection of antique sock knitting machines, the oldest dating back to 1803. Jacqui caught the 'sock bug' when given three old machines by an elderly couple from Timaru who'd had them for many years. Once bitten more and more machines joined the collection before Jacqui finally opened Sock World to the public.

Along with the collection, there is every conceivable type of sock available for sale alongside yarns for those who like to hand knit, and a range of possum/merino blend knitwear.

　93 Revell Street.
　03 755 7251
　www.autoknitter.com

17. Bonz 'n' Stonz

Bonz 'n' Stonz offers visitors the unique experience of creating their own pounamu creation (bone and paua options also available). After choosing a piece of pounamu, a master carver guides you through choosing a design and then working the stone into your own taonga, or treasure. No experience is necessary other than a good idea and, depending on size and complexity, the process can take from a few hours to a whole day. Also available are raw stone and personal ornaments.

　16 Hamilton Street.
　03 755 6504
　www.bonz-n-stonz.co.nz

18. Driftwood Beach Sculptures Hokitika

The beachfront at Hokitika is as wild as any stretch on the West Coast and, like most west coast beaches, is littered with all size and manner of driftwood. In typical inventive Hokitika style, the town has turned this into an advantage with the creation of unique beach sculptures using materials found on the beach. Visitors can just try their hand at creating something new, but it is bad form to pull down someone else's structure. Since 2002 the town has hosted the Hokitika Driftwood and Sand Sculpture Festival where creative types build sculptures that range from fantastical through to amusing and stylish.

19. Fossicking for Pounamu/Greenstone

In Maori legend there were originally two stones: Poutini (greenstone), belonging to Ngahue, and Whaiapu (obsidian), which belonged to Hine-tua-hoanga. Jealous of Ngahue's stone, Hine-tua-hoanga drove Ngahue out of Hawaiki to Aotearoa on the waka *Tahirirangi*, where Ngahue hid Poutini near Arahura. Still hidden under the protection of a taniwha, also named Poutini, occasionally small pieces of the stone break off and are washed down the river.

The importance of pounamu within Maori culture cannot be over-estimated; the very name of the South Island, Te Wai Pounamu, directly relates to this stone. Only found on the West Coast, pounamu in pre-European times was highly valued for both ornamentation and for weapons, and in particular, patu, or handheld clubs as pounamu is very hard and keeps a good edge. Pounamu patu were so valuable that the usually had individual names. Traditionally pounamu is given as a gift and is not acquired for oneself.

The Arahura River near Hokitika is the primary source of New Zealand pounamu and there are several outlets in the town where pounamu is sold and visitors can see it being carved into a variety of objects. However, be aware that much of the greenstone sold in this country is from Canada and China, and if you are keen to purchase pounamu, specifically ask if the stone came from New Zealand. Even 'New Zealand made' can disguise the fact that the stone came from elsewhere and was only carved in New Zealand.

There are four main types of pounamu, each with different names and properties: inganga (pearly, grey-green colour, often translucent);

kahurangi (very rare, translucent, light green and flawless); kakotea (dark green, streaky with black spots); and kawakawa (dark green).

In 1997 ownership of pounamu was handed back to Ngai Tahu, but anyone is still able to fossick for pounamu which can be found on beaches between Greymouth and Milford Sound. You may keep only as much as you can physical carry. Pounamu is more readily found after stormy weather and near river mouths and the distinctive green of pounamu is more visible when the stone is wet. Beware of serpentine, a stone similar in colour to pounamu, but which easily shatters when dropped.

20. Luminaries Walk

Published in 2013, Eleanor Catton's second book *The Luminaries* won the 2013 Man Booker prize. At twenty-eight, Catton was the youngest person to win the prize and at 832 pages, it was also the longest book to win the award.

Set in Hokitika 1866 during the peak of the gold rush, the main character Walter Moody arrives in the town to make his fortune but is instead caught up in a web of mystery involving several unsolved crimes. Not a fast-paced story, the book is infused with detailed description of Hokitika during that period. The BBC have produced a six-episode series based on the book.

After much demand from the book's many fans, the information centre and library now has a map of the town marked with locations from the book.

21. IaNZart

It started modestly enough with a wedding present, but today Ian Phillips has a flourishing business in Hokitika producing a huge range of handmade items from giant crayfish down to personal jewellery. Located on corner in the old Bank of New South Wales building (1905), wide windows open to the street, enabling visitors to watch Ian work on one his creations. (Ian still has old photos and the plans for the building).

Best known for his copper creations of birds, fish, plants and insects, Ian 'paints with a blow torch', the extraordinary colours coming from varying the heat and the texture. Now focusing on smaller jewellery items, Ian's unique approach ensures that the gallery has some of most inventive and individual creations in New Zealand.

📍 32 Revell Street, Hokitika.
🕐 Open 9 am to 5 pm but hours may vary.
📞 03 755 6336

22. Lake Kaniere

Much smaller than Lake Brunner and 195 m deep, Kaniere is 18 km inland from Hokitika and lies between Mt Graham (828 m) and Tuhua (1124 m), With an almost completely bush-fringed shoreline, the lake is popular for boating and canoeing and the nearby rivers and streams offer excellent fishing prospects for trout. There is a short fifteen-minute walk through kahikatea forest from the Sunny Bight picnic area, and for those looking for a longer stretch, the Lake Kaniere Walkway is a three-to-four-hour one-way walk from the same picnic area, following the western lake edge through lush native bush to Lawyers Delight Beach. The Dorothy Falls are a two-minute walk from the road on the eastern side of the lake.

📍 From Hokitika turn off SH 6 into Stafford Street and then into Lake Kaniere Road – continue on for 18 km.

23. Woodstock /Royal Mail Hotel

In 1864 gold was discovered near the Taramakau River north of Hokitika and quickly became one of New Zealand's largest gold rushes. By 1866 Hokitika was New Zealand's largest town with 25,000 people and at one point over eighty hotels jostled side by side in Hokitika's Revel Street, though many of these were little more than canvas tents with a wooden façade.

Three years later gold fever had peaked and gradually the people moved away and the hotels closed down. The remaining hotels in Hokitika are largely charmless with little attention paid to their unique history, but just outside the town, on the other side of the Hokitika River is a little gem.

When the bridge across the Hokitika River opened in March 1869, Harry Gaylor built a hotel at Woodstock to service the passing trade and modestly called it Gaylor's Hotel. Further down the hill from today's hotel, the pub was then only the size of the current public bar. When the road was extended south to Ross it was decided to move the hotel 200 yards to the new road and the entire pub was hauled uphill by cart horses using beer barrels as rollers. The new location also meant a new name and as the hotel now serviced the mail coaches travelling south to Ross, The Royal Mail Hotel was deemed appropriate.

Damaged by fire but never burnt down, the hotel has had a long and colourful history and, as the only place in town with cool cellars, frequently doubled as the local morgue. When the railway line was extended south in 1909, the mail service by horse drawn coach ended but the single lane bridge now handled both road and rail traffic ensuring the pubs survival. In the 1970s when new road and rail bridges were built at Hokitika, Woodstock became and remains a quiet backwater. Much later the hotel name changed yet again with the addition of the locality 'Woodstock', the only survivor in a township that once boasted twelve hotels.

There is nothing shabby about the Woodstock Hotel today. Typical of a goldfields hotel, the high façade shields a low wooden building opening out to the northwest on a wide wooden veranda with amazing views over river, farms, bush and mountains. Liberal use of polished wood for both fittings and furniture gives the pub a warm glow, while the log burner provides real warmth on chilly winter nights. Photos of old lost pubs, most now barely a memory line the walls and old bottles along with contemporary photographs and a lively mural behind the stage all add to the atmosphere.

The Woodstock hosts regular live music events and every Sunday the Hokitika Music Club meets at the hotel for a jam session that is open to locals and visitors, groups or individuals.

If you need more reason to visit the hotel, the pub is the home of the Woodstock Brewing Company producing both beer and cider that is only available at the pub.

📍 250 Woodstock-Rimu Road, Woodstock, Hokitika.
📞 03 755 8909
🌐 www.woodstockhotel.net

24. Lake Mahinapua

This shallow lake just 500 m from the sea was once a lagoon, but gradually the encircling dunes turned the lagoon into a freshwater lake. As early as 1907 the land around the lake was set aside as a reserve and today draws visitors attracted by the easy bush walks. The placid waters are particularly appealing to those wanting a gentle kayaking experience on a pretty bush-enclosed waterway. While most launch from the main picnic area, another option is to kayak up the Mahinapua Creek which enters the Hokitika River just below the bridge south of the town. The creek is slow moving, lined with native trees and flax, and passes under the historic Mahinapua Creek rail bridge built in 1905 and closed in 1980.

From the main picnic area there are several short flat bush walks and in the same area are the remains of the Lake Mahinapua steamer, built in Hokitika in 1883 to provide transport for those travelling between Hokitika and Ross. The longer Lake Mahinapua Walkway (two hours one way) begins opposite the famous Mahinapua pub just north of the picnic area.

West Coast Scenic Waterways offers both a cruise on the lake on their small boat the Eco Adventurer and freedom kayaking **(www.westcoastscenicwaterways.co.nz)**.

📍 On SH 6, 11 km south of Hokitika.

25. Jones Creek, Ross

Forget about Lotto and Big Wednesday, Jones Creek at Ross is the place to strike it rich! Gold was discovered at Ross in 1864, and the largest gold nugget ever found in New Zealand was discovered in Jones Creek in 1909. Named the 'Honourable Roddy' after the then Minister of Mines The Honourable Roderick McKenzie, the nugget weighed a hefty three kilograms. Good luck has it that this creek is now open to public gold panning, and what you find you can keep. If you don't have your own gold pan then they are available for hire from the friendly visitor's centre.

Panning for gold is best just after heavy rain, so if you strike the coast on a very wet day don't stay inside grizzling about the rain, head off to Jones Creek and find a nugget to beat the Honourable Roddy. Gold continues to be extracted at Ross, so your chances are still good. And if you have no luck you can always drown your sorrows like every other miner over the last one and a half centuries, just down the road in the 150-year-old Empire Hotel.

Jones Creek is right behind the Ross Goldfields and Information Centre. While you can drive past the centre, the road is very narrow, parking is limited and turning is extremely difficult.

26. Guy Menzies Park, Harihari

Crash landing upside down in a swamp doesn't sound that much of an adventure but that was the fate of the dashing Guy Menzies, the first person to fly solo across the Tasman Sea.

At 1 am on 7 January 1931, 21-year-old Menzies left Sydney in his biplane to cross the Tasman Sea with every intention of landing at Blenheim. He had told everyone that he was flying to Perth as he feared the authorities would deny permission for the flight. Nearly twelve hours later, and driven off course by bad weather, Menzies crash-landed upside down in the glamorous-sounding La Fontaine Swamp, which he had mistaken for level ground.

Menzies went on to be a squadron leader in the Royal Air Force and died on 1 November 1940 when his plane was shot down while en route from Malta to Sicily. Neither his body nor the plane were ever found.

Now a replica hangar in the lovely Guy Menzies Park on the main road in Harihari houses a reconstruction of his Avro Avian biplane, *Southern Cross Junior*, along with historic photographs.

 Guy Menzies Park, SH 6, Harihari.

27. Okarito

The area around Okarito sums up all the magnificence of southern Westland. To the east tower the Southern Alps, with Mt Ellie De Beaumont, Aoraki/Mt Cook, Mt Tasman and the Franz Josef Glacier all clearly visible on a fine day from vantage points such as the Okarito trig or lookout point on the Pahiki Walk.

Near the sea is the Okarito Lagoon, home to the famous kotuku, or white heron (*Egretta alba modesta*). Found throughout the South Pacific, Australia and Asia, but rare in New Zealand, this elegant bird gave rise to the traditional Maori proverb, 'He kotuku rerenga tahi' – 'A kotuku of a single flight' – referring to a once-in-a-lifetime event. The kotuku is the bird featured on the New Zealand two-dollar coin.

Okarito is also home to the rare Okarito brown kiwi, now identified as a separate species – and while often heard, it is only occasionally seen at night. Vast native forests stretch in every direction and the Okarito area has several good examples of virgin pakihi swamp. Peculiar to the high rainfall areas of the West Coast, the wetlands are almost permanently saturated and are characterised by low stunted vegetation, the result of nutrients being rapidly leached from the waterlogged soils.

Once used by Maori for seasonal harvesting, gold was discovered here in 1865 and a town sprang up on the southern shores of the lagoon. Today the township is a small collection of seaside cribs with a handful of historic buildings that include Donovans Store, built in 1865 and originally a hotel, along with the old school house dating from 1901. Extraordinary as it might sound, at one stage land was surveyed here for the Colonial University of Okarito.

There is a superb display of local history in the old Okarito wharf shed, built to accommodate as many as 500 miners arriving in one day, and all that remains of this once flourishing port. You could even take a boat directly from Okarito to Australia, but once the road went through in the 1920s, the port fell into disuse.

Okarito is the home of author Keri Hulme, who won the Man Booker prize in 1985 for her novel *The Bone People*. Award winning photographer Andre Apse is also based at Okarito and his gallery is open from December to March and the rest of the year by appointment (www.andrisapse.com).

Visitors wanting to see kotuku have two options. The breeding ground can only be accessed by tours operated between October and March by White Heron Tours (www.whiteherontours.co.nz) based in Whataroa. Another option is to see the birds feeding on the Okarito Lagoon either by kayak through Okarito Kayaks (www.okarito.co.nz) based at Okarito (morning is best, regardless of tide), or by boat operated by Okarito Boat Eco Tours (www.okaritoboattours.co.nz) based at Okarito and Franz Josef Glacier.

Okarito Kiwi Tours are the only licensed kiwi tour operators in the South Island and take small groups on walks beginning at dusk and lasting 3-5 hours (www.okaritokiwitours.co.nz).

Okarito is the base for several excellent short walks. The Okarito Trig Walk begins at the southern end of The Strand, and the one-and-a-half-hour walk to the trig is rewarded by spectacular views of Westland National Park. The Pakihi Walk is just thirty minutes return and leads through pakihi swamp to a platform with expansive views over the forest, sea and mountains. This track begins off the road to Okarito. Finally the Three Mile Lagoon track follows an historic pack trail over the Kohuamarua Bluff and through forest to the lagoon and then on to the beach. Access is the same as the Okarito Trig Walk and is around three hours return, slightly shorter if returning along the coast, though this option is determined by the tides (tides tables are very thoughtfully provided at the beginning of the track).

While there is plenty to do in Okarito, there is very little accommodation and no store.

📍 SH 6, 115 km south of Hokitika.

28. Shhhh Shed

Marked F for failure is an attempt to disguise a rather large wool shed right next to the main highway in south Westland. Cleverly painted in camouflage paint and with SHHHH written in metre high letters across the roof, the shed raises a smile and is a cheery diversion on the long trip down the coast.

📍 SH 6, just north of the Karangarua River Bridge.

29. Franz Josef Glacier Hot Pools

South Westland can be cold and wet so what could be better at the end of the a busy day than lounging in a hot pool?. Located on a quiet side street, on offer are public pools and private pools (as well as massage). Although not natural thermal water, the pools are set in landscaped grounds lush with ferns and with sails overhead offering protection from the elements with water temperatures ranging from 36°C to 40°C. The three main pools carry names gifted by the local Maori Iwi The Runanga o Makaawhio: Te Puna Mahaki – The pool of calmness; Te Puna Makoha – The pool of tranquillity; and Te Puna Marino – The pool of serenity.

📍 63 Cron St, Franz Josef Glacier.
 03 752 0099
 www.glacierhotpools.co.nz

30. Gillespies Beach

Beaches along the west coast were well known to hold large deposits of easily accessible gold (gold mining is still in operation at Ross to the north). Here at Gillespies, miners sluiced the gravel and sandy soil for flakes of gold and the occasional nugget. Little remains of the thriving township, now overgrown with the occasional relict found in the hummocks behind the beach. The light soils make for easy gold fossicking on the beach, but it is dangerous for swimming. Several walks branch out of the car park at the end of the road from which there are marvellous views back to the mountains. The walk to the lagoon is two hours return; to the pack track tunnel three hours return; and to the fur seal colony four hours return (there are more seals during the winter months). There is also a simple DOC campsite sheltered in the dunes.

📍 20 km west of Fox Glacier township. The road is narrow, winding and unsealed for half the length.

31. Munro Beach

If pristine Westland wilderness and wildlife is what you are looking for, then Munro Beach should fit the bill perfectly. The actual beach is a small sandy cove pounded by the wild weather straight off the Tasman Sea and backed by mature rainforest. While the beach is appealing in its own right, it is also favoured by fur seals and is the home of a colony of the very rare Fiordland crested penguin. Only 1500 pairs remain in the world, and like most penguins they are somewhat timid. The ideal time to see them is early morning or late afternoon, and it is best to sit still rather than wander all over the beach. Once disturbed they will return to the sea, leaving chicks unfed and the adult tired and unrested. The return walk to the beach is along an easy flat track through a beautiful coastal forest of magnificent rimu, and will take around ninety minutes return.

📍 Off SH 6, 30 km north of Haast at the southern end of Lake Moeraki.

32. Hunt Beach

Just a few kilometres off SH 6 at the mouth of the Manakaiaua River, Hunt Beach is a long stretch of sand and stone running between Makawhio Point and the much larger Karangarua river to the north. Just a few houses huddle behind the beach with even fewer visitors but this is a great place for collecting sea-sculptured driftwood and for rock hunting. Hunt Beach is littered with stones of every shape and size including small boulders of quartz, beautifully polished by the wild sea.

This is one of the few places in New Zealand where you can find kyanite, a rare blue mineral that occasionally washes up along this remote stretch of South Westland coast. Kyanite is very difficult to work but makes spectacularly jewellery.

 Off SH 6, 10 km north of Bruce Bay on SH 6.

33. Whitebait on the West Coast

The young of various species of the *Galaxiidae* family, whitebait come to the rivers on New Zealand's west coast between mid-August and mid-November. The most prolific of the whitebait species is inanga *Galaxias maculatus*, although it is hard to distinguish between the several species. After the adult lays its eggs on vegetation along the banks of a river in autumn, the newly hatched larvae are swept out to sea from where they return the following spring as whitebait. The fish then live out their adult lives in freshwater streams and rivers.

Fishing for whitebait is a long-established tradition on the West Coast and common along most of the rivers near the sea are whitebait 'stands'. Stands are platforms from which whitebait nets are cast and can vary between incredibly simple to wildly elaborate with movable gantries that drop down over the water. Consents to build a stand are issued by the local council and you NEVER use a whitebait stand without the permission of the owner.

Many places offer whitebait, but for the casual visitor to the West Coast one of the best places to try this delicacy is at Curly Tree Whitebait Company on the Waita River about 10 km north of Haast. The classic way to eat whitebait is simply served as patties on buttered fresh bread.

34. West Coast Sandflies

This is one creature to 'detour' away from and not towards.

Common on the wet West Coast is the sandfly/namu, which is also known as the blackfly. Small they may be, but it is guaranteed to make that walk in the bush or picnic hell. In all there are thirteen species in New Zealand (just two bite) and they vary between islands. In the North Island it is the New Zealand blackfly *Austrosimulium australense* while in the South Island is aptly name Westcoast Blackfly *A. ungulatum*. Only the female bites, requiring blood to produce her eggs, and since she lays these in water, it follows that sandflies are particularly prolific in the wetter bush areas. They most often bite in the morning (when the young hatch), the evening or on overcast days when they bite throughout the day. They are a persistent nuisance along the entire West Coast and the wetter the better. They pack a nasty bite that will leave you scratching for some time afterwards. The good news is that there are many insect repellents (including natural ones) that do a great job of protecting delicate skin from these ferocious blood-sucking insects.

35. Hapuka Estuary

Located south of Haast, this lovely short walk is often overlooked by visitors who don't venture south on the road from Haast to Jackson's Bay.

The estuary of the Hapuka River encompasses three interlinked ecosystems of forest, wetland and estuary. Starting through bush dominated by rimu and kahikatea, the first section of the walk is dense with the perching plant kiekie that gives the bushscape a subtropical feel. Some of the rimu here are estimated to be between 500 and 800 years old. Emerging from the shade, a raised boardwalk traverses a wetland thick with flax and manuka, and then finally the track follows the riverbank of the estuary back to the car park. The tea-coloured water is overhung with old kowhai trees, and whitebait are prolific in these tidal waters during the season. The loop walk takes just twenty minutes.

〔From Haast, head south along the coast towards Jackson Bay for 15 km. The walk begins on the left, 2 km after crossing the bridge over the Okuru River.

36. Jackson Bay

There is nothing quite like the end of the road and Jackson's Bay is as far south as you can drive in Westland, though most visitors begin or end their West Coast trip at Haast. Here Jackson Head protects a small fishing village from the worse of the weather off the turbulent Tasman. Once a significant whaling station, today the bay is home to a small fishing fleet. The short walk to Wharekai-Te-Kou through bush to the open sea will make you realise just how sheltered Jackson Bay really is. From the rustic wharf the views north along the coast are magnificent. Facilities are definitely limited and are confined to the Craypot, an old pie cart that has come to rest literally at the end of the road.

〔50 km south of Haast on a good sealed road.

37. Haast Pass Road from Haast to Wanaka

Covering a distance of 145 km, the road through the Haast Pass crosses the lowest of the passes through the Southern Alps at 563 m and follows an ancient Maori trail called Tiora Patea ('the way is clear') used to access pounamu on the West Coast. Gold prospector Charles Cameron was the first European to use the pass in 1863, followed a few weeks later by the explorer Julius von Haast, after whom the pass was named.

The pass was used extensively as the most direct route from Dunedin to the West Coast gold fields and later as a cattle trail, but work on the road did not begin until 1929 and reached Wanaka only in 1960. The road is now sealed and rarely blocked by snow and goes through the heart of Mt Aspiring National Park. Haast township, originally a workers' camp for the Ministry of Works, has limited accommodation and facilities.

Today the pass is a popular route with visitors in the summer months and most of the short walks are busy and the parking areas overcrowded. However, the two following walks are the least busy and usually overlooked.

Haast Pass Lookout Track is a steep uphill grind, which is probably why this walk attracts far fewer visitors than other points along the road. Actually, it's not that bad as the track is well formed and, as it zigzags up the mountainside, the gradient is fairly even. Beginning through beech forest, the trees gradually thin as you climb until you reach the lookout over the pass. The view down the bush-lined pass extends both east and west and snow-capped mountains soar in every direction. It's not a long walk and the quiet and solitude of the magnificent vista is worth a bit of sweat.

Makarora Bush at the Wanaka end of the road is all that remains of vast forests of beech, matai, kahikatea and miro that once cloaked the eastern foothills of the Southern Alps. Makarora grew as a mill settlement supplying timber to the Otago gold fields and the boomtown that was Dunedin in the nineteenth century. Now noted for its fishing, there is also a twenty minute walk through remnant forest, right on the climate line that divides the wet west coast with the arid inland of Central Otago. At Makaroa plants thrive that would not survive in Wanaka less than 30 kms away.

A curious remnant of the timber milling era is a double handed saw stuck in a log, in much the same way King Arthur's sword was locked fast in a stone, and no one is sure how long the saw has been there. Originally the pit below the log was much deeper and one man would work the saw from below while the other stood on the log above. Presumably the harder upward pull of the saw was compensated by the worker avoiding a face full of fine saw dust. Let's hope they took turns.

This is one place that visitors might be lucky to spot South Island kaka. The ancestors of the kea and kaka arrived in New Zealand around 20 millions years ago and kaka evolved to live in dense bush where it uses its powerful beak to pull apart decaying logs for any tasty insects it can find. Although the adult kaka can fend for itself, the kaka population has been devastated by rats, possums and stoats predating eggs and chicks.

KAIKOURA AND CANTERBURY
INCLUDING ARTHUR'S PASS

1. Crayfish
2. Fyffe House
3. Earthquake Reconstruction
4. Molesworth Station
5. Hanmer Springs Forests
6. Lewis Pass
7. Maruia Springs
8. Weka Pass Railway
9. Historic Hurunui Hotel and the Star and Garter Hotel, Waikari
10. North Canterbury Wineries
11. Inland Scenic Route 72
12. Kaiapoi Pa
13. The Kaiapoi Letterbox Sculpture
14. Blackwells Department Store, Kaiapoi
15. Oxford Butchery
16. Springfield Donut
17. Arthurs Pass
18. The Mt Cook Lily - Super-sized buttercup
19. Cave Stream
20. Glentunnel Library and Post Office
21. The Rakaia Gorge
22. Broadfield Garden
23. Ellesmere A&P Grounds, Leeston
24. Salmon Fishing in the Rakaia
25. Trotts Garden Ashburton
26. Ashburton Domain
27. Mt Somers
28. Lake Clearwater

Kaikoura

The physical location of Kaikoura is nothing short of spectacular. Within a short distance of the coast the rugged Kaikoura mountains rise to nearly 3000 metres, and off shore the seabed drops steeply into the Hikurangi Trench.

The Kaikoura peninsula and mountains have a long and vital Maori history beginning with the creation of the very land itself. This is where the mighty demigod Maui braced his foot on a seat of his giant waka in his titanic struggle to haul up his great fish Te Ika a Maui (the North Island).

The earliest Europeans were whalers and later fishers drawn to the area by the abundant sea life, and then farmers drawn by the rich soils land to the west. In more recent years the town has flourished, with the advent of whale watching, outgrowing the small attractive town centre sheltered beneath the peninsula and spreading northwards in an unattractive sprawl.

1. Crayfish

One of the local delicacies is crayfish (a spiny lobster-like sea creature without the claws), and renowned for its very sweet and delicate taste. Prolific along these rocky shores, the area takes it name from the crayfish – *kai* to eat, *koura* crayfish. Available at most restaurants (though usually at a fairly steep price) crayfish are also available at roadside stalls – usually at half the price and just as tasty.

2. Fyffe House

New Zealanders have always been good at making do. No doubt this stems from a pioneering spirit in both Maori and Pakeha, who both settled a long way from home and from where it was impossible to 'nip back' for anything forgotten! Kaikoura, occupied by Maori for over 700 years, attracted early European whalers, and what they had an abundance of in Kaikoura was whale bone. Not to let a good thing go to waste, when Captain Robert Fyfe, who established his whaling station at Waiopuka near Kaikoura, built his simple cottage by the sea in 1843 he very conveniently used that excess of whale vertebrae for the piles of the house. Later, in 1860, the house was extended by Robert's cousin George Fyffe (*his* surname had two 'f's), but this time he used more conventional timber piles. The house is virtually unaltered from that time and the whalebone vertebrae are clearly seen at the front. Imagine getting that past the Resource Management Act these days!

- 62 Avoca Street, Kaikoura.
- Open daily November to May 10 am to 6 pm, June to October 10 am to 4 pm.
- Entrance fee.

3. Earthquake Reconstruction

Just after midnight on 14 November 2016 a complex series of earthquakes with a combined magnitude of 7.8 hit the area and while only two people died, the earthquake destroyed all road and rail access to the town.

Damage to infrastructure was colossal. In all eighty-five slips covered roads and rail lines particularly north of the town. On the 40 km stretch of the road south of Clarence, around 400,000 cubic metres collapsed on the road and railway line below. Over 100,000 cubic metres covered SH 1 at Ohau Point alone. While reopening the road was a priority, roading engineers looked for more permanent solutions rather than just 'make do'. Long sections of both road and rail needed complete rebuilding and entire hillsides had to be stabilised, and before that could even start, the rocks and debris need to be removed.

The result is impressive, and when travelling down this stretch of the coast it is worthwhile to stop occasionally and admire the engineering work. Seven thousand concrete blocks weighing five tonnes each were used to create new sea walls. Huge pins have been driven into steep hillsides and vast areas of netting coat the land preventing rocks tumbling on to the road below. The highway north was finally reopened in December 2017, but work will continue for many years yet and is expected to top $1.5 billion.

4. Molesworth Station

New Zealand's largest station, covering over 180,000 ha of inland high country, has had a very mixed history. Established as a merino sheep station in the middle of the nineteenth century, farming initially flourished and in 1900 the run supported 50,000 sheep.

By 1925 the station's flock had dropped to just 1400 sheep. The cause was simply a plague of rabbits of such proportions that Molesworth and other runs like it were virtually turned into deserts. When the lease ran out on the station in 1938, Molesworth and neighbouring Tarndale returned to the Crown, and from 1949 these two stations (together with yet two more failed stations) have been managed by a government agency and today are under the care of the Department of Conservation. Through careful management of stock and land, Molesworth has slowly returned to production and now supports the largest herd of cattle in New Zealand, numbering over 10,000.

This is tough country at best. The climate is hot and dry in summer and very cold in winter with frequent snow, and frosts occurring over 200 days a year. Varying in altitude from 500 to over 2000 metres, the station is the source of the Acheron, Clarence and Waiau rivers, and much of the terrain is mountainous and rugged. While not as spectacularly alpine as the Southern Alps, this high country has a natural beauty and appeal all of its own, with a vast landscape empty of people, subtle vistas of muted colours, and a quiet solitude like few other places. At Acheron the historic guesthouse is open to the public. Built of cob in 1863, it was part of a number of such accommodation houses built between Canterbury and Nelson to provide shelter for men moving stock through the mountains (Tophouse south of Nelson still operates as a hotel).

Along the Acheron Road there is camping at both Acheron and Molesworth, and also at Lake Tennyson and Coldwater Creek, but no other accommodation or facilities. Make sure you also bring a fit passenger as there are plenty of gates to open and close!

Open only through summer, the public road from SH 1 just south of Blenheim runs 182 km through the heart of the station to Hanmer, and the 1437-metre-high Island Saddle is the highest point in New Zealand on any public road. While mostly gravel, and often winding and narrow, it is not a difficult road and it makes a comfortable day's drive with plenty of time for stops along the way.

If a long drive is not an option, the station is more accessible from Hanmer Springs on Jollies Pass Road. Just 80 km to Molesworth, the road a bit rougher and climbs steeply from Hanmer up and over the pass and down into the Clarence River Valley.

5. Hanmer Springs Forests

Constantly wrongly pronounced as 'Hamner', this busy resort is set in a high-country basin with extensive accommodation and facilities and is popular with Christchurch people looking for a weekend away lured by its famous hot springs. Surrounding the town is a mixture of exotic and native forest laced with walking tracks but it is the imported trees that grab the visitors attention.

In pre-European times the area around Hanmer was almost totally devoid of trees, but that radically changed in 1900 when the New Zealand government acquired over 200 ha as part of a forestry experiment to ascertain which imported trees would best replace the rapidly shrinking native forests. Using prison labour, the first plantings began in 1903, and included European larch, Douglas fir, radiata pines, Norwegian spruce, alder and Corsican pine as early foresters experimented with a surprisingly wide variety of species. While timber production was the primary aim, other species were planted purely for beautification purposes.

Silver birch were planted in 1904 and what makes the silver birch at Hanmer so unusual in New Zealand is that they were planted en masse as a forest tree when, most typically they are grown as single ornamental specimens or occasionally in very small groves. Here at Hanmer you can experience the feel and flavour of a northern European forest without having to leave the country.

The oldest plantings, now known as the Heritage Forest, are just a short stroll from the village and include a wide range of good walks, especially attractive in autumn when the deciduous trees are changing colour in the cool mountain climate. Short walks include Woodland Walk (forty-five minutes return), Conical Hill Lookout (one hour return), Majuba Walk (one hour return), Forest Walk (one hour return), and Dog Stream Track (one and a half hours return). Longer walks include Chatterton River Track (two and half hours return), Waterfall Track (three hours return), and, for the very energetic, Mt Isobel Track (five hours return). The information office has up-to-date information on all the walks, and if you have time for only one walk, Conical Hill is the pick, and if the uphill climb is not for you then the flat Woodland Walk is a good alternative.

6. Lewis Pass

At 864 m, Lewis Pass is lower than Arthur's Pass. This road follows an old Maori greenstone trail along the Lewis River south, and the Maruia River north of the pass. The main route from North Canterbury to the Buller region, this pass is only rarely blocked by snow and this area tends to have fewer visitors than many other South Island regions.

Straddling the main divide, the climate on either side of the pass couldn't be more different. To the west, dense beech forest thrives in the high rainfall, while to the east the landscape is open and dry with little forest and vast areas of tussock and grass.

There are a number of excellent short walks from the road including the Lake Daniels Track to a pretty mountain lake that will take around three hours return and for the more serious tramper, the 65-km St James Walkway (four to five days) is recommended.

7. Maruia Springs

Just west of Springs Junction are the Maruia Springs. Set in a forested mountain valley, the springs stand alone in a magnificent alpine setting, with the hot pools overlooking the Maruia River below.

Well known by Maori, the pools also drew European settlers who built cottages and a hotel adjacent to the springs. In the 1990s the springs were developed as a traditional Japanese Onsen and today the springs still retain elements of Japanese style.

The pools draw from a natural hot spring from the other side of the river, and the water is piped untreated to the complex. Free from additives, it is high in mineral content and reputed to have healing properties, particularly for the skin. Today the complex has private pools, outdoor rock pools styled to resemble a small mountain tarn, a cold plunge pool and two saunas. In addition to two dining areas, the springs also has a range of accommodation.

SH 7, 15 km east of Springs Junction.
  03 523 8840
  www.maruiahotsprings.nz

8. Weka Pass Railway

The Waiau Branch railway line, which first opened in 1884, was originally intended to be the main line north from Christchurch, but in 1945 the line via the coast was finally opened making this a branch line that serviced a sparsely populated district. Not surprisingly it closed down, though not until 1978, and in 1982 local people together with railway enthusiasts joined to preserve this piece of rail heritage and acquired the track and much of the rolling stock.

Today, the Weka Pass Railway owns five locomotives with A428, the steam engine, the darling of the fleet. Running 13 km between Waipara and Waikari, the highlight of the trip is negotiating the rugged open limestone country of the Weka Pass, after which the railway takes its name. Trains operate on the first and third Sunday of each month and on some public holidays. Best check the website for details before you go.

  Glenmark Station, Glenmark Drive, Waipara.
  www.wekapassrailway.co.nz.

9. Historic Hurunui Hotel and the Star and Garter Hotel, Waikari

Over the Weka Pass and into the Hurunui Valley, travellers will discover two classic New Zealand hotels very different from each other in style but both offering good Kiwi hospitality.

The oldest pub is the historic Hurunui Hotel, which was built in 1860 on a site near the Hurunui River. After a massive flood hit the region, it was decided to move the hotel to higher ground even though the flood had not directly threatened the hotel. Constructed of limestone blocks quarried from nearby Weka Pass, in 1868, the entire hotel was dismantled and then rebuilt on the present site.

In more recent years the hotel fell into disrepair, but in 1979 around 100 local shareholders rallied together and, with the help of the Historic Places Trust, they were able to return it to its former glory. Badly damaged by the 7.8 Kaikoura earthquake, it took almost two years for the hotel to reopen in time for the pub's 150th anniversary.

Today the two-storey hotel retains an exterior and interior that reflect a typical nineteenth century hotel. Simple in design, the hotel has a fine façade complemented by a veranda that runs the length of the hotel. Most older hotels have opened up the maze of rooms on the ground floor to form one large bar/dining room, but the Hurunui still retains most of the original floor plan. The main bar just inside the main door is tiny, off which two rooms led to the left and right. Today both are extensions of the bar, but originally they would have been sitting rooms or a ladies bar each complete with an open fireplace. Two garden bars flank the hotel: the one to the left a beer garden and the other a wine garden – the pub runs a small vineyard behind the hotel producing wine under the Hurunui Village label.

Down the road in Waikari is the Star and Garter Hotel, which is more typical of New Zealand country hotels in that it is built of wood and not stone like the Hurunui. The original hotel opened in 1863 and was the coach stop on the route from Amberley to Culverden.

A large two storey hotel, it boasted twenty-one rooms, two dining rooms and three sitting rooms, and was obliged under its licence to provide stabling for horses. It burnt down, and the new hotel, reopened in 1935, was like its predecessor a two storey wooden building. An attractive pub, it is the perfect place to experience country hospitality and an excellent base for those wanting to explore the area, particularly noted for its hunting and fishing.

10. North Canterbury Wineries

With its hot, dry summers and cool winters, North Canterbury now seems an obvious place to grow grapes but it wasn't until the early 1980s that local farmers looking to diversify began to consider producing wine. Now the region produces some of New Zealand's best pinot noir, along with aromatics, especially riesling.

Pegasus Bay Winery

One of the earliest vineyards in the region, Pegasus Bay produced its first vintage in 1981 and it was the wineries' pinot noir that drew attention to the Waipara Valley. Now a second generation of the Donaldsons are still actively involved in the vineyard and produce a wide range of exceptional wines. The restaurant has an equally impressive reputation and, like their wines, has also collected an impression stack of awards. Overlooking the gardens with a wide view to the north, its food style is influenced by contemporary European cuisine.

- 263 Stockgrove Rd, Waipara.
- Cellar door open daily 10 am to 5 pm.
- 03 314 6869
- www.pegasusbay.com

Torlesse Wines

Torlesse Wines exudes a rustic charm with its rich red corrugated-iron building, the old railway carriage that serves as a barrel room, and a friendly welcome at the cellar door. All its grapes are sourced from wide variety of terrain in the Waipara area, from valley floor to steep terraced hillsides from which are produced wines ranging from pinot and cabernet/merlot, through to pinot gris and tawny port.

- Loffhagen Dr, Waipara.

Cellar door open daily 11 am to 5 pm.
 03 314 6929
 www.torlesse.co.nz

11. Inland Scenic Route 72

If you are heading south from Kaikoura and Christchurch is not your destination, then seriously consider taking this alternative route south. Once an official highway, that designation was dropped in the 1990s, but old habits die hard and is now known as the Inland Scenic Route 72. It is an excellent road: 230 km long and a much more interesting drive than SH 1. Leaving SH 1 at Amberley in the north, the route skirts along low foothills through Rangiora, Cust and Oxford before crossing the Waimakariri River over a 30 m high bridge at the Waimakariri Gorge. Heading south, the road passes through Sheffield with its famous pies and excellent pub, and on past the old brickworks and potteries around Glentunnel to the spectacular Rakaia Gorge with its historic bridges and expansive views over the plains.

Much further inland than SH 1, the lower peaks of the South Alps, snow-capped in winter, rise directly above the road as it travels through Mt Hutt, Staveley and Mt Somers. Lakes Heron, Emma and Clearwater are just short drives off the road at this point. Progressing south the road crosses the Rangitata River near Mt Peel and on to Geraldine, a foodie heaven. From there it is just a short drive to Winchester on SH 1 and then on to Timaru.

12. Kaiapoi Pa

Kaiapoi or Kaiapohia was the main Ngai Tahu pa in the Canterbury area, built around 1700 when Ngai Tahu first migrated to the area. The pa was sited on a peninsula surrounded by deep swamp. A maze of waterways and lagoons protected the pa on three sides, and this was enhanced by deep ditches and stout palisading. A feature of the pa was a number of defended gates; the main entrance was located to the left of where the monument now stands. The pa had a population of around 1000 people and was considered unassailable – but all was about to change with the coming of Te Rauparaha.

Te Rauparaha visited Kaiapoi in 1828 on the pretext of trading pounamu, when in fact he was busily ascertaining the strength and defences of Ngai Tahu. Acutely aware of his real intentions, Ngai Tahu claimed that Ngati Toa had insulted them by dragging the corpse of a local woman through the swamp, and they used this insult as a pretext to attack the visitors. In the ensuring mêlée, eight Ngati Toa were killed and eaten, but – fatally for Ngai Tahu – Te Rauparaha escaped.

In the summer of 1831-32 Te Rauparaha returned to take revenge. During an inconclusive three-month period of skirmishes, Ngati Toa built a series of covered trenches up to the palisades against which they piled dry manuka, with the intention of setting fire to the wooden fencing. Realising their plan, the defenders within the pa decided to take advantage of a strong northwest wind blowing away from the pa and set fire to the manuka. As luck would have it, the wind suddenly switched to the south and the wooden walls burned, allowing Te Rauparaha and his warriors into the pa. The slaughter that followed was fearful, and fewer than 200 of the 1000 inhabitants escaped to Onewa pa on the Banks Peninsula.

Kaiapoi was never reoccupied, and even twenty years later the Reverend James Stack removed large piles of bones for burial. However, Ngai Tahu later reversed their losses and later still peace was made between the two enemies when Te Rauparaha returned many of those captured at Kaiapoi and Onewa.

Today little remains of this formidable pa. The swamps have been drained and now the site is surrounded by farm paddocks, while the formidable defences and gates have been reduced to grassy mounds. Near the road a towering white monument emblazoned with the simple words *Ngai Tahu* was built in 1898, but in the interests of reconciliation there is no reference to the fall of the pa. A wooden lookout point designed to give the visitor an overview of the site has unfortunately fallen into disrepair. However, the old pa holds an air of the past and, with a bit of imagination, walking over the old pa briefly takes the visitor back to times long gone.

 27 km north of Christchurch, 500 metres down Preeces Road off SH 1.

13. The Kaiapoi Letterbox Sculpture

Kaiapoi was badly hit the Canterbury earthquakes of 2010 and 2011, but in demonstration of resilience and determination, the local power company MainPower sponsored a unique sculpture by local artist Mark Larsen.

Standing in the centre of town, the tall sculpture consists of letterboxes and street signs from the parts of the small town's Red Zone following the earthquakes. Over 1000 home were destroyed in the earthquakes and the idea was inspired by a group of locals called 'Kaiapoi Rubble Rousers', wanting to brighten up their shattered town. The red and black colours signify both the 'Red Zone' and Kaiapoi's blackest day, and are also the traditional sporting colours of Canterbury.

 Cnr Williams and Charles Street, Kaiapoi.

14. Blackwells Department Store, Kaiapoi

Oh lucky people of Kaiapoi! So fortunate to have such an amazing shop as Blackwells, once typical of many department stores throughout New Zealand, most of which have long since closed down or been bought out by larger concerns.

Established in 1871 by George Henry Blackwell, who emigrated from England to New Zealand in 1840, this store has now been in the Blackwell family for five generations and these days is ably run by Andrew Blackwell. Not that it has been plain sailing all the way. A new store in Williams Street was built in the early 1920s and was, at the time, a grand affair with two floors of retail as well as elegant tearooms. Fire nearly destroyed the store in 1927, and then the 1930s Depression hit hard and the top floor closed, never to reopen.

Worse was to come over eighty years later when the Christchurch earthquakes damaged the store to the extent it needed to be demolished. Not a family to walk away, Blackwells rebuilt a new store on the same site and in a style that reflects the original store. Luckily the family managed to salvage from the damaged building a magnificent ornate till, originally purchased in 1885 and last serviced in 1893. It is still in use today – so even if the power goes off or EFTPOS crashes, Blackwells can keep trading. It is heartening to see such an establishment survive in the era of mass-market chain stores and 'box retail', and let's trust that the good folk of Kaiapoi continue to realise what a real treasure they have in their town.

 131 Williams Street, Kaiapoi.
 03 327 8029
 blackwellsdeptstore.co.nz

15. Oxford Butchery

Three generations of the Frahm family have run the local Oxford butcher's shop since 1953, so when Shane Frahm talks about doing things the traditional way he really means it. Sourcing all his meat from Canterbury farmers enables Shane not only to support his neighbours but also to maintain the quality that is essential to survive in this competitive retail environment.

The smoked bacon produced at the Oxford Butchers is a case in point. So much bacon and ham available in supermarkets is not only imported but full of water-retention agents and wrapped in sweaty plastic. When frying, the bacon not only cooks in the excessive water but also shrinks considerably.

The superb bacon from Oxford is very different. First, it is gently smoked using natural wood shavings then is allowed to cure and dry over time. The result is bacon that is full of flavour and less watery than supermarket varieties, and what goes in the pan is the same size as what comes out. As with all his other meats, a local farmer supplies the shop with pigs and these animals are bred outdoors, though later wean indoors with plenty of room to move about.

The butchery is also known for is superb sausages which contain no imported meat or bulking vegetable extract and, like the bacon, don't shrink during cooking.

Impossible to miss, the shop is also famous for its huge wall mural depicted early Oxford logging history.

   44 Main Street, Oxford.
   03 312 4205

16. Springfield Donut

Springfield New Zealand lies 68 km northwest of Christchurch on the main route to Arthurs Pass and the West Coast. This small farming community is not without a sense of humour and have built a huge donut within a children's playground right by the main road as a tribute to *The Simpsons*, the world's longest running TV cartoon which debuted on December 17, 1989.

   Unmissable in the middle of this small township on SH 73.

17. Arthurs Pass Huts

The most direct route from Canterbury to the West Coast, this road traverses some of the most dramatic mountain scenery in the country. From the dry tussock Canterbury region to the warm and very wet West Coast, the road in reality climbs two passes: the slightly higher Porters Pass in the east at 942 m and Arthur's Pass much further west at 920 m.

Of course, this highway is clogged with tourists, but one frequently overlooked feature of the small township is the old alpine huts. These are the mountain equivalent of the seaside bach and like the bach were small and simply built, often by the owners. While some were built for families, others were constructed for alpine clubs drawn to the area by climbing and skiing and were essentially bunkhouses. Corrugated iron was the exterior cladding of choice as it was cheap, light to carry, durable and fireproof. Frequently the fireplace and chimney were built in a manner where they were almost detached from the hut in order to provide more space inside the tiny building and to prevent fires.

18. The Mt Cook Lily - Super-sized Buttercup

With over 500 species, New Zealand is rich in alpine flora. Around 93 percent are not only endemic but also have no relatives anywhere in the world. Among the unique species are several species of ranunculus (buttercup) of which the misnamed Mt Cook Lily *Ranunculus lyallii* is the best known.

The world's largest buttercup, the Mt Cook Lily is a perennial plant that grows up to 1 metre high with dark glossy leaves up to 40 centimetres wide and startling pure white flowers on tall stems. The wide cup-shaped leaves collect enough water to afford a good drink. A true alpine dweller, this buttercup thrives in the subalpine environment, between 700 and 1500 metres, and is found throughout the South Island from Stewart Island to Marlborough but is completely absent from the North Island. Where the right conditions exist, the plant grows in huge swathes presenting a spectacular sight when flowering in late spring and summer.

The plant was misnamed a lily as the botanist David Lyall who discovered it only collected the leaves that resembled those of a lily. More than a decade later when flowers were collected it was realised that the plant was in fact a member of the ranunculus family, but by that time the lily name had stuck.

 An easy place to see this spectacular plant is at the Otira Viaduct Lookout, 5 km west of Arthurs Pass Township. There is a short loop walk through alpine plants on the south side of the road.

19. Cave Stream

If, like so many, you are not so crazy about narrow creepy caves, then this cave is the perfect adventure – challenging, but not too demanding. Almost 600 metres long, the cave is part of limestone country in the Castle Hill area and was created by an underground stream wearing away the soft limestone. This is great fun for those with no caving experience: it takes about an hour to work from one end to the other, following the stream for the most part but with a little climbing as well.

That said, this cave is not to be taken lightly, and every precaution should be taken before entering the system (people have died in here). While it is easily accessible to anyone moderately fit, you will get wet and the water can be very cold, especially in winter. Warm clothing is essential, as is a torch along with a back-up. Do not enter the cave after heavy rain or if the water is discoloured.

On SH 73, 3 km west of Castle Hill, on the road to Arthur's Pass.

20. Glentunnel Library and Post Office

If this isn't the smallest library in the country, then it must be close. Built in 1886, the Glentunnel Library is beautifully constructed of bricks and tiles made at the nearby Homebush Pottery. With handy sources of coal in the vicinity, the Homebush Pottery was just one of many such potteries that thrived in the Glentunnel and Coalgate area up until the 1980s, producing bricks, ceramic pipes and domestic pottery.

The library's proportions are perfect, with ornate tiles decorating the external walls, while still surviving inside is a wonderful original fashion poster taken from the 'Supplement to the Young Ladies Journal' in 1894. Today the library still operates and doubles as the local post office. Just up the road from the library are the old stables that once housed the pit ponies, and just beyond that are the remains of a small kiln.

📍 The library is on SH 77 at Glentunnel.

21. The Rakaia Gorge

The Rakaia River leads deep into the mountains via the Lake Coleridge basin, and has good access to numerous fishing rivers with a reputation for small numbers of big fish, including brown and rainbow trout, and salmon. Here at the Rakaia Gorge the river squeezes through two narrow channels before fanning out over the plains to the sea. On either side broad terraces step away from the river and the narrow gorge is spanned by two bridges over a small rocky island in the middle of the river. A ferry service operated at this point until the two bridges linking both banks and Goat Island were built in 1884. The views both up into the mountains and down into the plain are expansive.

A lovely walk upstream from the bridge takes around five hours return, but an appealing option is to take the jet boat, located just below the bridge, to the end of the track and walk back.

📍 SH 77, 16 km north of Methven.

22. Broadfield Garden

There is something extraordinary and maybe a bit crazy about a person who can look at 3.5 ha of flat Canterbury farmland and envisage a garden like no other. Just the mere thought of it would make most of us reach for a cup of tea and lie down.

Not David Hobbs, though, when he stood in those empty paddocks more than twenty-five years ago, and with vision and courage he set about creating Broadfield Garden. While much of the area is old riverbed or waterlogged swamp, this land is rich and productive Templeton silt loam, fertile and well drained. Clearly inspired by a European style, David did not just recreate an English garden with European plants. Right from the beginning he cleverly used New Zealand plants to create the effect he was after. Totara is every bit as good as yew for shelter and hedging and a good deal more disease resistant. The result is a wonderful blend of native and exotic plants in a mixture of formal and less managed settings.

The Oak Lawn, Cricket Oval, Camellia Garden and Rose Gardens are equally balanced by the Kowhai Walk, Lowland Forest and Kauri Forest; while the New Zealand Conifer and Daffodil Walk is a marriage between Northern and Southern Hemispheres.

Ultimately the two hemispheres come perfectly together in New Zealand Border. A stickler to the design of the traditional herbaceous border of the north in its use of colour, form and texture, here all the plants are New Zealand natives and the result is perfectly stunning.

To cap off this great gardening experience is a clamber up the five metre high Viewing Mound which, as the name suggests, has a wide vista over the gardens and far beyond to the Southern Alps.

📍 250 Selwyn Road (between Cross and Waterholes Roads) Rolleston.
🕐 Wednesday and Saturday 8 am to 4 pm or by arrangement.
📞 027 433 4099

23. Ellesmere A&P Grounds, Leeston

Agriculture and Pastoral Shows (better known just as A&P Shows) were an integral part of colonial life. They were huge events, frequently the highlight of the social calendar and almost every town and city had showgrounds, ranging from not much more than a bare paddock to elaborate complexes.

The first A&P Show was held in Auckland on 14 December 1843 and here the focus was purely on livestock and the breeding of stud animals in particular. By the 1860s the shows had grown to encompass a wider range of rural enterprises, and as the crowds grew larger so did the shows, to include fairground entertainment and food stalls. Many shows have ceased to exist partly in favour of more sophisticated entertainment or by rural depopulation. However, where they have survived, they are still a big day out.

Established in 1870, the Ellesmere A&P Show held in Leeston is one of the district's largest events. It attracts tens of thousands of visitors and is very typical of the modern metamorphosis of the old agricultural show. Held every year in October, there is still a focus on rural activities, livestock and local produce, but the show also offers craft stalls, wood chopping, vintage and modern machinery, wine tasting, wearable arts and, of course, fair ground rides. In all it's a great Kiwi day out.

 1650 Leeston Road, Leeston.

24. Salmon Fishing in the Rakaia

You can't mistake Rakaia townships' passion for salmon fishing. A huge five metre high leaping salmon right by the main road is really hard to miss, and right next to the jumping fish is a café offering salmon-based delicacies and an aquarium for an up-close look at this amazing fish.

Salmon were introduced into New Zealand around 1907 in the Waitaki River and today are found primarily off the east coast of the South Island between Kaikoura and the Otago Peninsula. In this area nearly all the fish are taken in the lower reaches of the rivers between SH 1 and the sea. On the West Coast salmon fishing is primarily on lakes, while the inland lake population of Canterbury is sustained by fish released by Fish and Game as these populations are not self-supporting. Occasionally fish are caught in the North Island, but salmon are not established north of Cook Strait.

Salmon require very specific conditions including an adequate water flow. Several Canterbury rivers, including the Ashburton River, were once highly productive salmon waters but today have water flows so low that there is no salmon fishing at all.

The wide braided Rakaia and Rangitata rivers are the country's two best salmon rivers and the fishing season from October to the end of April attracts thousands of anglers to the Canterbury region. The Rakaia Salmon Fishing Contest during the peak season of February/March is the highlight of the salmon fishing year.

25. Trotts Garden Ashburton

Spectacular is a good word to start any description of Trotts Garden and it is no surprise that this is a New Zealand Garden of International Significance and was awarded the highest six-star category by the New Zealand Gardens Trust. But every story starts somewhere and this begins in late 1978 when Alan and Catherine Trott purchased an old house in a bare paddock of 4 ha on the outskirts of Ashburton. Six years later, and with three small sons in tow, planting began between the road and house and by the following year a full plan was drawn up for the entire 4 ha.

Plans change and today the garden is a series of different areas that include woodlands, formal plantings, a fabulous perennial border, and a knot garden. There are just under 700 rhododendrons and the more recent red border is inspiring.

In 2017 the Trott's Charitable Trust took over the garden to ensure that future generations continue to enjoy this national treasure.

 371 Racecourse Road, Ashburton.
 Open Monday to Friday 10 am to 4 pm
 03 640 4094
 www.trotts.co.nz

26. Ashburton Domain

Once described as a 'miserable wilderness of scrubby broom, spear grass and tussock', the Ashburton Domain is one of New Zealand's finest public parks. Unlike many other parks, which are essentially gardens, this domain combines outdoor recreation in almost every conceivable form.

Laid out as part of the Ashburton town plan in 1864, a formal Domain committee was established ten years later. Two dams created smalls lakes and in 1878 an area was cleared for a cricket ground. By 1889 the domain hosted, in addition to the cricket club, a bicycle club, the Caledonian Society, running tracks, swimming baths and formally planted areas. Over the years the Domain has continued to improve and any attempt to encroach on its space has been fiercely opposed by locals.

Today the Ashburton Domain is 37 ha of formal gardens, lawns, arboretum and sports fields, and is well worth the stop along the long stretch of SH 1 between Christchurch and Timaru. Particularly appealing are the magnificent trees, a mixture of natives and exotics with some well over a century old, of which the conifers are especially impressive. The two small lakes are packed with fat, happy, well-fed ducks. In addition to the gardens, there is a children's playground, aviary, skateboard park and plenty of good places for a picnic, and it is all beautifully maintained. It really is impossible not to stop and take a stroll.

📍 Cnr SH 1 and Walnut Ave, Ashburton.

27. Mt Somers

The cool beech forest of the Canterbury foothills around Mt Somers and Staveley are in direct contrast to the open plains below and the dry tussock mountain country inland.

In contrast to the nearby Southern Alps, Mt Somers, at 1688 m, is actually an old rhyolite volcanic dome formed by magna forced up through a crack in the rock rather than by an eruption. The forest is mainly beech, with occasional southern rata, and on the lower slopes there is rimu and kahikatea. Bellbirds are common in the bush. The tramp to the top is a demanding seven hours return, although the lower peak of the Duke Knob (739 m) is a more manageable option that will take around three and a half hours. More manageable is the intriguing walk up to the abandoned Blackburn Coal mine which still has left over machinery and great views. This walk begins from the end of Jig Road, off the road to Lake Clearwater.

 SH 72, 'Inland Scenic Route'.

28. Lake Clearwater

Covering 2 sq km, this small lake is set amongst specular alpine scenery and is place of quiet and solitude. In the winter, on a clear still day after a snow fall, it is magical.

The lake is located in the Hakatere Conservation Park, which covers 60,000 ha between the Rakaia and Rangitata Rivers and is part of a group of small lakes collectively known as the Ashburton Lakes. Most are easily reached by gravel road and are relatively shallow (Lake Clearwater is only 19 m deep) so they frequently freeze in winter, but in summer are warm enough for swimming. The Northwest winds are particularly fierce in this area. A small village of mostly modest cribs has developed since 1925 between Clearwater and nearby tiny Lake Camp and is mainly used by those fishing and duck shooting.

As a reserve, no dogs are permitted and motor-powered craft are forbidden, making it ideal for kayaking, rowing, windsurfing and kitesurfing. A 10.3 km walking & mountain biking circuit track follows the lake shore, and a tramping track to the summit of Mount Guy starts at Lake Clearwater.

The reserve was established primarily to protect the Great Crested Grebe, a relatively large diving bird with striking plumage and intricate mating behaviour. An excellent swimmer, it pursues fish underwater. Once down to just 200 birds the current population is now around 1000.

There is a basic camping ground and toilet facilities but no shop.

> Lake Clearwater is 38 km west of Mt Somers and the last half is unsealed gravel.

CHRISTCHURCH CITY AND
THE BANKS PENINSULA

1. The Arts Centre of Christchurch
2. Ice Cream Charlie, the Home of the Vanilla Ice
3. New Regent Street
4. Margaret Mahy Playground
5. Kate Sheppard Memorial
6. 185 Empty White Chairs
7. A Tale of Three Cathedrals
8. Quake City
9. Velocity Karts
10. Riccarton Market
11. Show Week
12. Cabbage Trees, Burnside High School
13. Three Boys Brewery
14. Dame Ngaio Marsh's House
15. Taylors Mistake
16. Orana Park
17. Steam Scene – Canterbury Steam Preservation Society
18. The Whare, Halswell Quarry Gardens
19. Kaituna Valley Scenic Reserve
20. Birdlings Flat and Kaikorete Spit
21. Bridal Path Walkway
22. Port Hills Rest Houses
23. Lyttelton Harbour
24. Quail Island/Otamahua, Lyttelton Harbour
25. The Thornycroft Torpedo Boat Museum
26. Ohinetahi Garden
27. Allandale Gaol
28. Two-thousand-year-old Totara Tree
29. French Peak Winery
30. Barrys Bay Cheese Factory
31. Onawe Peninsula, Akaroa Harbour
32. Okains Bay Maori and Colonial Museum
33. German and Portuguese Akaroa

1. The Arts Centre of Christchurch

Originally the home of the University of Canterbury, as well as Christchurch Boys' and Girls' High Schools, the earliest buildings were constructed in 1877. Designed by Benjamin Mountfort, the stone buildings reflect the Gothic Revival style popular during the Victorian era. More buildings were added over the years, but the university rapidly outgrew the site during the 1950s and 60s, and in 1974 the last of the departments moved to the new campus at Ilam.

These handsome buildings didn't stay empty for long and were quickly developed into a lively and an attractive combination of retail and entertainment known as the Arts Centre. It included specialty shops, art galleries, live theatre, an art-house cinema, as well as bars and cafés. On the weekend a bustling market operated with great international food, fresh Canterbury produce, and unique New Zealand craft as well as live entertainment.

All this came to a crashing halt during the Canterbury earthquakes of 2010 and 2011. The stone buildings were extensively damaged, though none had actually collapsed, and so began the long process of repair and restoration. Still continuing today most of the buildings have been reopened in stages depending of a range of factors such as heritage significance, damage and cost.

This is New Zealand's largest collection of historic buildings by far and of the twenty-three separate buildings on site, twenty-two are listed by Heritage New Zealand, and twenty-one of those are Historic Category 1.

These three parts of the complex are unmissable:

The Great Hall

Originally the classics lecture room dating from 1882, it is as British as it gets, but there is a more subtle tip to local influences in the extensive use of native timber with rimu and kauri wall panels and matai, rewarewa and totara uses in the detail. The room is lined with memorials to university notables, and especially impressive is the huge memorial window created by Martin Travers in 1938. This wonderful building is now used for concerts and exhibitions.

Rutherford's Den

New Zealand's most famous scientist, Ernest Rutherford, was born at Brightwater, Nelson in 1871 and studied mathematics and physics at Canterbury University in the early 1890s. Rutherford left New Zealand in 1895 to study at Cambridge University and he is best remembered for his pioneering work in nuclear science, for which he is often called the 'father of the atom'. He died in 1937 and is buried in Westminster Abbey near two other great scientists, Sir Isaac Newton and Lord Kelvin. Ernest Rutherford appears on the New Zealand $100 note.

At the Arts Centre is a series of superbly preserved rooms that Rutherford once used, reflecting university life in New Zealand around 1900. The lecture theatre comes complete with desks absolutely covered in student names and doodles carved in the wood over many decades, while downstairs is a tiny basement room where Rutherford conducted his experiments. It is amazing that these rooms have survived all these years virtually unaltered, and it really is like walking back into the past. In addition to the lecturer theatre and the Den, there is an extensive exhibition detailing the importance of Rutherford's work to modern science.

$ Entry fee.

Tecce Gallery

Opened in May 2017 this exceptional small museum is the home of the extensive University of Canterbury Logie Collection and is New Zealand's only museum dedicated to classical antiquities, with a focus on Greek, Roman, Egyptian and Near Eastern cultures. The Collection covers no less than 7000 years of human history beginning with Neolithic pottery in 6500BC through to the later years of the Roman Empire.

Professional curated, each exhibition is different and great care is taken to make displays accessible and interesting. Even if your interest in classical cultures is minimal, you are guaranteed to find something of interest and the size is such that thirty minutes is all you need. The only permanent exhibits are the Roman floor mosaics.

Appropriately, the Teece Museum of Classical Antiquities is located in the old University of Canterbury Music and Classics Departments.

📍 Arts Centre,
Worcester Boulevard, Christchurch City.

2. Ice Cream Charlie, the Home of the Vanilla Ice

The Vanilla Ice cart first appeared on central city streets in 1903 as a handcart pulled by Sali Mahomet. The family were either from Afghanistan or Northern India and, after spending some time in Australia, Sali came to Christchurch with his father Sultan (Sali's brother stayed in Australia working as a camelteer). For some unknown reason Sali became known as Charlie, hence the name 'Ice Cream Charlie'.

He married a local woman, and the couple had three daughters before Sali finally gave up the cart in 1926 (by then he had a horse drawn cart). The cart was taken over by Vic Wilkinson, a former competitor, and then taken over again in the 1950s by Vic's son-in-law, Ken Burns, who only died recently. By that time the cart had a permanent spot in Victoria Square where it stands today. A Christchurch tradition, the cart is frequently visited by families who are loyal customers across several generations.

Vanilla ice is distinctly different to ice cream and was called 'ice' as didn't have a high enough cream content to qualify as ice cream. Still made to the original recipe, the ice has a lighter taste than traditional ice cream as it has a much lower fat content.

📍 Armagh Street, Victoria Square.

3. New Regent Street

Built in the 1930s, New Regent Street is very rare in New Zealand in that the entire street is in the same Spanish Mission style with the pastel-coloured buildings complementing the architecture. Originally a pedestrian mall, the narrow street was reopened to cars in the 1940s but has reverted back to a pedestrian precinct in recent years, with only the Christchurch tram running down the middle. Somewhat overrun by tourists, the street is now home to an eclectic and interesting mix of small shops and cafés.

4. Margaret Mahy Playground

Covering 2 ha and billed as the largest children's playground in the Southern Hemisphere, this is one place that will have the adults grizzling that they are tired and want to go home. Working on the principle of mixing 'play with managed risk', with favourites such as a four-metre-wide slide, a giant sandpit and a flying fox, the playground has the perfect summer attraction: water cannons, splash pad and timed sprinklers. For the very little one there is a crawl tunnel, rockers and gentle swings; for patient adults there are food and drink stalls, seating, BBQs, shade and a talking toilet.

Margaret Mahy was the much-loved award-winning author of more than 140 books for children and young people with an enormous sense of fun. Born and raised in Whakatane, Mahy spent most of her adult life in Christchurch, publishing her first book *A Lion in the Meadow* in 1969.

The playground wasn't without controversy, particularly in the cost which, when the playground opened, was said to be $3 million. What wasn't mentioned at the time was the $19.6 million for land purchase, $1.3 million for demolition of existing buildings, and $17 million to prepare the land for the modest $3 million playground. Fortunately, none of that seems to matter to happy, gleeful children.

 Corner of Manchester and Armagh Streets, Central Christchurch.

5. Kate Sheppard Memorial

Unveiled in September 1993 by New Zealand's first female Governor General, this memorial commemorates 100 years since women in this country won the right to vote, and in particular honours the leading campaigner, Kate Shepherd.

Throughout the second half of the nineteenth century the movement to grant women the right to vote grew throughout the world and New Zealand was at the forefront of that movement. Led by various male politicians such as Robert Stout, Julius Vogel, John Balance and William Fox, several bills in favour of votes for women narrowly missed passing in 1878, 1879 and 1887, though from 1876 women who paid rates could vote in local government elections. One of the complicating factors was that votes for women and the Temperance Movement were often viewed as much the same thing and that votes for women would inevitably lead to prohibition (a fear very nearly realized in 1919).

Elsewhere in the world, women had limited voting rights in The Isle of Man, Pitcairn Island and in several US territories including Wyoming (1869), Utah (1870), Washington (1883), Montana (1887) and Colorado (1893).

In 1891 the Liberal government under John Balance, a firm supporter of votes for women, came to power and at the same time women mobilised under the leadership of Kate Sheppard to present parliament with huge petitions. Electoral bills in favour of women's suffrage were passed by the lower House of Representatives in both 1891 and 1892, only to be defeated in the upper and more conservative house, the Legislative Council.

When Balance died, Richard Seddon became Premier. Seddon, closely aligned with the liquor industry, was antagonistic to the third bill which easily passed through the lower house, though it was expected to be defeated in the Legislative Council. Seddon and his supporters attacked the legislation but their underhand tactics were their downfall. Two councillors, previously opponents of change, voted for the bill just to antagonize Seddon and the bill was passed 20 to 18.

On September 19 1893, New Zealand became the first self-governing country to grant women the right to vote for members of parliament. What is frequently forgotten is that while women were able to vote from 1893, they were not allowed to stand for parliament until 1919.

When it comes to women politicians it was women from the South Island who led the charge.

Elizabeth McCombs finally won the Kaiapoi seat in 1933 after the death of the previous member who was her husband James. Elizabeth's majority was 2600 where her husband had a very slim majority of just 31.

The first woman elected under the National Party banner was Mary Grigg in 1942 for the Mid-Canterbury seat and, like Elizabeth McCombs, stood in an electoral seat formerly held by her husband. The first Maori woman MP was Iriaka Ratana, elected in 1949 for Western Maori.

Mabel Howard was New Zealand's first woman Cabinet Minister holding the Labour seat of Sydenham. In April 1947 she was appointed the Minister of Health and Minister in Charge of Child Welfare. Not only was Mabel the first woman to serve as a Cabinet minister in New Zealand but also in a Commonwealth country.

In December 1997 Jenny Shipley became New Zealand's first female Prime Minister and first female leader of the National Party. Born in Gore, Shipley was MP for Rakaia and served under the National Government as Minster for Social Welfare, Minster for Woman's Affairs, Minster of Health and Minister of Transport before becoming Prime Minister.

Shipley lost the 1999 election to Labour's Helen Clark, New Zealand's second female Prime Minister.

The stone wall memorial features life size bronze sculptures of Sheppard along with five other suffrage leaders: Helen Nicol, Ada Wells, Harriet Morrison, Meri Te Tai Mangakahia and Amey Daldy. They are pushing a small cart containing the suffrage petition to Parliament. Other panels illustrate scenes from women's lives in the nineteenth century.

 Kate Sheppard National Memorial Reserve, Oxford Terrace.

6. 185 Empty White Chairs

Sometimes the simplest ideas are the most powerful and this collection of 185 empty white chairs, each representing a person who died in the February 2011 earthquake, is incredibly moving.

Artist Pete Majendie was inspired by Van Gogh's painting of empty chairs representing the owner's personality. Each of the chairs is different, but all are ordinary everyday chairs, and all have been thickly coated in stark white paint. Lounge chairs, kitchen chairs, office chairs, a baby's high chair, a rocking chair and even a wheelchair. It is the plainness and everydayness of the chairs that really touches the heart. A simple chair that is no longer occupied conveys an enormous and enduring sense of loss. Every visitor will find one or more chairs that they can identify with.

Originally planned as a temporary, the installation is now looking for a permanent home and is currently located in Manchester Street.

236 Cashel Street, Christchurch.

7. A Tale of Three Cathedrals

The Canterbury earthquakes left in ruins two of New Zealand's finest cathedrals and struck at the heart of Christchurch's identity. The earthquake also provoked a long a bitter discussion of the fate of both churches, both churches with the Anglican Cathedral to be rebuilt, while the Catholic building is demolished.

Consecrated in 1905, the Catholic Cathedral of the Blessed Sacrament is the grandest of all Francis William Petre's New Zealand churches. Built over a period of four years in the Roman Renaissance style, the massive dome rose more than 40 m above the city and the magnificent stained-glass windows came from both Chartres in France and Munich in Germany. Inside the church, the altar contained the relics of four saints: Severinus, Lucidus, St Anthony Mary Zaccaria and Peter Chanel. When George Bernard Shaw visited the city in 1934 he was full of praise for the Petre's church while dismissing the Anglican Cathedral as a mere copy of every other Anglican Church. It was Shaw's comments that put this church on the map.

Petre also designed similar but smaller churches for Invercargill, Waimate and Timaru. It is likely that the entire Christchurch cathedral will be demolished.

Lying isolated and forlorn in the middle of Cathedral Square is ChristChurch Anglican Cathedral, and it is this building more than any other that made the city appear so 'English'. It was the most traditional of buildings, constructed in the English Victorian Gothic style with a soaring nave, fine wall mosaics and stained-glass windows. Building began on the cathedral in 1864, but after the foundations were laid funds quickly ran out, and when novelist Anthony Trollope visited in 1872 he described the 'vain foundations' as a 'huge record in failure'. However, by 1881 the nave was complete and opened, though the church was not finished until 1904. Severely damage in the earthquakes, it took many years to reach an agreement to restore the cathedral, but work is yet to start.

The 'cardboard' cathedral was the Anglican churches' response to a city without its main Cathedral. Cleverly designed by Japanese architect Shigeru Ban, noted for his 'disaster' buildings using recycled cardboard tubes, the Transitional Cathedral was quickly built and opened in August 2013.

The phrase 'cardboard' cathedral comes with the heavy expectation of a church constructed from a stack of grocery boxes. Instead this a very solid building with huge tubes of heavy industrial grade cardboard filled with concrete and complimented by a very clever and extensive use of plywood. The atmosphere is intimate and welcoming.

 Cathedral of the Blessed Sacrament: 122 Barbadoes Street.
ChristChurch Cathedral: Cathedral Square.
Transitional Cathedral: Latimer Square.

8. Quake City

Quake City is a temporary exhibition by Canterbury Museum. The display includes extensive videos not only of the event, but also on seismic activity and earthquake engineering. There is a detailed and lucid explanation on liquefaction, a phenomenon that affected large areas of the city. On display are numerous damaged artefacts from some of Christchurch's most iconic buildings.

The reaction of visitors is surprising. The atmosphere is quiet, respectful and one of intense concentration, and the mostly younger crowd are totally absorbed.

  299 Durham Street North, Christchurch
  Open daily 10 am to 5 pm.
  03 365 8375
     www.canterburymuseum.com
  Entry fee.

9. Velocity Karts

Located in the bizarre empty streets of Christchurch's devastated eastern suburbs, Velocity City brings a welcome spark of life to this barren area. Wind is definitely not a problem in the open flat space near the sea. This Kiwi invention is very simple and takes the concept of sailing on water and moves it on to land. Those who have experience with sailing dinghies will feel right at home here. However, the blokarts are very easy to use for even the complete novice and in no time first timers are zipping around the simple course like old hands. The world record for a blocart is a snappy 124 kph but the average speed is more modest, around 50 kph.

More unusual are driftkarts, which are also a Kiwi invention. These small vehicles are front wheel driven which allows the rear end to smoothly slide and spin in a wide angle around sharp bends and tight corners.

Still want more? Then try Human Foosball, which is just like the tabletop version but here you have to kick the ball.

Bookings are essential.

 Bexley Reserve, 499 Pages Road, Christchurch
 02 3888 222
www.velocitykarts.nz

10. Riccarton Market

This large bustling market with over 300 stalls operates on a Sunday morning (except Easter Sunday when it operates on Easter Monday), and sells everything from fresh vegetables and food through to clothing and craft and a lot more besides. What makes this market so appealing and different is that, unlike most other markets, Riccarton is not stuck in some ugly car park, but situated in an attractive leafy park alongside Riccarton Racecourse with plenty of space and parking. The friendly atmosphere under the trees on a warm summer's days, while munching on a tasty treat and looking for that special bargain is a great way to idle away a Sunday morning in the 'Garden City'.

 Riccarton Racecourse, Racecourse Road.
 Every Sunday 9 am to 2 pm.

11. Show Week

A&P shows are a common part of New Zealand life especially in rural areas, but 'Show Week' in Christchurch is unique in New Zealand.

Show Week combines a series of horse races with the traditional A&P Show and includes the public holiday of Canterbury Anniversary Day. The city is packed as town and country enjoy a week of parties, dinners and picnics (and accommodation is at a premium).

The actual Canterbury A&P Show is held for three days at Canterbury Agriculture Park in Wigram Road and combines trade shows, produce and animal competitions, equestrian events and wood-chopping contests with the ever-popular carnival sideshows and rides.

The racing part of the week includes gallops, trotting, and greyhounds at Riccarton and Addington racecourses, and the highlights are Guineas Day, New Zealand Trotting Cup Day, Mile Race Day and the grand finale, The New Zealand Cup Day.

12. Cabbage Trees, Burnside High School

In the grounds of Burnside High School is a group of cabbage trees/ ti kouka that date back to pre-European times. They were used both as a reference point and a resting place by Maori travelling from pa on the Banks Peninsula through swamp land to the major pa at Kaiapoi. Known as Te Herenga Ora, the trees became tapu as travellers performed certain rights at the trees to ensure a safe journey. Recognising the trees' significance, early European settlers fenced them off to prevent damage and now safe within the grounds of Burnside High School their future is secure. The cabbage tree forms the school's crest and the school's Latin motto *Recte soc dirige cursum* also links to the trees' important as a landmark. It roughly translates as 'Take the right path'.

9 Corner Memorial Avenue and Greens Road, Christchurch.

13. Three Boys Brewery

Three Boys Brewery started in a small garage in 2005 and now, four moves later, it is housed in a purpose-built state of the art brewery. Still very much a hands-on family brewery, the beer is brewed in small batches and close attention is paid to every stage from selecting the best ingredients to bottling. The beers are neither filtered nor pasteurised and taste reigns supreme: the Oyster Stout actually contains oysters, not just flavouring.

This is not a cosy wood-lined bar for an evening out, but a working industrial brewery with a tasting and drinking area attached (the tasting room only operates during working hours, see the website for details). Here you can experience the rattle of the bottling machine just a few metres away. That said it is an excellent place to end a busy day. It is relaxed and friendly and has an upper mezzanine floor with comfortable chairs overlooking the entire operation.

There are always five staple beers on tap and five others which constantly change, along with cider and non-alcoholic drinks for your driver. An excellent place to start the tasting is with a flight of beers. You can also fill your own bottles.

  592 Ferry Road, Woolston.
  03 940 5621
    www.threeboysbrewery.co.nz

14. Dame Ngaio Marsh's House

Born in 1895, Dame Ngaio Marsh lived in this house for seventy-seven years from the age of ten until her death in 1982, and during this time she cast a wide and domineering shadow over Canterbury literary and theatrical life.

The house is not large, but beautifully proportioned and full of family treasures, books and paintings, including the famous portrait of the Dame by Olivia Spencer Bower painted in the early 1950s. Ngaio Marsh was also an accomplished painter in her own right, and some of her early works are on display in the house.

However, it is her detective fiction for which she is best known and Ngaio Marsh stands among the 'Great Ladies' of the English mystery novel, such as Dorothy Sayers and Agatha Christie. Her first novel, *A Man Lay Dead*, was published in 1934; her last novel, *Light Thickens*, was published shortly after her death in 1982; and only four of her novels were set in New Zealand. Curiously, she always wrote with a Waterman pen in green ink. In all Ngaio Marsh wrote over thirty novels from 1934 to 1978, as well as numerous articles, short stories, plays and works of non-fiction. Her popularity peaked in 1962, when one million copies of her books were sold.

Marsh's autobiography *Blackbeech and Honey Dew*, first published in 1965 and revised in 1981, is still in print.

While her mother was a New Zealander, Ngaio's father was English, and during her later life she spent considerable time in England. It is not surprising, then, that the house is very English in style, with a beautiful wood-panelled dining room, a very chintzy bedroom, and a wonderful period kitchen. The living room, complete with a grand piano and known as the 'Long Room', is both stylish and comfortable and the scene of many an elegant party. In the Long Room hangs a very fine Ngaio Marsh watercolour painting *In The Quarry*. Samuel Hurst Seager, who pioneered the style of the New Zealand bungalow, built the house for the family between 1905 and 1906. Later extended, the house still retains the interior colour schemes chosen by Ngaio Marsh.

The house is only open by appointment, but it is well worth making the time to visit the home of this extraordinary woman.

- 📍 37 Valley Road, off Sherwood Lane, Cashmere.
- 🕐 Guided tours daily (except Monday), by appointment only, discount for groups.
- 📞 03 337 9248
- 🌐 www.ngaio-marsh.org.nz
- 💲 Entrance fee.

15. Taylors Mistake

As hard as it is to believe, this bay takes its name from the incredible coincidence that three sea captains, all with the unlucky surname Taylor, wrecked their ships on this short stretch of sand just over the hill from Sumner. While the details of the first wreck are cloudy, the name was in use as early as 1853. However, the name finally stuck after the unfortunate

Captain Taylor of the American ship the *Volga* apparently mistook the bay for the entrance to Lyttelton Harbour and came to grief here in 1858.

Today the beach is best known for both its collection of home-built cribs, some of which are nestled right into the rocky cliffs, and for its very lively surf (check out the live webcam, www.taylorssurf.co.nz). It is also a start point for the very popular Godley Head Walkway.

 Taylors Mistake is 10 km from central Christchurch.

16. Orana Park

Set on 80 ha, Orana Park is an open-range zoo with more than 400 animals from over seventy species. The openness of the park might come as a surprise to people more used to the zoo and botanical garden combination of many city zoos, but the space allows animals the freedom not found in smaller urban zoos. Here you will see not one or two rhinos, but a small herd of six grazing in a huge paddock.

The real secret to enjoying a visit to Orana Park is to time your visit to take advantage of the numerous animal encounters, as this is a great way to see the animals up close and learn more about them from the park's staff. The encounters are timed roughly 30–40 minutes apart so there is plenty of opportunity to see the animals and then stroll on to the next encounter. It is an amazing experience to hand-feed the giraffes, get within a metre of the massive rhinos, watch the 'cheetah chase', and, for the very young, pat and cuddle the farmyard animals. Recently the zoo has acquired gorillas and orangutans and you can easily while away a few hours just watching our nearest primate relatives going about their daily business. Go to the website and figure out what animals you want to see and time your visit accordingly, but start early as you are most likely to end up being at the park all day.

Operated by a charitable trust, the Park is also heavily involved in breeding programmes for both New Zealand and exotic endangered animals. In particular they are boosting numbers for the highly endangered who/blue duck and the orange-fronted kakariki of which there are less than 100 left in the wild.

Orana Park is a vastly different experience from a zoo and while an enjoyable day with children, it is also a great adult experience, so don't feel you have to come with youngsters. On your own is just as satisfying as you can spend your time seeing what you want and not have to cope with bored and tired young ones.

A shuttle service runs around the park if your legs become weary and there is a good café for a sit down and a cup of tea.

 McLeans Island Road.
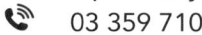 Open daily 10 am to 5 pm. Closed Christmas Day.
 03 359 7109
www.oranawildlifepark.co.nz
$ Entrance fee.

17. Steam Scene – Canterbury Steam Preservation Society

Established for over fifty years, Steam Scene is a huge 30 ha property on McLeans Island which started off with a bush railway and still operates on 1.2 km of track. Run by volunteers, most of the machines and related material come from the Canterbury region and, along with the restored engines, there are many 'works in progress'. Included in the collection is the unique McLean engine, specifically built for the University of Canterbury as a test engine. Naturally there is also a model railway and, if Steam Scene isn't enough, right next door is another organisation called Everything Steam.

Check the website for opening times and open days when many of the machines are working.

 621 McLeans Island Rd, Waimakariri River Regional Park, McLeans Island.
 www.steamscene.co.nz

18. The Whare, Halswell Quarry Gardens

Halswell was once the site of an extensive quarry, providing stone for many of Christchurch's best-known buildings including Canterbury Museum. Opened in the late 1850s and known as Rock Hill, the quarry finally closed in 1990. Today the 55-hectare site is gradually being transformed into extensive gardens, though the quarry itself remains largely untouched. Newly established, six of the gardens represent Christchurch's various sister cities, while another garden focuses entirely on the Canterbury region's native plants.

Below the quarry, near the entrance is a small stone building known as 'The Whare'. Constructed in 1922 of locally quarried stone (naturally) to replace a wooden building that burnt down, this small low building was the single men's quarters and provided accommodation for up to twelve quarrymen at any one time. While The Whare is simple and sturdy, it was not exactly homely, with the men sharing two large bedrooms and a single living area. The highlight is the huge deep bath – a necessity for what must have been a very dirty job but, constructed entirely of concrete, must have taken an age to heat up.

The building also has excellent displays regarding the quarry and buildings and the coffee truck in the car park is worth a visit.

 The main entrance is off Kennedy Bush Road, Halswell. Usually open 8 am to 4 pm but hours may vary.

19. Kaituna Valley Scenic Reserve

Canterbury brings to mind open plains, wide vistas and trees either laid out straight in long lines as shelter belts or in immaculate English style gardens. However, it wasn't always like that. Maori extensively burnt lowland forest and what was left was efficiently hooved up by European settlers for timber or cleared for farming.

A rare glimpse into times past is this reserve in the Kaituna Valley. A mere 6 ha, this tiny bush remnant escaped the adze and the axe and has very fine examples of mature matai and kahikatea along with groves of large titoki. Despite its size tui, ruru and bellbird can be found here and the flat easy loop walk winds through the bush and alongside the pretty Kaituna River. By the entrance is a large sheltered swathe of grass, ideal for picnics.

> Kaituna Valley Road, 5 km off SH 75.

20. Birdlings Flat and Kaikorete Spit

Lake Ellesmere, as much a lagoon as a lake, is New Zealand's fifth largest lake covering an area of almost 200 sq km. At its deepest point, the lake is only two metres deep and is protected from the open sea by the Kaikorete Spit, a long thin finger of land that extends from Banks Peninsula and along the Canterbury Bight for 25 km. The entrance to the lake is frequently blocked by the constantly shifting shingle of the spit and although the lake (along with nearby Lake Forsyth) and the spit have been severely compromised they are still and important habitat for native flora and fauna including native eels.

Birdling's Flat, located near mouth of the Lake Forsyth, is a huge open sweep of beach build up by small stones that have been washed down the Rakaia River and then swept along the coast by tides and currents. A rock hound's paradise, most of the pebbles on the beach are greywacke, but it is also common to find agates, carnelian, petrified wood, jaspers, quartz and volcanic stone.

Definitely leave your swimming gear at home as this coastline is very exposed and very dangerous with huge powerful waves that rush a very long way up the beach. Despite that it is also incredibly beautiful.

> Just off SH 75 10 km south of LIttle River township.

Port Hills and the Banks Peninsula

21. Bridal Path Walkway

In 1851 this track was the main access from Lyttelton to the fledgling Christchurch settlement and, today, the Bridal Path is still a challenging walk. For the early settlers laden with baggage this track must have been daunting indeed and a monument commemorating the endurance of pioneer women can be found on the summit. An alternative to walking the uphill track is to take the gondola to the top and walk back down to either the Heathcote Valley or Lyttelton where the track ends near the entrance to the road tunnel.

- From the Christchurch side, the track begins from the gondola carpark at the end of Bridal Path Road.

- From Lyttleton, the track begins at the end of Bridle Path, which is just left of the Lyttelton Road Tunnel.

22. Port Hills Rest Houses

Henry Ell, an early-twentieth-century Liberal politician, envisaged a series of rest houses along the Summit Road as stopping points for walkers and travellers, though only four were ever built. The Sign of the Takahe, completed in 1949 (long after Henry died), was the most ambitious of the rest houses. Constructed of volcanic stone with stained-glass windows in the ornate Victorian Gothic style, the Sign of the Takahe became a popular restaurant. This building was badly damaged in the earthquakes and, although still standing, it is currently closed.

The Sign of the Kiwi at the summit of Dyers Pass Road is a more modest structure and is now a lovely tearoom, but the Sign of the Bellbird in Kennedy's Bush, and the Sign of the Packhorse at Mt Bradley are little more than stone shelters.

23. Lyttelton Harbour

Like Akaroa, Lyttelton Harbour is the crater of a very ancient volcano formed 12 million years ago, and the rugged hills and dramatic sea cliffs are testament to aeons of geological turbulence. The area around the harbour has been occupied for over 1000 years, first by the Waitaha people, and later by Ngati Mamoe and then Ngai Tahu. Quail Island in the upper harbour was for a considerable period the quarantine station, and even at one time, in the early 1920s, a leper colony. Tiny Ripara Island is an historic pa site and at the end of the nineteenth century was fortified against attack from Russia, which was at that time expanding into the Pacific. The rare Hector's dolphin is frequently seen both in the harbour and around the entire Banks Peninsula.

Christchurch's port, Lyttelton quickly became an important settlement when the only access over the steep Port Hills was by a difficult road. A rail tunnel was vital, and this was opened in 1867, though a road tunnel had to wait almost 100 years and was eventually opened in 1964. The town has many historic buildings, though the port lost many of these in the Canterbury earthquakes including the unique Timeball Station (built 1860).

With a sizeable local population Lyttelton has a well-deserved reputation for live entertainment, good food and excellent coffee and while the town attracts visitors, unlike Akaroa it is not overrun by tourists

 Black Cat Cruises operate the ferry service to Diamond Harbour across from Lyttelton.
 www.blackcat.co.nz

24. Quail Island/Otamahua, Lyttelton Harbour

Windswept and exposed in Lyttelton Harbour, this island has fascinating geological, natural and human history. Built up by three distinct volcanic eruptions, the oldest stone of the island dates back to an eruption at the head of the harbour 14 million years ago. A second eruption 11 million years ago added more lava to the island, while yet more was added during the third six million years ago. The volcanic origins of the island are very clear from the steep cliffs of distinct columnar basalt on the eastern side. Pre-European Maori used the island, known as Otamahua, both for food and as a source of good workable stone.

Otamahua takes its European name from a native quail that appears to have been confined to the island and that quickly became extinct once the land was cleared for farming. Interestingly, Californian quail are common on the island today, so perhaps the name is still appropriate after all. The island is best known as a quarantine station for both people and animals. Once extensive, only a few buildings survive from this period, the oldest being the single men's barracks built in 1874 and occupied from 1875 to 1910. The island was then used as a sanatorium, a hospital during the 1918 influenza epidemic, and for a period from 1907 to 1925 as a leper colony. The grave of the only leper to die on the island occupies a lonely headland overlooking the harbour.

On the western side of the island is a shipwreck graveyard where eight old vessels are clearly visible, especially at low tide. These ships were dumped here rather than wrecked, the largest being the *Darra*, built in 1865 and wrecked in 1951, and the oldest the steamer *Mullogh*, built in 1855 and scuttled in 1923, still with its boiler intact.

Today the island is virtually devoid of native trees but is slowly being replanted by volunteers, though these plantings are still at an early stage. The exception is the area around the old quarantine station where superb old trees offer both shade and shelter and a large grassy area ideal for a picnic (the beach here is good at high tide). The complete circuit of the island takes around two hours, with a shorter walk taking about fifty minutes.

 Black Cat Cruises runs regular trips to the island through the summer.
 03 328 9078
 www.blackcat.co.nz

25. The Thornycroft Torpedo Boat Museum

Mad or brilliant? The Torpedo Boat Museum is not easy to find, but this curious slice of naval history is well worth the effort of hunting out. Torpedo boats had their heyday in the late nineteenth century, originating in the American Civil War and further developed for the British Navy in the 1870s. These extraordinary, small, semi-submerged vessels were equipped with a charge that was designed to explode against a ship below the water line. The charge itself was fixed to the end of a 10-metre-long pole that was rammed against the enemy ship while at the same time the torpedo boat rapidly reversed to avoid being overwhelmed by the blast from the explosion.

During the 1880s, the British Empire felt threatened by the rapid expansion of the Russian Empire and in particular the Russian interest in a warm-water port on the Indian Ocean. Colonies such as Australia and New Zealand suddenly realised just how defenceless they were and rushed to arm themselves against any naval invasion (the 1886 Tarawera eruption was initially thought to be a Russian invasion). New Zealand's response, among much fanfare and flag waving, was to acquire four torpedo boats in 1884, each costing £4000 pounds – one each for Auckland and Port Chalmers and two for Lyttelton, including the *Defender*. But the technology was not a great success. Their low sleek lines, partially to make them hard to see but also to avoid the blast of the explosion, also made them very unstable in rough water. By 1900 the development of the modern destroyer, that could easily defend itself against the torpedo boat, finally made the semi-submersibles redundant.

Eventually sold off, for many years the *Defender* lay abandoned and ended up buried at Purau Beach on the side of the harbour. Rediscovered and recently rescued, the partially restored boat is housed in the old Powder Magazine Building (built 1874 and itself an interesting building). The museum is small and contains not only the remains of the only surviving torpedo boat, but also a working engine from the Dunedin boat, and some amazing archive film showing the boats in action. It is well sign posted to the museum, but it can be confusing – but persevere, as it is worth seeking out. Best to park by the yacht club.

- Charlotte Jane Quay, Lyttleton.
- Open 1 pm to 3 pm, summer: Saturday, Sunday, Tuesday and Thursday, winter: Saturday and Sunday.
- www.lytteltonheritage.co.nz
- Entrance fee.

26. Ohinetahi Garden

The first garden was established here in 1865 by T Potts, but the garden fell into decline after his death in 1888 and all that remained were a few large trees and the lawn on the north side of the old house. In 1977, now in the ownership of Sir Miles Warren, a new garden was designed for the property and expanded again in 2008. The historic house along with the walls, tower and paths were all badly damaged in the Canterbury earthquakes, but have since been restored.

Sloping down to the tidal shore of Lyttleton Harbour, this marvellous garden is a blend of native and exotic plants. Around the house are the more formal gardens with beds of rose, a long border, a wall garden with intricate box hedges and the perfect lawn. On higher slopes, paths weave through woodlands which combine native trees with rhododendrons, camellias and magnolias. A tall tower above the house overlooks the gardens, while below the house towards the sea, the gardens slope down to an amphitheatre.

Throughout the garden are a number of sculptural works by contemporary New Zealand artists.

- 31 Governors Bay Road, Teddington Bay.
- Open September to March, Daily 10 am to 4 pm.
- 03 4299852
- www.ohinetahi.co.nz
- Entrance fee.

27. Allandale Gaol

All that remains of the Allandale settlement is an old gaol, and while an old gaol is not unusual in New Zealand, what is curious is why this gaol, along with an enormous police station, was built in the first place.

Allandale was on the coach road from Lyttleton to Diamond Harbour, but was more rural then than it is today. A constable had been stationed in the area intermittently since 1866, but in 1876 the local MP Thomas Potts (the very same Mr Potts who established the Ohinetahi Gardens mentioned above!) convinced authorities a police station was urgently needed, though the project doesn't seem to be have been backed by any evidence of a crimewave sweeping Allandale. At the cost of PDS300, six acres were purchased and in the following year a further PDS1000 was spent building a substantial two storey, seven room house, a large stable block and a two cell gaol. In July 1877, Constable George Dance moved in. Possibly Constable Dance did a great job, or the police department realised their folly, as just three years later the station was closed down as a permanent police presence was no longer needed.

This, however, was an era of 'waste not, want not' and in 1882 Mr William Teape set up a coach and Royal Mail business in the police buildings. Today just the gaol is left standing.

> 11 km south west of Lyttleton on the Governors Bay-Teddington Road.

28. Two-thousand-year-old Totara Tree

Before the arrival of humans 700 years ago the entire Banks Peninsula was covered in dense forest that supported a wide range of birds including kiwi, weka, kaka and moa. Only 2 per cent of the bush remains, in scattered fragments that include a grove of nikau palms that are here at their southern limit, making these trees the most southerly growing palms in the world.

With the forest remnants are ancient totara trees high on the steep hills that survived both the adze and the axe as they were too inaccessible, small and of irregular form to be of any use. The most impressive of these is a 2000-year-old totara making this possibly the oldest totara in the country (and the world). Bound to a rocky slope by massive roots this tree is not so tall and looks every bit its incredible age. Distinguished by its twin trunks, the totara also has suffered some wind damage with the protection of other forest trees long gone.

> Montgomery Park Scenic Reserve.
> From Hilltop on the Akaroa Road, turn left into Summit Road; the reserve is on the left, 500 m from the intersection.

29. French Peak Winery

Tucked away in French Farm, this small vineyard of just 3.5 hectares is run on organic principles by Renan Cataliotti. Hailing from southern France, Renan produces wine in the drier Provencal style including pinot noir, pinot gris and chardonnay. He also produces a pinot rosé and has a Champagnoise style wine planned for the near future.

Surrounded by vines and set in a lovely small garden is a timber-framed barn containing both the wine-tasting room and self-contained attic accommodation. Just a short drive off the main road, this is a small vineyard and your host is very likely to be the winemaker himself. The really French experience is here and not in Akaroa.

> 79 French Farm Valley Road
> Open 11 am to 5 pm. November to March, Tuesday to Sunday, April – October, Friday and Saturday.
> 021 02956043
> www.frenchpeakwines.com

30. Barrys Bay Cheese Factory

Producing a wide variety of cheeses made in the traditional manner and using only natural ingredients, the Barrys Bay Cheese Factory is the only remaining dairy factory of the many that were once scattered around the peninsula. Established in 1895, the original factory was on the other side of the road by the sea. When this burnt down in 1952, the existing building was constructed closer to the road. Said to be one of the oldest cheese factories in the country, Barrys Bay still only uses locally produced milk. Cheeses include havarti, maasdam and Canterbury red, and Barrys Bay have a strong reputation for aged gouda and mature cheese. Recently cold smoked cheeses have been added to the range.

Monday to Thursday during the season (usually September to May), cheese making can be viewed through wide windows into the factory with helpful signs indicating the type of cheese being made. Available for tasting and purchase, the retail outlet also sells local wines and produce.

 5807 Christchurch-Akaroa Rd (SH 75), Barrys Bay.
 03 304 5809
 www.barrysbaycheese.co.nz

31. Onawe Peninsula, Akaroa Harbour

Onawe Peninsula, shaped like a giant teardrop, juts out into waters of the upper Akaroa harbour and rises to a height of over 100 metres. Linked to the mainland by a narrow strip of land and virtually cut off at high tide, at first glance this was an ideal position for a fortified pa – in fact, the early French settlers called it 'Mount Gibraltar'.

After the fall of Kaiapohia, Te Rauparaha turned his attention to Onawe, the only remaining Ngai Tahu pa in the area and the refuge for many of the survivors. There he cut off the pa by dividing his forces to cover both sides of the narrow isthmus linking the pa to the mainland. The pa had some disadvantages: the terrain allowed for the attacking force to take a position on the hills above the pa where they could easily observe both the defenders and the defences within the pa; the peninsula was large, with no steep cliffs to protect it; and, more importantly, with the isthmus sealed there was no escape route. Te Rauparaha found the pa difficult to capture, but once the opportunity arose, he was very quick to take it.

Seeing Te Rauparaha's frustration during the long siege, Ngai Tahu forces under Tangatahara decided to press their advantage and harry Ngati Toa. However, the attack went wrong and Ngai Tahu retreated back to the pa. Ngati Toa warriors quickly followed, using captives from Kaiapohia as a screen. Reluctant to fire on the attackers for fear of hitting their relatives, the defenders left the gates open too long and Ngati Toa poured into the pa. The well defended pa now became a trap and few inhabitants escaped the terrible massacre, which was followed by a cannibal feast at Barrys Bay.

When peace was finally established in 1839, Ngai Tahu returned to the peninsula, but they were a shadow of their former force and never recovered from the deadly raids in 1831–32.

The track starts to the right of the carpark and skirts around the beach (not over the bluff); it is difficult right on high tide. From there it is an easy walk through open grassland to the top. Today, details of the pa are hard to discern. The rocky outcrop at the summit is called Te Pa Nui Ohau and has marvelous views over the harbour. Do not eat or drink on the summit, it is considered disrespectful. The walk takes around one hour return.

 At Barrys Bay turn into Onawe Flat Road. The track starts from the carpark at the end.

32. Okains Bay Museum

One of the most extraordinary collections anywhere in the country, this originally began as the private collection of Murray Thacker and is now housed in the old cheese factory (built 1894). The Maori collection alone rivals any of New Zealand's major museums, and in addition to a complete meeting house includes an 1840 kareto, or puppet, a god sticking dating back to 1410, a pre-European waka huia from the East Coast, superb greenstone tiki, and even a Chatham Island dendroglyph – human figures carved into the bark of a tree. In fact a whole room is given over to the Chatham's Island collection.

Not content with the small stuff Murray was also busy collecting buildings, most due for demolition. These include the old Akaroa Grandstand, a totara slab cottage built in 1884, and a complete 1871 blacksmith's workshop.

The Colonial Room houses artefacts relating to the history of the bay, and among a vast array of items includes an impressive collection of tobacco-related objects such as matchboxes, cigarette packets and tobacco tins. Murray's private collection of firearms is now on display, and where else would you find a collection of fencing wire? An old whaling gun and oil pots date from the era when the peninsula was a major whaling station.

Murray died in 2017 but his collection is in safe hands and is now run by a trust.

Okains Bay is worth a visit in its own right. Maori settled here drawn by seals and the sheltered beach, though their main pa was on Pa Island, a short distance along the coast. After the incursions by Te Rauparaha in 1830, the pa was abandoned and most of the population fled south.

Settled by Europeans in the early 1850s, Okains Bay flourished on the back of a timber industry supplying the growing town of Christchurch. Farming followed on from timber, but the isolation of the bay led to a declining population and to the small seaside settlement that it is today. Unspoiled Okains Bay has a very good swimming beach and, near the beach, two large caves large enough to picnic in. There is a very large camping ground near the beach.

Along with the museum, the tiny settlement boasts a number of historic buildings including the schoolhouse, the tiny library and the rustic shop and garage hardly altered over the years.

Tihi Arapata Wharenui and waka shed is directly opposite the museum.

 Okains Bay is about 20 km from Akaroa. Okains Bay Road runs off the Summit Road and a short section of the road immediately below the intersection is particularly steep, very narrow and with several sharp turns.

📍 146 Okains Bay Rd, Okains Bay.
🕐 Open daily 10 am and 5 pm. Closed Christmas Day, Good Friday and half day Anzac Day.
📞 03 304 8611
🌐 www.okainsbaymuseum.co.nz
💲 Entrance fee.

33. German and Portuguese Akaroa

In 1838 Captain Langlois, a French sea captain who had visited Akaroa, established the Nanto-Bordelaise company, and in 1840 set sail for New Zealand with the intention of establishing a French colony. By the time they arrived in August 1840 on the ship *Comte de Paris*, the Treaty of Waitangi had been signed, and the new arrivals found themselves in what was now a British colony. Not wishing to return, the settlers established themselves around Akaroa Harbour and were a short time later joined by British immigrants.

Understandably, much is made today of the French settlement of Akaroa. However, very little distinctly French remains from this period, apart from place names and one or two buildings. The town has numerous historic buildings all within a short walking distance and the Rue Jolie and Rue Balguerie are particularly notable for their Victorian cottages. Akaroa in the summer is a popular day trip from Christchurch and is very busy, but when you have an eatery called La Thai Restaurant you know that the faux French Style is well overdone. That said it is a lovely to town to visit especially in the off season.

What is usually forgotten is that French were not the only settlers and there were also a good number of Germans on that first ship (Takamatua was originally German Bay), and British settlers quickly followed. Two old hotels in the town owe their existence, not to the French but to settlers from Germany (The Grand Hotel) and Portugal (Madeira Hotel).

Jacob Waeckerle, a German migrant, arrived with the first group of settlers in 1840 and after working at German Bay, moved to Akaroa and to set up a blacksmith shop. Ever one to recognised an opportunity, Jacob set up a flour mill in 1848 and in 1860 he obtained a hotel licence and built the French Hotel on the main road. In 1878 Jacob Waeckerle served two years as the mayor of Akaroa.

Clearly fond of name changes, he renamed his hotel Waeckerle's Hotel, and it was one of three hotels on Rue Lavaud burned down by an arsonist. Rebuilt by his son-in-law Robert Bayley, the hotel reopened in 1883 with a name to say it all: 'Waeckerle's New Grand Commercial Hotel'. In 1918, as a response to anti-German sentiment, the hotel reverted to its original name and has remained the Grand Hotel ever since. The current hotel honours the original founder of the hotel with Jacob's Bar and Waeckerle's Restaurant.

In contrast the Madeira Hotel has had few name changes from when it was opened in 1871 by Antonio Rodrigues. Born in Funchal on the island of Madeira, Rodrigues first arrived in London in 1857 and then set sail for New Zealand, where he arrived in Lyttleton with his wife Adelaide in 1858. Moving immediately to Akaroa, Rodrigues first set up a bakery before working at the Commercial and Criterion hotels. Finally he built his own hotel in 1871 and named it after his birthplace. Why Rodrigues came to New Zealand is unclear as, apart from a handful of early Portuguese whalers from the Azore Islands, New Zealand has had very little connection with Portugal. In 1888 he built a small cottage for his family of eight children and this still stands today. After running the hotel for thirty-four years Rodrigues died in 1905 and was buried in St Patrick's Catholic Cemetery. After his death a new hotel was built next door and opened in 1907 with the same name, and both hotels are still standing today.

 The Grand Hotel, 6 Rue Lavaud, Akaroa.
The Madeira Hotel, 48 Rue Lavaud, Akaroa.

SOUTH CANTERBURY/ MACKENZIE COUNTRY

1. Peel Forest Park
2. The Giant Jersey
3. Geraldine Vintage Car and Machinery Museum
4. Barker's Preserves and Talbot Forest Cheese Geraldine
5. South Canterbury Blackcurrants
6. Temuka Pottery
7. Caroline Bay
8. Aigantighe Art Museum
9. Richard Pearse Aeroplane Replica
10. York Street Gallery of Fine Art
11. Timaru Botanic Gardens
12. Kakahu Escarpment and Lime Kilns
13. McKenzie and his Dog Statue Fairlie
14. Mackenzie and Hakataramea Passes
15. Aoraki Mackenzie International Dark Sky Reserve
16. Tasman Glacier, Aoraki/ Mt Cook National Park
17. Black Stilt Country
18. Upper Waitaki Power Project
19. The Rock Piles of Omarama
20. The White Horse Monument, the Hunters Hills, Waimate
21. Waimate Parks
22. Dr Margaret Cruickshank Statue
23. St Augustine's Church
24. St Patrick's Church
25. Waimate Silo Murals and the Empress Flour Mill
26. Kapua Moa Swamp
27. Ted's Bottle, Waihao Forks Hotel
28. Paterson Cob Cottage

1. Peel Forest Park

Covering over 700 ha on the southern bank of the Rangitata River in the foothills of the Southern Alps, Peel Forest Park is a remnant of a much larger forest. The area has a climate distinct from the plains, with a much higher rainfall and heavy snowfalls in the winter that supports a rich and diverse flora and fauna – including a large number of native birds and giant totara, matai and kahikatea trees. Much of the bush was felled to supply timber and in 1909 just 94 hectares remained and was set aside as a reserve which protected a huge totara, estimated to be over 1000 years old. With a girth of 8.5 metres and 31 metres tall, over the years the rough bark on the lower trunk has been polished to a smooth sheen rubbed by the hands of the many visitors who have walked to the tree. The variety of ferns is especially surprising, and a third of all native fern types can be found here.

Mt Peel also figures large in the history of New Zealand forestry for it is was at Mt Peel Station that the first radiata pine was planted in 1859, followed by Douglas fir the following year.

The park has a wide range of walking tracks, and jet boat and raft companies provide trips through the Rangitata Gorge. The walking tracks, short and easy, start at two main areas, Blandswood and Te Wanahu, both clearly sign-posted and within 2 km of Mt Peel village.

 Mt Peel Village is 10 km off highway 72 at Arundel.

2. The Giant Jersey

Geraldine is home to the Giant Jersey, now housed in the i-SITE building in the main street. The largest knitted jersey in the world as confirmed by the Guinness Book of World Records was clearly not made with anyone in mind. Measuring over 2 metres high and 5 metres across and 5.5kg, the jersey was made from smaller knitted squares of every conceivable colour and then stitched together.

📍 Geraldine i-SITE, 38 Waihi Terrace, Geraldine.

3. Geraldine Vintage Car and Machinery Museum

Considerably expanded in recent years, this museum has a very extensive and well-displayed collection of vehicles spread through seven large sheds (over 1400 items on show). Originally the museum had a strong emphasis on tractors and farm implements, but today houses a much larger collection of cars ranging from vintage through to more recent 'muscle' cars.

A favourite item here is the incredible 'Wilcox Special'. Designed and built by Reid & Gray in Invercargill in 1939, this enormous plough was produced especially to 'plough the unploughable', and it did just that. This huge and tough plough literally turned over swamp and scrubland, ripping its way through manuka and heavy soil and eventually turning marginal land into productive usable farmland (an accompanying photograph shows the plough in use).

Alongside the cars and farm machinery, the museum is home to an 1877 horse-drawn fire engine, a 1913 Sanderson & Mills tractor, a 1929 International truck restored and rebuilt by John Britten as a gypsy caravan, plus just one aeroplane – the rare, English-built 1929 Spartan.

📍 178 Talbot Street, Geraldine.
🕒 Open daily 9.30 am to 4 pm 1 September to 1 June, 10 am to 4 pm weekends only June to end of July.
📞 03 693 8756
$ Entrance fee.

4. Barker's Preserves and Talbot Forest Cheese Geraldine

Geraldine has become a compulsory stopping point for any foodie on a South Island tour and the main destination is Four Peaks Plaza in the heart of the town. Numerous quality food outlets cram this small location of which the two main highlights are Barker's Preserves and Talbot Forest Cheese.

Established in 1969 by Anthony and Gillian Barker, initially to create fruit based wines, this business grew from modest beginnings to become a highly respected company producing fruit-based products by focusing on innovation, and at the same time never being relaxed about quality.

One of Barker's signature products, the blackcurrant syrup, was developed when local growers approached Anthony Barker with a problem – too many blackcurrants. Seizing an opportunity, Anthony developed a high-quality syrup that remains market leader. Today Barker's offers a wide range of syrups, preserves, fruit pastes, dressings, chutneys, jams and marmalades. The lemon curd and ginger beer syrup is personally recommended. All Barker's products are still made on the site of the original family home and the Barker family are still actively involved.

Talbot Forest Cheese was established by Paul Fitzimmons and partner Angela Veales, when Paul returned to his hometown of Geraldine after working extensively for major cheese producers. In 2000 they produced just ten tonnes of cheese, but they were riding the speciality cheese boom which was sweeping New Zealander's taste buds after a life time of living off great blocks of mass-produced cheddar. Sourcing cow and goat milk from local farms, Talbot Forest produces a wide range of high quality and uniquely flavoured cheeses that scoop up both awards and loyal customers throughout New Zealand. The shop in Geraldine is also the factory where visitors can not only taste the cheese but see them being handmade through huge windows overlooking the production area. Talbot Forest was the town's original name and many of the cheese varieties are named after local places.

Four Peaks Plaza, 76 Talbot St, Geraldine.

5. South Canterbury Blackcurrants

It has always been known that blackcurrants in whatever form are good for you and now it is official: South Canterbury produces the best blackcurrants in the world. Short, cold winters followed by long, hot summers produce fruit with exceptional flavour that are high in vitamin C and antioxidants. Recent studies, however, have now labelled New Zealand blackcurrants as the new super food.

One study showed that within forty-five minutes of drinking New Zealand blackcurrant juice, there was a complete reduction in the enzyme that degrades the 'happiness' hormone dopamine. Another study showed those who consumed New Zealand blackcurrant juice not only exercised longer but also enjoyed it more. Yet more research has also shown that our juice significantly improved recovery after exercise, improved immunity and minimised muscle damage.

It is believed that the high levels of ultra-violet light in New Zealand significantly enhances the natural properties of the blackcurrant and now the company Curranz is producing supplements primarily for athletes using only New Zealand blackcurrant extract.

6. Temuka Pottery

Once every large New Zealand town and city had its own clay works, producing bricks, very basic domestic pottery and in some cases industrial products such as electrical insulators. Most now have long gone, including the most famous of all, Crown Lynn.

Temuka Pottery has an unusual history, not only that is has survived, but its first pottery items, manufactured in the 1930s, were company Christmas gifts for NEECO (National Electric and Engineering Company) and included teapots, vases, tobacco jars and mixing bowls.

Production was severely cut back during WW2 to electric jugs, mixing bowls, chamber pots, hot water bottles and teapots, and its customers oddly enough included the Indian Army. Small decorative pieces were still made as gifts for staff at Christmas.

After the war, production expanded and the company commercially produced mixing bowls, basins, teapots, jugs and vases and even the famous and indestructible New Zealand Railways cups and saucers. Cable Price Downer took over NEECO in 1966 and curtailed the production of domestic pottery, but not for long. In the 1970s Temuka pottery burst upon the New Zealand market with highly fashionably stoneware dinner, tea and coffee sets and storage jars, and a Temuka casserole dish could be found on the gift table at every New Zealand wedding. The range was extensive, unlike the colour, which was only available in various shades of brown.

Since then Temuka has kept up with ceramic fashions, in 2002 they began exporting to Britain and in 2012 provided Hobbiton Movie Tours with tableware for their café Green Dragon Inn.

Today Temuka Pottery produces a wide range of domestic pottery with a focus on striking colourful every day dinnerware. Naturally the shop has the full range, but also has older 'pre-loved' pottery, making it a compulsory stop for Temuka collectors.

57 Vine St, Temuka.
Open 9 am to 4.30 pm, Monday to Friday; 10 am to 4 pm Saturday and Sunday.
03 6155651
www.temukapotteryretailshop.com

Timaru

7. Caroline Bay

In 1890 the creation of a lengthy breakwater for Timaru Harbour changed the sea currents sufficiently to start washing sand of pulverised shingle from the harbour entrance into Caroline Bay, creating, in a very short time, a safe sandy beach. In 1911 the Caroline Bay Association was formed to popularise the bay as a resort along European lines. To this end, formal gardens, promenades, a sound shell and playgrounds were built linked by a grand set of stairs to a piazza on the bluff above the bay. Today the area still retains its original Edwardian flavour, but with many more attractions designed to appeal to newer generations. The piazza has recently been redeveloped into a lively café strip.

The first Caroline Bay Carnival was held in 1911 and still today is a major annual event beginning on Boxing Day. The Carnival draws people from all over the South Island attracted by two weeks of non-stop seaside entertainment, ranging from ever-popular talent quests through to sideshows and, of course, the Miss Caroline Bay competition. In the past, Caroline Bay was always up there with Whangamata and Mt Maunganui as a New Year 'hot spot' but things have settled down and now a more family festival, the Carnival highlight is the New Year's Eve concert and spectacular fireworks display.

Long a part of the carnival is the historic merry-go-round, now restored and the only one of its kind in New Zealand. Built in France in 1920 by a showman named La Retle, the ride has carved German horses, a German organ and hand-painted roundings. The merry-go-round was first shipped to England for the Crystal Palace Show in the early 1920s, then transported first to Australia, finally arriving in New Zealand in 1928. Acquired by the Caroline Bay Association in 1973, the merry-go-round is such a carnival institution that parents who rode on it as children are now bringing their children back to experience the unique showground ride.

8. Aigantighe Art Museum

Housed in a wonderful old Edwardian house (built 1908), this small but lively art gallery offers the perfect combination of traditional and contemporary art and will appeal even to those who rarely set foot in an art gallery. Including a substantial European collection dating from the sixteenth century, Aigantighe also has a significant holding of works by New Zealand artists including CF Goldie, Frances Hodgkins, Petrus Van der Velden and Colin McCahon, who was born in Timaru and whose parents lived in Geraldine. In addition to the permanent collection, the gallery hosts innovative art from both New Zealand and around the world.

The gallery also has a substantial collection of sculptures from both New Zealand and international artists in the garden surrounding the house, which are open to view at all times. Aigantighe is pronounced 'egg-and-tie' and means 'at home' in Scottish Gaelic.

- 49 Wai-iti Road, Timaru.
- Open Tuesday to Friday 10 am to 4 pm, Saturday and Sunday 12 noon to 4 pm.
- www.aigantighe.co.nz
- 03 688 4424
- Koha/donation.

9. Richard Pearse Aeroplane Replica

Suspended from the high roof of the South Canterbury Museum is a replica of Richard Pearse's aeroplane, designed and built by him from bamboo and calico (his nickname was 'Bamboo Dick'). While the debate whether Pearse flew before the Wright Brothers will never be settled in New Zealander's minds, the argument really hinges on whether or not Pearse achieved 'controlled' flight. Several witnesses saw him fly his plane on 31 March 1903, but he was unable to land and ended up in a gorse hedge. Pearse himself never claimed it was controlled flight.

Born and raised in Upper Waitohi, about 18 km northwest of Timaru, Pearse was an inveterate inventor but was considered by many locals to be a crank. While he worked away at other inventions, flight was his passion, though developments in aviation quickly overtook Pearse's backyard efforts. He died in 1953 in relative obscurity, his achievements recognised only long after his death.

The replica hanging in the museum is so flimsy and basic that you would have to agree that one of his other nicknames 'Mad Pearse' is not far off the mark. Basic the plane might be, the design of his plane was surprisingly sophisticated and Pearse had in place most of the elements for controlled flight. Pearse is certainly an early aviation pioneer worthy of respect and remembrance.

- Perth Street.
- Open Tuesday to Friday 10 am to 4.30 pm, Saturday, Sunday and public holidays 1.30 pm to 4.30 pm.
- www.museum.timaru.govt.nz
- Koha/donation.

10. York Street Gallery of Fine Art

Small, stylish and welcoming, the York Street Gallery is both the sculpture studio of Debbie Templeton and a place to both view and buy carefully selected, exceptional works of art by both established and emerging New Zealand artists.

An accomplished sculptor, Debbie moved to New Zealand from her native Tasmania in her early twenties. The gallery opens out to a courtyard, partially enclosed by the sculpture studio and featuring an intriguing ground level water feature.

- 21 York Street, Seaview, Timaru.
- Open Thursday to Saturday only, 11 am to 3 pm.
- 03 634 4795
- www.debbietempletonpage.com

11. Timaru Botanic Gardens

Dating from 1864, one of the earliest established botanic gardens in New Zealand, these gardens tucked away just south of the city centre have retained a wonderful Victorian and Edwardian flavour. Covering 19 ha, the surprisingly large grounds contain over thirty different plant collections as well as formal flower beds, an aviary, children's playground, fern house and rose gardens. The borders are especially attractive and dedicated to one type of plant including iris, dahlia and of course perennials. But it is the older structures that give the gardens a special feel. The very grand war memorial was originally erected to commemorate the First World War, and the Edwardian band rotunda was built in 1911 to celebrate the coronation of King George V and Queen Mary (which, of course, is then not strictly Edwardian). Another gem is the former tea kiosk, a small elegant building delightfully remembered as 'Erected in 1923 by the Floral Fête Committee'. The gardens were declared Gardens of National Significance in 2014.

- Corner King and Queen Streets, Timaru.
- Open summer 8 am to dusk; winter 8 am to 5 pm.

12. Kakahu Escarpment and Lime Kilns

The limestone landscape around Kakahu is an area of fascinating rock formations combined with a rare lowland bush remnant. Like a giant high tidal wave of rock about to break over the surrounding farmland, the Kakahu Escarpment is a wonderful smooth and weathered limestone cliff 30 m high. Sculptured by wind and water, long striped patterns run down the rock face and huge mushroom-shaped boulders lie at the base of the escarpment. The short track can be very muddy in places. Just down the road are historic lime kilns built in 1876.

In the same area is the largest colony in the eastern South Island of the New Zealand long-tailed bat *Chalinolobus tuberculatus,* one of just two surviving native bat species.

- From Geraldine take SH 79 for 15 km towards Fairlie/Mt Cook and then turn left into Hall Road. The escarpment is 3.5 km down this gravel road.

The Mackenzie Country

13. McKenzie and his Dog Statue Fairlie

In February 2003, locals turned out to witness the unveiling of a statue of James McKenzie and his dog Friday. Cast in bronze by sculptor Sam Mahon, the statue weighs 450 kg and depicts the both the dog and McKenzie, moving forward into the unknown. The statue is mounted on stone from the Mackenzie Pass.

The statue was not without controversy. In particular some locals objected to its placement in the centre of town as it was inappropriate to have 'a statue of a thief in the main street', while others said the statue was irrelevant as McKenzie never even came through Fairlie. Finally one of the councillors remarked at the time 'it has to go somewhere' and so the statue stayed in the main street.

 Fairlie town centre

14. Mackenzie and Hakataramea Passes

For those who like a different driving route, these two passes are an interesting and not difficult detour from the usual route through South Canterbury, though it does involve a considerable stretch of gravel road.

Mackenzie Pass

The pass through which James McKenzie drove his stolen sheep lies on a rugged stretch of road just to the south of the more frequently travelled Burkes Pass. Born in Ross Shire, Scotland, McKenzie (better known as Jock) emigrated first to Australia and then on to New Zealand, coming to fame in March 1885 when he 'acquired' a flock of 1000 sheep. According to McKenzie, he came by the flock by legitimate means, but not so according to the law, and he was apprehended near a pass leading to a previously unknown high-country basin. McKenzie's dog, Friday, was equally legendary, and apparently capable of moving the entire flock of sheep without command.

McKenzie, whose native tongue was Gaelic, sat silently throughout the trial, was found guilty, and sent to jail. He twice escaped and was last seen in Lyttelton before vanishing from history altogether. Both the pass and the basin now bear his name (though spelt differently), and a plaque at the spot where he was apprehended written in English, Gaelic and Maori commemorates McKenzie's exploits.

Hakataramea Pass

After travelling through the Mackenzie Pass the road joins the sealed route from Tekapo. Turn left on this road and after a few kilometres turn left into the Hakataramea Pass. Again, this road is gravel and although it involves a number of shallow fords and closed gates is navigable by the average family car. This is lost and lonely tussock country of rolling hills and stark beauty – much like Central Otago, but without all the people. At one point the road travels right through the middle of the stockyards and homestead of a high-country station. Eventually the gravel runs out and back on sealed the road meanders down the Hakataramea Valley to Kurow on the Waitaki River.

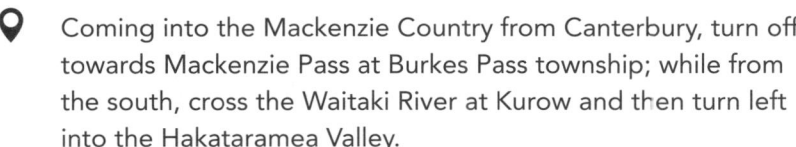

> Coming into the Mackenzie Country from Canterbury, turn off towards Mackenzie Pass at Burkes Pass township; while from the south, cross the Waitaki River at Kurow and then turn left into the Hakataramea Valley.

15. Aoraki Mackenzie International Dark Sky Reserve

Fed by the icy waters of the Godley River, Lake Tekapo is quickly becoming an alternative holiday destination to the more commercial Queenstown and Wanaka. At 700 m the climate is definitely alpine, but the rainfall is low, the sunshine hours high and in summer it can be very hot.

On the main route from Christchurch to Mt Cook, Tekapo is overrun by tourists during the warmer months, but now there is a very good reason to come here in the winter. In 2012, 4300 square kilometers were declared to be the Aoraki Mackenzie International Dark Sky Reserve, one of only eleven in the world and the only one in the southern hemisphere.

With a tiny permanent population, outdoor lighting control was introduced nearly forty years ago and is now strictly controlled in the area. These controls, together with the unpolluted air and clear skies, make the vast night sky an amazing sight especially in winter. From horizon to horizon the entire sky is full of stars and constellations, and it is not surprising that New Zealand's leading astronomical observatory is located on the summit of Mount John overlooking Lake Tekapo.

16. Tasman Glacier, Aoraki/Mt Cook National Park

At over 30 km, the Tasman Glacier is the longest glacier in the country and reaches far into the mountains at the base of Mt Cook and terminates in the Tasman River. But don't come looking for a spectacle of sparkling white ice. The glacier has been slowly shrinking over the past 10,000 years, leaving a thick layer of rocks and gravel covering the ice, and it looks more like an abandoned quarry than the spectacular glaciers of the West Coast on the other side of the Alps. However, beneath the scruffy surface the ice is much deeper than it appears, going down over 100 metres and still grinding its way down the valley, through a vast landscape of rock torn apart by the power of moving ice. Small, slowly melting icebergs drift in the icy green water of the glacier's terminal lake. The walk to the lookout is relatively easy, apart from a rocky scramble at the end, and takes around forty minutes return.

> Just before Mt Cook Village, turn right into Tasman Valley Road and continue 8 km to the car park. The road is gravel but in good condition.

17. Black Stilt Country

The black stilt, found only in New Zealand, is one of our most endangered birds and its habitat is now severely restricted to a handful of rivers in the Mackenzie basin. In 1981 the birds numbered a mere twenty-three, and in 2005 the population had still only risen to just fifty-five adults. Despite a huge effort to increase the population, by 2018 numbers had only risen to 135. The birds nest on the ground on the banks of rivers and streams rather than islands, and not only are the birds, eggs, and chicks an easy meal for predators, but their habitat is very difficult to protect.

The jet-black plumage and long red legs of the adult bird are very distinctive, and while the birds are rare, there is a very good chance of spotting one as they are not shy and feed in shallow water throughout the basin including the hydro canals.

18. Upper Waitaki Power Project

This extensive power project, begun in 1968, links lakes Tekapo, Pukaki, Ruataniwha and Ohau through a series of massive canals and power stations to Lake Benmore. The town of Twizel, taking its name from the nearby Twizel River, was created to service the project and was, at the time, the most modern of all the hydro towns. The intention was to remove the town once the project was completed, but it survived and is now the centre of a thriving tourist industry. The hydro lakes have become destinations in themselves, popular for fishing and boating, and Mt Cook/Aoraki is not far away.

 The best place to get an idea of the extensive nature of the Upper Waitaki scheme is just south of the town, where a viewpoint overlooks the complex of canals and one of the power stations.

19. The Rock Piles of Omarama

Clearly, the trip through the Lindis Pass has a strange effect on people. Along a 10-km stretch of the long lazy road from the pass to Omarama stand numerous rock piles built by passers-by just for the sheer hell of it – much like building sand castles, but more permanently, out of stone. Some are just mere piles, others are created in stylish geometric patterns, while yet others are delicate geological balancing acts, though it is doubtful these last for long in the howling nor'westers that frequently blow through the Mackenzie basin.

Some cairns are clearly little roadside shrines, though the deity to which those topped by a beer bottle or an old broken jandal are dedicated remains a mystery. The etiquette of pile construction is also unclear. Do you reuse previously collected stones or do you gather fresh ones? While it probably doesn't matter, plainly it would be in bad form to actually destroy a still-intact pile, but collapsed piles are surely fair game. Happy building!

Waimate

Although just a few kilometres off SH 1, quaint Waimate is often bypassed by busy tourists rushing between Dunedin and Christchurch. It is worth the short detour from the main road as the town has numerous attractions for those looking for the quirky and different.

Norman Kirk, New Zealand's second prime minister to die in office (Michael Joseph Savage was the first), was born here in 1923, attended primary school in the town, and is buried in the local cemetery.

Another handsome historic building is the old courthouse in Shearman Street and now the Waimate Museum. One of the country's most appealing small buildings, the courthouse was constructed in 1879 and still contains the magistrate's bench. Alongside the museum are a cob cottage and a pit-sawn totara cottage and jail, both built around 1880.

20. The White Horse Monument, the Hunters Hills, Waimate

The White Horse Monument high on Mt John (446 m), dedicated to the work of the humble Clydesdale horse, is best appreciated from a distance. Constructed from rough blocks of concrete in the 1960s, this is a quaint piece of New Zealand folk art which owes more to Kiwi enthusiasm than to any form of high art. It is easy to see that the materials to construct the horse only cost $240. Behind the project was retired farmer Norman Hayman who, while on a visit to the Netherlands, was inspired by a statue of a Friesian cow to establish a similar tribute to the stoic Clydesdale.

But the good folk of Waimate also have a sense of humour, and at times the horse has been repainted with black stripes to turn it into a zebra, while at others it has been painted a vivid pink. The views from up here are worth the effort, whether you come by road, via the walkway, or on mountain bike.

📍 End of Centrewood Park Road, Waimate.

21. Waimate Parks

In addition to its many historic buildings, the town has two very fine public parks. Established in 1881, Victoria Park is appropriately Victorian with formal gardens, playgrounds and an aviary. An unusual feature for a small town is the park's banked cycle track, built in 1891 and still in use. Also within the park is a small enclosure housing Bennett's or red-necked wallabies. Imported from Tasmania in 1870 and released into the Hunters Hills west of the town, these wallabies quickly became pests and today are still a fine trophy for local hunters. The other park, Knottingley, established in 1874, is a combination of sports fields (cricket was first played here in 1902) and arboretum and now contains over 3000 trees.

📍 Victoria Park: 22 Naylor Street, Waimate.
Knottingley Park: Waihao Back Road, Waimate.

22. Dr Margaret Cruickshank Statue

The first two women to graduate from the University of Otago Medical School did so within a year of each other; Emily Siedeberg in 1896 and Margaret Cruickshank in 1897. However, it was Margaret Cruickshank that first registered as a doctor in May 1897 with Emily registering the following year. Both women commented that although there was some reluctance to accept women into the medical professional, there was in fact a good deal of support and no hostility from men.

Margaret went into practice with Dr Barclay in Waimate where she tragically died during the 1918 flu epidemic. A commemorative statue of Dr Cruickshank now graces the main street of Waimate inscribed with the words 'The Beloved Physician/Faithful unto Death'.

📍 Seddon Square, Waimate.

23. St Augustine's Church

This extremely attractive church was built in 1872 of locally milled matai and totara on land donated by settler Michael Studholme. The very handsome lantern tower was added in 1883, giving the church a distinctive and unusual roof line. The stand-alone bell tower was added in front of the church in 1903, and a rare stained-glass window features Sir Galahad's vision of the Holy Grail, which in this case is a chalice.

📍 John Street, Waimate.

24. St Patrick's Church

Built in 1909, this church seems far too big for a town the size of Waimate. Tall and grand in style, the design is distinctly the work of FW Petre, who built several other Catholic churches in the South Island. The three bells of the church were cast in Belgium in 1922, the largest weighing over half a tonne, and the organ was one of the last built by renowned organ builder Arthur Hobday, in 1916.

 6 Cameron Street, Waimate.

25. Waimate Silo Murals and the Empress Flour Mill

Dominating the southern end of the main street are two enormous silos in front of which is the modest historic building, the Empress Flour Mill. Once a major wheat producing area, the Empress Flour Mill built in 1892 is the last mill left standing.

The four huge silos, standing 35 m tall and holding over 3000 tonnes of wheat, were constructed in 1934. However, the silos were left unused for over forty-five years as the concrete was not properly cured and due to sweating ruined the wheat.

Transport Waimate now use the old mill as a transport depot and the owner Barry Sadler arranged with local artist Bill Scott to use the silos to depict Waimate history. Not yet complete, so far the silos are adorned by giant murals of Dr Margaret Cruickshank, World War II hero Eric Batchelor, Chief Te Huruhuru, Michael Studholme and former Prime Minister Norman Kirk.

 172 Queen Street, Waimate.

26. Kapua Moa Swamp

In all honesty you don't need to stop here and in fact it is not even worth slowing down that much, but this low stretch of land on the southern side of the Waimate Gorge has contributed more to our understanding of the extinct bird the moa than any other location in New Zealand.

During the unusually dry of summer of 1895 local famer T MacDonald was anxious to find a better water supply for his stock and spotting a likely spot started to dig. Very soon he began to find bones – and a lot of them – but dismissed the finds as 'bits of one of Studholme's bullocks'. His neighbor, Mr Frederick Sevicke-Jones, noticed the bones and pointed out to MacDonald that they were moa bones. On closer inspection MacDonald agreed that the bones were unlikely to belong to a bullock. The find caught the attention of Frederick Hutton, curator of the Canterbury Museum who then paid PD40 for a 'claim' to work the area.

Over the years Kapua swamp yielded bones belonging to no fewer than 800 moa and the number of birds and type of species led to a great leap forward in our understanding of this unique animal. Moa used this swamping ground for grazing and occasionally a hapless bird stepped into deep watery sink hole from which it was impossible to escape. Once dead and decomposed, the bird's bones sunk deeper into the sink holes. The deaths occurred singularly over a long period.

In all there were nine species of moa with an estimated total number of birds of around 160,000 when Maori arrived around 1280. In less than 150 years, all species were extinct.

  SH 82, 8 km south of Waimate.

27. Ted's Bottle, Waihao Forks Hotel

A word of warning before reading this – get your hankie out now.

LeTour Mollet D'Auvergne, known by his nickname Ted, grew up and farmed at Waihao Forks, 10 km south of Waimate, and enlisted in the New

Zealand Army on 19 September 1939 (his family were originally from Jersey in the Channel Island, hence the unusual French name). As part of the 27th Machine Gun and Infantry Battalion, Ted was due to go overseas on 27 December 1939 and, after spending some time with his family decided on a few beers at this local pub, the Waihao Forks Hotel, before the train left for Waimate and then on to Burnham Military Camp near Christchurch.

Stories vary somewhat, but the most popular version is that Ted had lined up two bottles of his favourite brew, Ballins XXXX ale, but after finishing the first, the train whistle blew and Ted left the second bottle with publican George Provan to keep on the shelf for when he came home. Other versions of the story have Ted drinking in the pub a few days earlier and leaving the extra bottle with the publican, as the train he caught to Waimate would have left just after 7 am and it was unlikely that the pub would have been open at this time. Whatever the story, Ted never returned for his second bottle, as he died in battle among the vineyards of Crete on 2 June 1941, aged thirty-five.

However, in 1947, Ted's father received a letter from Yakovos Kalionzakis, a Cretan partisan who was only seventeen in 1941 and who found Ted wounded by a shot in the chest in the vineyard. Unable to move the badly wounded soldier, who was a big man, Yakovos managed to hide him from the Germans and brought him food for two days before he died. Sadly, the tragedy doesn't end there, as Ted's sister, with the very Kiwi name Rata, served in London during the war driving fire engines and died there in 1945.

Today, Ted's bottle is an official RSA war memorial, and each Anzac Day locals gather at the pub to ensure that Ted and other men and women like him who never returned are not forgotten.

 The Waihao Forks Hotel is about 10 km south of Waimate on the road to Kurow.

28. Paterson Cob Cottage

This tiny cottage on the long stretch of road between Waimate and Kurow was once the centre of busy stopping point in the nineteenth century.

Thought to have been built by Henry LeCren in 1880, the land was purchased by James Paterson in January 1883 and he moved there with his wife, three sons and a daughter. Stables once existed just 50 metres away and these were used to change the horses for coaches travelling between Waimate and Kurow. As small as the cottage is, it is likely that the Paterson's also provided accommodation for drovers moving stock along the wide valley, along with paddocks to hold stock overnight. Nearby was a wool wash and the cottage possibly accommodating the men working there.

Eventually the cottage was abandoned, but early preservation efforts saved enough of the structure that is was fully restored by 1990 when the Paterson family held a reunion that was attend by 100 people.

📍 SH 82, 40 km from Waimate on the road to Kurow.

NORTH OTAGO

1. Benmore Dam
2. Waitaki Valley Wineries
3. Nicol's Forge, Duntroon
4. Waitaki Valley Limestone and Fossil Country
5. Maori Rock Drawings, Duntroon
6. Danseys Pass
7. Historic Oamaru
8. Criterion Hotel
9. Janet Frame House
10. Whitestone Cheese
11. Yellow-eyed Penguin/Hoiho Colony
12. Totara Estate and Clarks Mill
13. Oamaru Dog Trial Grounds, Waianakura (North Otago)
14. Katiki Point
15. Shag Point
16. Puketapu Summit – Palmerston
17. Macraes Gold Mine
18. Matanaka
19. Evansdale Cheese Factory
20. Huriawa Pa, Karitane Beach
21. Mapoutahi Pa

1. Benmore Dam

The Waitaki River has the fourth-largest water flow of any New Zealand river and the narrow valley of the upper Waitaki River was ideal for the construction of hydro-electric power schemes. There are, in all, three hydro lakes: Waitaki, Aviemore and Benmore, the latter dam being the largest of the three. Construction on the oldest dam, Waitaki, began in 1928 and was completed in 1934. The last dam in New Zealand to be built using picks and shovels, before the advent of earthmoving machinery, over 1200 workers were on site at the peak of construction. The Aviemore dam, built in 1968, is a combination of earth and concrete and features a 1-km-long spawning race that allows fish to migrate upstream.

Benmore, built between two natural rock outcrops, was begun in 1958 and completed in 1965 and is the largest earth dam in New Zealand. Constructed of clay-like gravel and supported by two shoulders of river gravel, the volume of water behind the dam is one-and-a-half times the capacity of Wellington Harbour. The Benmore Track begins at the carpark above the dam and is a short climb to a viewpoint over the Waitaki Valley and to the mountains, including Mt Cook.

The area is fast becoming a popular holiday destination, especially for boating and fishing both in the lakes and on nearby rivers.

- 📍 Benmore Information Centre open daily 10.30 am to 4.30 pm
- 🕐 from mid-October to end May.
  From June to mid-October open 10.30 am to 4.30 pm weekends only. Tours are at 11 am, 1 pm and 3 pm.
- 🚫 Not recommended for people with pacemakers.
- 📞 03 438 9212
- 💲 Entrance fee.

2. Waitaki Valley Wineries

Waitaki is New Zealand's smallest and newest grape growing area with less than 60 ha in production. Just eight small vineyards, all close to Kurow, specialise in cool climate wine especially pinot noir, pinot gris, Riesling and gewürztraminer. With variable climatic conditions harvests differ considerably from season to season, but in a good year it produces superb wine.

Pascale Winery was the first to grown grapes in the Waitaki Valley and its vineyards lie adjacent to the river with the grapes grown on deep silt and gravel. Pinot noir, pinot gris, gewürztraminer and riesling are their specialities with their Alma Mata wine a blend of all three wine varieties fermented together.

Right next door is River-T Estates Wines established in 2007 and producing riesling, chardonnay, pinot noir, pinot gris and rosé. Making it easy for the visitor, River-T, in addition to their own range of wines, also stock wines from all other Waitaki Valley wineries, along with local craft beers. The cellar door opens onto a wide terrace beyond which the vineyard slides away on a gentle slope down to the Waitaki River.

  On SH 83, five km south of Kurow.
  River-T Estate Wines: 021 292 4081
  www.rivertwines.co.nz

3. Nicol's Forge, Duntroon

Anywhere else this building would have been pulled down long ago, but the smart locals of Duntroon know what a little gem they have on their hands in this place. Looking much the same as when it was established in 1898, the corrugated-iron shed that is Nicol's Forge looks ready for the smithy to walk straight in and start work. Nicol's was typical of country forges which operated as blacksmiths, wheel wrights, farriers and later as motor garages.

The business was run by Nicol Muriden from 1930 to its closure in the early 1970s and a promotional calendar produced by NS Muirden still hangs on the office wall. Faced with demolition, in 1975 four local farmers bought the building and chattels and in 2006 Nicol's Blacksmith Historic Trust was established to preserve the building and open it to the public.

The grimy interior, the tools, and even the tiny front office with its ancient typewriter and narrow fireplace all look at least a hundred years old, while outside is a collection of old farm machinery. Nicol's Forge is a real peek into New Zealand's pioneering past and it is a category 1 Historic Place.

Opening hours depend on the local smithy, a tall, genial woman who makes a fantastic guide. When it is open, make sure you stop as you are in for a treat. Other times you can look into the interior from the open doors. Handmade items made in the forge are for sale.

- Nicol's Forge is on SH 83.
- Opening hours vary considerably, but during winter it is only Saturdays and Sundays from Queen's Birthday weekend through to Labour weekend.

4. Waitaki Valley Limestone and Fossil Country

North Otago has some of New Zealand's most interesting geology and, around Duntroon in particular, there are fascinating rock formations and fossils that are easily accessible from the road.

The Vanished World Centre is an excellent starting point with a collection of impressive fossils up to 30 million years old and including ancient penguins, whales and dolphins, some species of which are unknown to science. Even better, the centre has a kids' table where youngsters (why do they have all the fun?) can crack open rocks and find their own fossils to keep. Available for purchase from the centre is a brochure 'Vanished World Fossil Trail' which details a self-guided tour of the most interesting geological sites in North Otago. And don't forget to check out the mysterious 'rattling rocks'.

A short loop drive from the Centre at Duntroon takes around two hours including walking and these are some of the highlights:

- Anatini Whale Fossil: a short walk from the road through a landscape looking like a movie set takes you to the fossil of a baleen whale.
  The fossil is very clear and protected by perspex from prying fingers and has an interpretive board explaining which parts of the whale are visible.
- Elephant Rocks: Fascinating limestone formations shaped by erosion stand out starkly in the open farmland.
- Awamoko Stream – Valley of the Whales: Exposed limestone contains the fossils of whales, dolphins and shells.
- Earthquakes: Huge rocks have broken away from the cliffs to expose fossils of an ancient seabed. Take care as rocks still fall and there are crevices in the area.

📍 Duntroon is on SH 83, 20 km from Kurow and 34 km from SH 1.

5. Maori Rock Drawings, Duntroon

Over 500 Maori rock drawing sites have been found in the South Island, and around 100 in the North Island. It is possible that the art form was common throughout Aotearoa and that more drawings have survived in the Waitaki area because of the relatively dry climate and the location of the drawings in dry sheltered caves and overhangs. Rock art can be either scratched into the surface or drawn and painted on. The paint was usually made from animal fat mixed with various other mediums such as soot or charcoal, kokowai and yellow ochre.

Over twenty Maori rock art sites have been found in the Waitaki Valley, but most have since disappeared. Of the three remaining sites, Maerewhenua and Takiroa near Duntroon are the most accessible.

Maerewhenua is a substantial rock shelter lined with simple drawings. This shelter was occupied over hundreds of years but is unlikely to have been permanently occupied – this would have been a seasonal food-gathering area. In addition to the drawings, there is evidence of cooking fires, bird bones and fishhooks. It appears that the drawings were added to, altered and improved over the years, and the subjects range from extinct birds such as moa and Te Pouakai (Haast eagle), through to nineteenth-century sailing ships and names.

The location is in a long shallow cave stretching over 30 metres. Many of the drawings are initially difficult to make out but spend some time and gradually the scale of the drawings is revealed. To reach the site there is a short steep walk uphill from the road.

Like Maerewhenua, Takiroa is a limestone cliff that would have been a temporary shelter as Maori travelled from their settlements on the coast to inland hunting grounds. Many of the best paintings have been removed or damaged and a large rock fall has obscured others, but there are still substantial drawings in both red and black. Painted between 1400 and 1900, of particular interest is the depiction of a European sailing ship.

 Maerewhenua : 500 metres east of Duntroon on the Livingstone–Duntroon road off SH 83 (Dansey's Pass Road). Takiroa: 3.5 km west of Duntroon on SH 83.

6. Danseys Pass

If you're looking for a yesteryear driving experience, then a trip over the Danseys Pass is for you. Linking the Waitaki Valley to Central Otago through to Naseby, this was originally a coach road supplying the goldfields of the Maniototo basin – and, quite frankly, the road hasn't changed much since the coaching days. The first section after leaving Duntroon is sealed and winds gently through the handsome limestone farmland along the Maerewhenua River. Once off the seal (after about 15 km), the road is narrow, winding and gravel for the next 45 km, with enough corrugations to shake your brain loose (though it has improved over recent years).

But don't let any of that put you off the trip. The countryside is wild, empty and beautiful, and twists and turns through stunning wild tussock country before dropping down into Naseby. The pass itself is just shy of a thousand metres (at 934 m) and was named after William Dansey, who had a run on the Waitaki side of the pass.

For a reward on the southern side, near Naseby, call in at the historic Danseys Pass Coach Inn. Built of local stone and beautifully restored, this is a popular stopping point, offering refreshments and accommodation. The inn was built in 1862 (legend has it that the stonework was paid for in beer) and serviced the nearby Kyeburn Diggings, a goldfield that at one stage supported a population of 2000 people. The road is occasionally closed by snow in the winter.

From the Waitaki Valley, the turnoff to the pass is at Duntroon; and from the south, via Naseby.

7. Historic Oamaru

Oamaru is an unusual townscape in that it has New Zealand's most extensive area of Victorian buildings and it has been largely constructed in a single building material, Oamaru stone.

Naturally sheltered from the worst of the southerly weather by Cape Wanbrow, Oamaru attracted early Maori and was also home to sealers and whalers in the first half of the nineteenth century. With the construction of the breakwater beginning in 1871 Oamaru quickly became an important port town, especially after the development of refrigerated export meat shipments in 1884. The town boomed. Around the harbour arose grain stores, warehouses and shipping offices while along the main street rose more grand buildings including banks, an Opera House and grand hotels. The good times did not last and as improved rail links replaced the port as a means of transport, the town became a quiet backwater. With a small and stable population throughout the twentieth century, the lack of development in the town through this period no doubt saved these fine buildings.

The working area for the port, Harbour Street, is totally Victorian in character and has an appealing intimate feel. Historic buildings in the harbour area include Smith's Grain Store (1881), Union Bank (1878), New Zealand Loan and Mercantile Warehouse (1882), Customs House (1883), Harbour Board Office (1876) and the Criterion Hotel (1877).

Thames Street, Oamaru's main thoroughfare, has the finest collection of Victorian buildings in New Zealand and the grandest of these are along a short section of Thames Street. Most were built between 1870 and 1885 and include Bank of New South Wales (1883 and now the Forrester Gallery), National Bank (1871), St Lukes Anglican Church (1876), First Post Office (1864 and now a restaurant), Post Office (1883 and now the Waitaki Council offices), Courthouse (1882) and Athenaeum (1882 and now housing the very fine North Otago Museum). All are within an easy walking distance of each other.

Grainy in texture and creamy white in colour, Oamaru limestone comes from quarries working a 40 m thick seam inland from Oamaru. Cut into blocks with huge saws, the stone is soft when first quarried but hardens when exposed to air. It is however porous and susceptible to polluted air, so it doesn't do so well in wet, urban environments. Easy to work, it is also widely used for carvings and sculptures. Frequently the light stone was used together with the hard bluestone basalt, creating a striking effect that can be seen in buildings such as the Christchurch Arts Centre and Dunedin Railway Station. Easily to handle and readily available, the stone was extensively used in Oamaru and in the case of Harbour Street, nearly all the buildings are constructed with this one material.

In keeping with the town's Victorian style Oamaru has, over the years, developed one of the best heritage festivals in the country. Held in November over a number of days the festival features a wide range of events such as The Servants and Swaggers Dance, the National Stone-Sawing Competition, a Victorian High Tea, the highly entertaining New Zealand Penny-farthing Championships, the Grand Victorian Street Parade, the Garden Party and the Victorian Ball and, on the final Sunday, the whole historic area is closed off for the Victorian Fête.

However, this is not a town to only dwell on the past, and in recent years Oamaru has embraced Steam Punk, with is own Steam Punk HQ, and declares itself Steam Punk Capital of New Zealand.

8. Criterion Hotel

Standing proud in the heart of Oamaru, this handsome old hotel is a rare survivor of New Zealand's roller-coaster liquor laws. Through the second half of the nineteenth century the temperance movement grew from strength to strength, and in 1893 the government allowed individual electorates to decide whether their area was to go 'dry' (that is, ban the sale of alcohol) or stay 'wet' (or continue the sale of alcohol). The vote needed a two-thirds majority, and no doubt influenced by the strong Presbyterian presence in the south and the fact that women could now vote, Clutha was the first electorate to go dry in 1894. A raft of other electorates followed suit in 1902, 1905 and 1908, accompanied by hotel closures in each of these areas.

Built of Oamaru stone in 1877, the Criterion closed its doors in 1906 after the area went dry the previous year. For other hotels, that was usually the end, as the old buildings were either pulled down or radically reshaped for other purposes. Not so the Criterion, which extraordinarily not only retained its original facade and fittings, but also reopened in 1998.

Having been lovingly restored, the Criterion is today one of New Zealand's most authentic old watering holes and offers food, drink and accommodation.

📍 3 Tyne Street, Oamaru.
📞 03 434 6247
🌐 www.criterion.net.nz

9. Janet Frame House

This modest dwelling, a short walk from the centre of Oamaru, was the home of Janet Frame – one of New Zealand's best-known authors – who lived here between 1931 and 1943. Janet attended Oamaru North School and Waitaki Girls High School, and her time in Oamaru made a deep impact on the young writer (her three-part autobiography, beginning with *To the Is-land*, is particularly worth reading).

The house has altered very little from the time Frame lived here, though the weatherboards have since been rough-casted over and the windows altered. Today it is simply furnished in the style of the period as well as containing Frame memorabilia. Incredibly, a collection of childhood writings was recently discovered under the floorboards, hidden away for over sixty-five years.

📍 56 Eden Street, Oamaru.
🕐 Open daily 1 November to 30 April, 2 pm to 4 pm.
🌐 www.jfestrust.org.nz
$ Entrance fee.

10. Whitestone Cheese

Feeling hungry? Then drop by Whitestone Cheese for a spot of cheese tasting. Established in 1987, and creating cheeses from both goat's and cow's milk, Whitestone now produces a range of around eighteen varieties – the awards this company has won would fill a small hall. At the 2019

New Zealand Food Producer Award, Whitestone took out nine medals including a gold medal for their signature cheese, Vintage Windsor Blue.

Still in the original factory, around the back of the building is a viewing area with large windows offering a great view of the cheeses being made. In addition to their cheese, the café at Whitestone has a fabulous baked cheesecake and excellent coffee. Whitestone also offer a cheese making tour with cheese and wine pairing.

---

 3 Torridge Street, Oamaru.
 Open daily 9 am to 5 pm.
www.whitestonecheese.co.nz

11. Yellow-eyed Penguin/Hoiho Colony

While folk flock to Oamaru to see the blue penguins' evening parade, a short distance away is a colony of yellow-eyed penguin, and it doesn't cost a cent.

The hoiho, or yellow-eyed penguin, is much larger than the blue penguin and much less sociable, preferring nesting spots isolated from other penguin neighbours. At Bushy Beach, a small colony of these rare birds has established itself in the low-growing vegetation above the beach and a special hide has been constructed to allow public viewing. These penguins come ashore late in the afternoon (the blue penguin comes ashore at dusk), and the beach is closed after 3 pm as the birds will not come ashore if they are disturbed by people positioning themselves on the shore between the sea and their nests.

 To get to Bushy Beach from Oamaru town, follow Tyne Street to Bushy Beach Road and continue to the car park at the end of the road.

12. Totara Estate and Clarks Mill

Comprised of four historic farm buildings constructed of Oamaru stone, three of these buildings date from the 1860s, and the carcass shed from 1881. It was from here that the first cargo of sheep meat was prepared to be sent frozen to Britain on the ship *Dunedin* in 1882, though the meat was frozen on board, and the ship left from Port Chalmers, not Oamaru.

In addition to the restored nineteenth-century farm buildings, there are early New Zealand sheep breeds and an audiovisual presentation on the New Zealand meat industry. Totara Estate also hosts the Harvest Home Festival, a traditional autumn harvest festival, though with modern twists such as lamb burgers.

Clarks Mill is just south of Totara Estate and was once the grain mill for the estate until it was sold to the three Clark brothers in early 20th century. Built of stone to a Scottish design in 1866, the four-storeyed mill processed mainly wheat but also rolled oats, two crops that flourished in north Otago. Later expanded, the mill employed the latest technology, but times change and so does farming and eventually the mill closed in 1976.

What make this place so special is that most of the roller milling machinery, installed in 1893, is still in place and working, painstakingly restored by dedicated volunteers. Even if you have not a shred of interest in Victorian agricultural machinery this is still worth a stop, made more enjoyable by the friendly and knowledgeable hosts.

- Totara Estate: Maheno, SH 1 8 km south of Oamaru.
- Open 10 am to 4 pm. September to May.
- www.totaraestate.co.nz
- Entrance fee.

- Clarks Mill: Maheno, SH 1, 10 km south of Oamaru.
- Opening hours vary considerably so check the website.
- www.clarksmill.co.nz
- Entrance fee.

13. Oamaru Dog Trial Grounds, Waianakura (North Otago)

Dog trialing as a sport had its origins the sheep farming boom of the nineteenth century in Australia and New Zealand, and like the dessert Pavlova, the origins of the sport are claimed by Australia whereas the honour should go to New Zealand. It is widely regarded that the first dog trials were held in Bala, New South Wales Australia in 1873, but in the July 9 1869 edition of the Oamaru Times, the paper reported that the third dog trial had been held at Wanaka in June of that year. By 1900 the sport was well established with regular trials being held in both North and South Islands, though the first national championships were not held until 1936 in Hawera. Today there are 161 New Zealand clubs and while the rules have been formalised, the sport is still solidly grounded in pratical shepherding skills. Internationally the sport is confined to New Zealand, Australia, Scotland, Wales and England, and competitions are divided into four classes – two heading (long head and short head), and two hunt-away (zig-zag hunt and straight hunt), though a more recent development has been the running of show and yard trials throughout the year, and televising events to ensure great public interest.

The Oamaru dog trial grounds are as kiwi as it gets. Established in 1949, the grounds are on the farm of Ross McMillan who also donates the crossbreed sheep for the trial. Consisting of a wide flat paddock along the road, the grounds lead up to steeper terrain that is essential for some of the events. Trials are held here for two days once a year in the middle of April as part of the North Otago circuit and attracts competitors from all over the South Island. Recognised as one of the strongest dog trialing areas in New Zealand, North Otago has produced some notable dog trialers such as Jack Warkworth, Andy Gibson, Bert White and Angus Fergussion. The buildings are 'homely' verging on the ramshackle (but not rundown), including the bar known as *The Dog Triallers Retreat* where apparently the biggest lies are told. The toilets created out of water tanks donated by the local council are a fine testament to kiwi ingenuity. (for dates visit www.sheepdogtrials.co.nz)

 Waianakarua Road, 3 km from the Mill House, where SH 1 crosses the Waianakarua River.

14. Katiki Point

There's much more to Moeraki than a quick stop at the famous boulders. This short forty-five minute walk is a gem usually bypassed by the busy tourist, but one which has it all – great coastal views, an old pa site, an historic lighthouse, and a great hide for watching wildlife. The walk begins at the elegant wooden lighthouse constructed in 1878. Originally intended for Hokitika, numerous shipwrecks along this wild coast convinced authorities to build it at Moeraki instead. The views are amazing: north to Cape Wanbrow near Oamaru and south to Shag Point, and beyond that, even further south, a glimpse of the Otago Peninsula.

Just below the lighthouse is a large fenced area of coastal vegetation and a short track which leads down to a small sandy cove overlooked by an excellent hide complete with binoculars! Both blue and yellow-eyed penguins nest here and the beach is home to fur seals as well. A short way south of the lighthouse is a superb pa site located on a narrow spur of land and almost surrounded by sea.

Though little remains, the pa, known as Te Raka a Hineatea, was established in the eighteenth century as the principal base for the Ngai Tahu invasion of Ngati Mamoe territory. The pa was built by Taoka, the son of Ruahikihiki, who had his main pa at Taumutu. Taoka became embroiled in a bitter feud with his nephew Te Wera at Huriawa, a conflict that led to the famous siege of Huriawa and the destruction of Mapoutahi near Waitati. The pa resisted many attempts to capture it and once the conquest was completed, it fell into disuse.

Turn off SH 1 at Moeraki and then turn right into Tenby Street, which becomes Lighthouse Road. Drive 3 km to the end of this gravel road.

15. Shag Point

This high bluff to the north of the Shag (or Waihemo) River is high in both natural and human history. Rich forest, flocks of moa, and a bountiful sea drew early Maori to settle this area, and even after the moa were hunted to extinction the local iwi flourished here. Whalers were the earliest Europeans to settle on this coast in the early 1830s, and it was they who first noticed the dark seams of coal right at sea level. Coal mining began as early as 1863, mostly below sea level, and reached a peak in 1880 when over 170 people were employed in its extraction. Originally, coal was shipped out by sea, but in 1879 the railway line reached Shag Point and followed what is now the road that runs along the north side of the bluff. In 1902 the underwater mining came to an end, but the mines only finally closed in the 1970s.

Surprisingly, considering the relatively recent closure, very little remains of the coal-mining era, though the string of small houses – that at first glance appear to be cribs – are in fact mainly old miner's cottages. The main attraction today is the colonies of fur seals and yellow-eyed penguins that now make Shag Point their home. The small narrow coves, offshore rocks and reefs make the point an ideal playground for seals and a sheltered spot to raise their pups. Walking tracks weave along the windswept bluffs giving several excellent views of the seals lounging on rocky ledges or ducking and diving in the rolling waves below.

📍 Shag Point is 2.5 km off SH 1, 9 km north of Palmerston.

16. Puketapu Summit – Palmerston

A steep climb leads to an unusual monument erected on the summit of Puketapu (343 m) in the memory of local politician Sir John McKenzie. McKenzie was a champion of the small farmer and, as a politician, instrumental in breaking up the huge landholdings of the late nineteenth century. Built in 1931 (an earlier monument collapsed) of local bluestone, the cairn is 13 m high and has an internal staircase. The walk is two hours return and the view from the top is spectacular. For the very fit, a race to the top is held in October in memory of Albert Kelly the local policeman who, during the Second World War, hiked to the top of the hill every day to scout out the local coastline for signs of the enemy.

Once covered in dense bush, Puketapu was also a favoured haunt of the patupaiarehe and, according to Maori tradition, the heavy mists that often shroud the summit allow the patupaiarehe to reclaim the hill and play music undetected. Maori workers helping construct the monument refused to work on the very summit of the hill.

It's a steep climb and the return walk will take around one hour, fifteen minutes.

 From SH 1 just north of the Palmerston shops, turn into Stour Street, cross the railway line and go 500 metres. The track begins on the left.

17. Macraes Gold Mine

Gold was discovered round here in the 1860s and small-scale mining continued through to 1954, when all the operations closed down. Then, in the 1980s, when the price of gold escalated, the area was investigated for a new mining operation which eventually opened in 1990. Now New Zealand's largest gold mine, Macraes produces on average over 50 per cent of the country's production, though the number of pits varies from time to time.

The scale of this operation is impressive. The main pit goes down over 200 metres and the huge machinery – the biggest in New Zealand – is reduced to toy dimensions. The largest dump trucks are capable of up to 330-tonne loads when full, and the massive excavators scoop an amazing 40 tonnes in one go. But this equipment doesn't come cheap – the dump-truck tyres cost $28,000 each and the excavators use 250 litres of diesel per hour.

The mine has been active in restoring the local wetlands and heritage sites, and has a rainbow trout hatchery that releases over 150,000 fish per year into local streams. The mine no longer offers tours, but Macraes is still worth a detour as there is a marvellous viewing platform that looks deep into the heart of the pit.

📍 From SH 85 2 km north of Dunback turn in Macraes Road Road and continue 18.5 km to Macraes Flat.

18. Matanaka

These plain wooden farm buildings set on a bare hill have a surreal quality about them. Minimalist in style and simple and rectangular in structure, all the buildings are painted a uniform deep red colour, with only the faded and lightly rusting iron roofs (which are original) offering any contrast. The long tawny-coloured grass around the buildings is offset by the two-tone blue of sky and sea in the distance. On a still summer's morning this place is magical, with the only sound being the distant surf far below.

Believed to be the oldest surviving farm buildings in New Zealand, they were originally built during the 1840s by Johnny Jones, a Sydney wheeler and dealer involved in whaling at nearby Waikouaiti who later bought land to the north of the bay on which the buildings stand today. Once more extensive, still standing are the stables (complete with old leather horse harnesses), the granary, a schoolhouse and a barn that houses an old boat – an echo of Johnny's connection to the sea. The stylish old buildings provide a strong contrast with the utilitarian but charmless modern farm sheds nearby.

An extra bonus on this detour is the marvellous views over Waikouaiti Beach and the verdant country inland. There is an easy ten-minute walk from the car park through farmland to the buildings.

Matanaka is signposted from SH 1 at Waikouaiti. The road is mainly sealed but becomes narrow and gravel on the uphill stretch to the farm.

19. Evansdale Cheese Factory

It started with a cow ... Beginning in 1977, with the Dennison family cow that produced more milk than the family could use, Evansdale Cheese was the first artisan cheese-making factory in New Zealand.

Gradually expanding, twenty years later the factory moved to a new site 22 km further north at Hawkesbury on the site of the old Cherry Farm Psychiatric Hospital. An interesting location, though now most of hospital buildings have gone, the residential buildings remain and are occupied.

Still going strong today, the Denniston family are still the cheese makers and the focus remains on quality and not quantity. Evansdale makes a range of ten cheeses and are best known for manuka smoked brie and Farmhouse brie. They also regularly produce cheesecakes as a wedding cake.

 4 Duncan Ave, Hawksbury Village , SH1, 4 km south of Waikouaiti.
 03 465 8101
 www.evansdalecheese.co.nz

20. Huriawa Pa, Karitane Beach

Huriawa peninsula was the perfect location for a fortified pa – volcanic in origin, with steep cliffs and sea on three sides. Defenders of the pa had uninterrupted views both north and south along the coast and over the estuarine marshes to the east. A Ngai Tahu stronghold, Huriawa was the scene of an epic siege in the eighteenth century.

The rangatira of Huriawa was Te Wera, who became embroiled in a family feud with his nephew Taoka, though the cause of the conflict has long been forgotten. Tension escalated between the two and finally Taoka decided to attack Huriawa. Te Wera had anticipated the attack and had vastly improved the defences of Huriawa and had the pa well stocked with food. Even under siege the defenders could go out fishing from a small cove on the north side of the pa called Te Awamokihi (Raft Cove). Usually the weak point in any pa was the lack of water, and here Huriawa was fortunate to have a small spring that provided the pa with just enough water. After the siege this spring became known as Te Punawai a Te Wera (Te Wera's Well).

Taoka camped on the sandspit just to the north of the main land gate, Te Kutu o Toretore. His forces assaulted the pa and raided the surrounding countryside; any hapless stragglers were immediately consigned to the hangi pits.

In order to demoralise and weaken the defenders, Taoka devised a daring plan to steal the wooden carving of Kahukura, the god of war, who also appeared in the form of a rainbow and whose image was under the close guard of the tohunga Hatu. In the dead of night two warriors entered the pa at low tide through the sea caves on the southeastern corner and stole the precious carving.

In the morning Hatu discovered the theft and, while pandemonium swept through Huriawa, outside Taoka's men performed haka, called insults about the poor protection of the pa and waved Kahukura above their heads. However, their bravado was not to last long. Hatu, invoking all the gods, pulled together his considerable powers and stretched out his arms towards the enemy, crying out 'Return to us, O Kahukura.' The carving flew through the air and came to rest at the feet of Hatu.

Now it was the turn of those within Huriawa to celebrate; and to Taoka's men, the signs were clear that the gods favoured Te Wera. Thoroughly discouraged, Taoka gave up the siege of Huriawa which had by that time lasted six months, and turned his fury towards Mapoutahi just a little way to the south.

The entrance to the pa is through a beautifully carved gateway and the track meanders gently to the end of the peninsula, with great views along the coast in both directions. The convoluted nature of Huriawa is such that specific evidence of terraces and defences is not so easy to spot, but Te Wera's Well is still visible, and the great blowholes through which the thieves stole into the pa can be found on the south side of the pa.

📍 From SH 1 turn off towards Karitane and take the road right to the beach. At the beach turn left along Sulisker Street and continue 500 metres uphill to the entrance.

21. Mapoutahi Pa

Like Huriawa Pa to the north (see above), Mapoutahi was located on an inaccessible peninsula, protected by steep cliffs and superbly fortified. Taoka could make no impression on the impregnable fortress. The attack took place in the middle of winter and on one particularly cold night, the sentries of Mapoutahi set up dummies to the entrance to the pa and then retreated to the warmth of the fires in the huts. Alerted to the ruse, Taoka attacked, quickly seized the pa and then proceeded to massacre the inhabitants. The pa was never reoccupied and the peninsula then became known as Mata-awhe-awhe, 'the dead gathered in a heap'.

While today the fortified ditches and terraces have largely disappeared, the site of the pa is nothing short of perfect. Steep cliffs and a very narrow access point made it easy to protect, while the sea and wide lagoons both north and south provided an excellent food resource. In either direction the views are extensive: Orokonui Lagoon and the Otago Peninsula to the south, and Purakaunui Inlet immediately to the north, with Huriawa pa glimpsed in the distance.

There are two ways of getting to the pa. The most picturesque involves walking along the beach and around Doctors Point. From the carpark, walk down the beach and head south (right) and around Doctors Point, passing through sea caves on the way. This walk can only be undertaken at mid to low tide, and even on those tides there is a short scramble over a rock slide that has tumbled down from the coastal cliffs. If the tide is not right, the northern access to the pa is via Osborne Road, and from there a short walk through the sand dunes to the pa. The Doctors Point route will take one hour return and the Osborne Road twenty-five minutes return.

📍 Doctors Point: Turn off SH 1 at Waitati and turn left into Doctors Point Road. Follow this road to the end and park by the beach.

📍 Osborne Road: Turn off SH 1 at Waitati and the, take the road to the Orokonui Ecosanctuary. Turn left into Purakanui Road and then left again into Osborne Road and drive to the carpark at the end.

CENTRAL OTAGO

1. Naseby
2. Maniototo Curling International, Naseby
3. Ranfurly Art Deco
4. Bonspiel at Oturehua
5. Hayes Engineering Works
6. Ophir
7. Chatto Creek, New Zealand's Smallest Post Office
8. Earnscleugh Historic Tailings, Alexandra
9. Flat Top Hill and Butcher Dam
10. Mitchell's Cottage
11. Jimmy's Pies
12. Lake Onslow
13. Somebody's Darling
14. Bendigo Goldfields
15. Cromwell Chafer Beetle Reserve
16. The Sluicings and Stewart Town
17. Highlands Motorsport Park and Museum
18. Jackson's Orchard
19. Shrek Museum
20. Lindis Pass Road
21. Lake Wanaka Islands
22. That Wanaka Tree
23. Glendhu Bay Motor Camp Ground
24. The Paddock, Lake Hawea
25. AJ Hackett Bungy
26. Edith Cavell Bridge
27. Oxenbridge Tunnel
28. The Road to Skippers
29. Queenstown Hill/Te Tapunui
30. Moke Lake
31. Little Paradise Lodge, Mt Creighton, Glenorchy
32. Glenorchy, the Dart Valley and a Lost Railway Shed.
33. Central Otago Vineyards

1. Naseby

If you have ever wondered what Arrowtown was like before all the tourists arrived, then Naseby is the place for you. Situated in the northern Maniototo under the Kakanui Mountains, gold was discovered in the Hogburn in May 1863, and by the end of the year the diggings were home to over 5000 men. Four years later the rush was over, but gold could still be extracted by hydraulic sluicing – effective, but with a ruinous impact on the landscape. Fortunately, conifers were later planted over the old tailings and today Naseby is an attractive forested township.

Originally the area was known as 'Parkers', after two brothers involved in the initial gold discovery, and later changed to Mt Ida, and finally to Naseby. The small cosy town has a number of historic buildings including two of Central Otago's oldest pubs, both of which were built in 1863. The elder by just three months is the Ancient Briton, an atmospheric old stone building, while just around the corner is the fine wooden Royal Hotel.

 Naseby is 10 km north of Ranfurly off SH 8.

2. Maniototo Curling International, Naseby

No doubt most people have seen curling on television at some time or other. You know, those half-frozen individuals in woolly tam-o'-shanters sliding great chunks of stone along the ice while their teammates furiously sweep a path with witch-like brooms. Originating in Scotland, the game found a natural home in Central Otago, with winters cold enough to freeze small lakes and ponds. Traditionally, a bonspiel (or curling) tournament was held outdoors in winter on frozen lakes and ponds throughout Central, but here at Naseby, summer or winter, you can try your hand at this ancient sport.

Maniototo Curling International has both an outdoor rink for winter and a brand-spanking-new indoor rink for all-year-round sport. If you have never tried the game, no worries, the friendly people at Naseby provide not only all the equipment but full tuition as well. You will need to bring flat-soled shoes and warm clothing, as the indoor rink is maintained at a chilly 4°C (ideal on one of those scorching hot Central afternoons!). Curling also holds a unique New Zealand record, in that the Baxter Cup was first contested in 1884 and is the country's oldest national sporting trophy.

 Maniototo Curling International.
1057 Channel Road, Naseby.
 03 444 9878
 www.curling.co.nz

3. Ranfurly Art Deco

Today the little Maniototo town of Ranfurly is best known for its small collection of Art Deco buildings. What makes Ranfurly so unique is that the architecture came in response to a number of suspicious fires in the early 1930s and just one builder, JM Mitchell and Sons, constructed all of the buildings and continued building in the art deco style long after its popularity had waned elsewhere.

While there are only about ten Art Deco buildings in total, the pick of them are the Ranfurly Lion Hotel and the very stylish Centennial Milk Bar. The milk bar was the refreshment rooms for the rail passengers and today houses a great collection of 1930s and 1940s crockery, period clothing, furniture and memorabilia. The town also hosts a lively art deco festival in February each year.

One burning question remains unanswered – just who was playing with matches in Ranfurly around 1930? The town wasn't that big, but the fires destroyed, among other structures, the town hall and a hotel. No one was ever charged, nor does there seem to be much speculation about the culprit – but surely in a town the size of Ranfurly someone must have had some idea. And why did the fires stop? Possibly, as is typical in a small town, the local coppers had a good idea just who this bad egg was, but did not have enough hard evidence to take it further. Perhaps they either kept a close eye on the pyromaniac or 'suggested' the evildoer leave town. Either way, the legacy of the fire-happy ratbag is a small town with a big Art Deco heart!

The old railway station is still standing and is now the i-SITE and even the old railway goods shed has survived along with several carriages.

Making a stop in Ranfurly even more appealing are the towns excellent cafés including Fantail Café with its famous homemade pies in mouth-watering flavours such as pork belly, venison and mutton.

4. Bonspiel at Oturehua

Bonspiel is a Scottish word for a curling match usually held over a weekend. In Central Otago a bonspiel is announced if a body of water is properly frozen over.

It does get cold here. New Zealand's lowest temperatures have been recorded in this region: -25.6°C at Ranfuly on 17 July 1907 and -21.6°C at Ophir on 3 July 1995. The lowest North Island temperature was a toasty -13.6°C at Chateau Tongariro, while Kaitaia in the far north has never recorded a frost. Central Otago also holds the record for the driest twelve months on record when just 167 mm fell between November 1963 and October 1964.

Oturehua Railway Hotel is the home of the Bonspiel, and Idaburn Dam just 2 km to the south is one of the best-known natural ice-skating and curling waters in the area. Manorburn, a larger lake, a further 50 km south is also a popular spot but freezes over less frequently.

Another event at Idaburn Dam to coincide with the cold weather is the famous Brass Monkey Rally. A motorcycling institution, this rally is held annually on the Queen's Birthday Weekend and attracts over 3500 motorcyclists to this mad winter campout. The Brass Monkey is famous for the most ingenious inventions to keep warm and a large continuous bonfire is the natural heart of the rally.

 Idaburn Dam is 7.5 km off SH 85 at Idaburn.
 www.brassmonkeyrally.org.nz

5. Hayes Engineering Works

The modest mud-brick and corrugated-iron buildings that form Hayes Engineering are representative of the Kiwi knack of being able to make everything from anything. From this remote workshop established by Ernest Hayes in 1895, issued forth a wide range of simple but effective agricultural innovations that, by his death in 1933, had gained a worldwide reputation. In particular, the Hayes Wire Strainer invented in 1905 was widely exported internationally and is still used today throughout New Zealand. The company moved to Christchurch in 1952 (and is still in operation and owned by the Hayes family), and today this unique collection of buildings is much the same as when they were fully operational in the 1930s.

All the buildings have survived including the stables and a simple shed stacked with spare lengths of timber and bits of old iron – you just never know when they will come in handy.

What is so appealing about the engineering works is that not only does much of the equipment still work, but so many of the original tools still remain in place. Everywhere are lathes and drills, while the benches and walls are covered in tools that elsewhere would have long since disappeared. Even after all these years, the rich warm aroma of motor oil still pervades the old shed. For those aficionados of the home workshop, this place is the backyard mechanic's heaven.

More recently, the 1920s homestead has been restored and is now open to the public, and is a real gem of domestic architecture. Much larger than it looks, the house comprises four bedrooms and three living areas. When constructed it would have represented state of the art technology for the time including electricity supplied by the factory. Many of the Hayes family's furniture and personal belongings add a final touch to this fine homestead. Out the back in a shed built from homemade mudbrick is the dairy, cool and dark, and a vegetable garden protected by a sturdy rabbit proof fence.

The tiny cob cottage, formerly a worker's home, is now an award-winning café complete with its own cosy parlour.

A detour down the quiet Ida Valley is a lovely trip in its own right. A good sealed road, the Ida Valley-Omakau Road is just 40 km long but has added bonus of fantastic views from the top of the Raggedy Range just before the road drops down to Omakau. Rocky tors crown the summit and in summer the scent of wild sage hangs in the air.

📍 39 Hayes Road, off the Ida Valley/Omakau Road, Oturehua.

🕐 Open daily November to April, 10 am to 5 pm, Wednesday to Sunday, September, October and May, 10 am to 5 pm, Closed, June to August, Christmas Day and Boxing Day. Pre-booked guided tours are an option, check website for details.

📞 03 444 5801

🌐 hayes@heritage.org.nz

6. Ophir

A gold boom town named after the biblical King Solomon's mine, gold was discovered here in 1863 and the population quickly rose to 1000 people. Originally known as Blacks, only a handful of buildings remain, including the court house, police station and the post office. The post office is particularly notable and is now owned by the Historic Places Trust. Built of schist stone in 1863 it still has most of its original furnishings, and the internal configuration is unchanged from the time it was built. Today, the building still functions as a post office for the tiny population of only fifty people, and by a strange twist of history has been run by women since the 1890s.

While there, drop by the classy Blacks Hotel, the only building that bears the original name of the town. Unlike the other old hotels in the area, Blacks is a stylish Art Deco building as the first hotel burnt down and was replaced in the 1930s.

📍 Ophir is 2 km off SH 85 at Omakau.

7. Chatto Creek, New Zealand's Smallest Post Office

Hang on to all your postcards and then mail them at New Zealand's smallest post office at Chatto Creek, just north of Alexandra. Opened in 1892, this post office was originally little more than a canvas tent a few metres square with just one window. Later, the building went very upmarket and had corrugated iron nailed over the canvas – and in fact the original cloth material is still visible on a section of the inside wall. In keeping with the style of the period, the internal walls are lined with both old wallpaper and magazine spreads, and today you can still read the news from the *Otago Witness* on 23 July 1919.

This tiny building was the domain of the legendary Miss Kinney, who ran the post office for over forty years and knew everyone and everything in the district. Using only a butter box for a chair, Miss Kinney was a woman of strong opinion and biked the 4 km from her home daily. Often, when the weather wasn't so great, she was offered a ride by local motorists, but being a woman of firm principle only accepted a lift from Catholics and never from Anglicans, Methodists, Presbyterians or any other denomination.

The post office was closed in 1975, but with the support of locals reopened in 2004 complete with old typewriter, wooden telephone and the old post boxes housed in a tiny leanto. Standing just a few metres away is the old longdrop, which fortunately is no longer in use.

It is administered by the Chatto Creek Tavern, built in 1886, which is right next door and worth a visit on its own.

📍 Chatto Creek is 14 km north of Alexandra on SH 85.

8. Earnscleugh Historic Tailings, Alexandra

There isn't that much to see here other than a ruined landscape, but the tailings are a most bizarre attraction in their own right and a testament to human ingenuity and determination. Covering hectare after hectare, these piles of shingle and stone are the remains of an industry that boomed in the early twentieth century.

Gold was discovered here in 1862, and once the easily worked ore was exhausted, dredges moved into the riverbed with varying degrees of success. In 1895 the invention of the tailings elevator that allowed dredges to stack the tailings behind them – and therefore work in to the river bank rather than just the bed – radically changed things. At its height, twenty dredges worked the riverbed between Alexandra and Clyde, leaving behind a moonscape of debris. The tailings are part of the Otago 50th Anniversary Walkway that runs from Alexandra to Clyde.

From Alexandra, cross over the Clutha River Bridge and turn right into Earnscleugh Road, and then after 3 km right into Marshall Road.

9. Flat Top Hill and Butchers Dam

Flat Top Hill is a rare example of dry short-tussock grassland and has its very own natural history with distinctive plants, animal life and geology adapted to this harsh environment. Gold was discovered at Butchers Gully in 1862 and the dam itself was built from 1935 to 1937 for irrigation. A loop walk takes around thirty minutes with excellent interpretive panels along the way, but it is worth continuing further up the slope to the summit of Flat Top Hill from which there are great views over Alexandra and the Clutha River.

On SH 8, 5 km south of Alexandra.

10. Mitchell's Cottage

While there are plenty of stone cottages scattered throughout Central Otago, Mitchell's Cottage stands out from the crowd. For a start it has the most impressive location, set among rocky tors and facing north high above the Clutha Valley and exposed to the elements, with marvellous views. The cottage itself is perfectly built into the landscape it occupies, and it is doubtful whether any other New Zealand building has been constructed so sympathetically with the surrounding environment.

A natural rock slab forms the foundation of the house, the front step, and at the same time acts as a stone terrace in front of the small building. The cottage, the outhouses and the fence are constructed of local split schist rock, carefully shaped and crafted and then fitted together with a precision that even today is impressive. Experienced with building in stone in their native Shetland Islands, the Mitchell brothers John and Andrew built numerous cottages in the district before completing this house in 1904, which became the home of John and his wife Jessie who raised ten children in the two-bedroom cottage. The interior of the house is lined with tongue-and-grove wood and is currently unfurnished with just a lovely old photo of John and Jessie hanging on the kitchen wall.

Just below the cottage is a sundial cut into solid stone and several hardy trees planted by the Mitchells around the turn of the nineteenth century. Just below that again and built into the rock wall is a small forge, while behind the house are small outbuildings including a stone chook house. It's a wonderful place, often bypassed, so there is a good chance you will have the place to yourself.

 End of Symes Road, 1 km off SH 8, 8 km north of Roxburgh. There is just a small sign from the main road so it is easy to miss.

11. Jimmy's Pies

Jimmy Kirkpatrick started a business in Invercargill making mixes for cakes and biscuits just after the Second World War. The idea was a bit ahead of its time and not overly successful, so in 1960 Jimmy and his family moved to Central Otago, taking over a small bakery in Roxburgh. This time he focused on pies and over time developed a flourishing wholesale business supplying outlets throughout the region. Today the business is run by his son Dennis and his two sons, and now you can find Jimmy's famous mince and cheese pies everywhere in Central Otago and Southland. But what the locals know is the tastiest pies are only available at the original bakery in Roxburgh and the standout of these is the exceptional lamb shank pie.

The fresh lamb shanks are first oven-baked, then simmered for two to three hours with vegetables and stock and then left for a day to maximise the flavours. Excess fat is skimmed off, the bones removed, and the thickened mixture is then poured into pastry cases made on the premises. The result is a superb-tasting pie full of meat and thoroughly infused with the most delicious baked lamb shank flavour.

Only available in Roxburgh are these equally tasty flavours: venison and blackcurrant, chicken and mushroom, and chicken and curry. If that isn't enough, Jimmy's also makes two superb mutton pies, one hot and one cold. The cold mutton pie is very similar in style to the traditional pork pie and is very meaty and so, so delicious.

But wait, there is more. Jimmy's also makes a great vanilla slice (custard square) and grain breads from its own recipes. Jimmy's bakes its own hams, which are then cut with a knife (and not thinly cut in a bacon slicer) to make fresh ham sandwiches. Add to this takeaway coffee and free hot water for those who want to brew their own tea – how's that for service?

If the day is fine and the kids need to run around, right across the road is a grassy park with shady trees (and clean toilets) – just the spot for a picnic. (Roxburgh is halfway from both Dunedin and Invercargill on the way to Wanaka and Queenstown).

If tasty food isn't enough, Jimmy's Pies might just be the secret to long life, especially if you are a parrot. In June 2018, Guinness World Records confirmed that Roxburgh cockatiel Buddy is, at the ages of thirty-two, the longest living cockatiel in the world. Buddy replaced a previous bird in 1986 when that bird named John Wayne flew off Anne Walder's shoulder when mowing the lawn. Now Buddy has his own place at the dinner table when he regularly enjoys a Jimmy's pie and a cup of coffee.

 143 Scotland Street, Roxburgh.
 03 446 9012
 www.jimmyspies.co.nz

12. Lake Onslow

The drive to Lake Onslow, east of Roxburgh, is as appealing as the lake itself. Although the idea of travelling 40 km on a winding gravel road may not sound like a lot of fun, the trip passes through wonderful open, high tussock country slashed by deep gullies and looking every bit like a Grahame Sydney painting.

The man-made lake was originally known by the very evocative name 'The Dismal Swamp', no doubt due to the open and windswept nature of the area. Flooded in 1888 to provide water for mining operations, the dam was later raised several times, and from 1924 provided water for irrigation and power. Now covering an area of over 800 hectares, the lake has excellent fishing (brown trout) and boating facilities. A handful of small cribs nestle amongst the tussock, along with the attendant 'dunnies' that are firmly wired down to stop being blown away in the relentless wind.

Initially the lake is not so easy to find, as it is not signposted from Roxburgh.

 From the main street of Roxburgh (SH 8), turn down Jedburgh Street (signposted Roxburgh East) and cross the Clutha River. At the T junction turn right, and after 1 km turn left into Wright Road. From this point on it is reasonably signposted.

13. Somebody's Darling

The legend of Somebody's Darling is a good deal more appealing than the truth, but as the old saying goes, 'Don't let truth get in the way of a good story'. According to the popular tale, in February 1865 the unidentified body of a young man was found washed up on the riverbank by local man William Rigney. Rigney then buried the drowned man not far from the riverbank and provided a headboard for the grave inscribed 'Somebody's Darling Lies Buried Here'. When Rigney died in 1912 he was buried next to Somebody's Darling, with his inscription reading: 'Here Lies the Body of William Rigney, The Man Who Buried Somebody's Darling'.

In fact, William Rigney never claimed to have either found the body or to have buried it, but merely provided the gravestone. As for being unidentified, it is reasonably certain that the dead man was Charles Alms, a butcher from the Nevis Valley who drowned in the Clutha on 25 January and was subsequently washed downstream. While the truth is less endearing than the legend, isn't it still rather odd to want to be buried next to someone you never knew?

> From SH 8, turn over the Clutha at Millers Flat then turn right and follow the river for 9 km. The last section down Beaumont Station Road is unsealed.

14. Bendigo Goldfields

In 1873, Thomas Logan discovered gold in this area and, like so many others, promptly named a town after himself. Logantown is just one of the many old townships, mineshafts, water races and ruined stamper batteries that are spread among the rocks and tussock of the Bendigo Goldfields. What makes this area particularly appealing is that the dry climate has preserved many of the mining relics and the high altitude provides a magnificent backdrop to the picturesque ruins.

Not too much remains of Bendigo at the foot of the hill that climbs to Logantown, which today consists of just a ruined cottage and a surprisingly well-preserved wooden cart. Just beyond Logantown are Welshtown and the Matilda Battery, which are considerably more substantial. Opened in 1878, the shaft at Matilda went down 178 metres and the 16-stamper battery, powered by steam, crushed the ore hauled up from the depths. The mine closed in 1884, and in 1908 ten of the stampers were relocated to the nearby Come In Time Battery where they remain today.

Welshtown has some of the best-preserved miner's huts in Central Otago (several of which are only missing the roof), as well as old rock walls and the remains of the Matilda Battery itself. Just across the valley is the incredibly tiny Pengelly's Hotel, with rooms so small it is hard to imagine how the patrons actually squeezed in.

The Loop Road from SH 8 is a dramatic illustration of the impact of the wine industry in this area. Ten years ago not a single vine was planted in this arid landscape; today vines stretch in every direction and driving along this road is like a roll call of famous local labels.

 To get there from Cromwell, take SH 8 towards Tarras, and after 14 km turn right into Bendigo Loop Road. Continue down this road for 2 km then turn right at Bendigo township to Welshtown. The road beyond Bendigo is narrow and gravel but has much improved in the last few years. There is parking at the end of the road at Welshtown.

15. Cromwell Chafer Beetle Reserve

Those travelling from Cromwell en route to the Bannockburn wineries may not consider this worth a detour at all – but let's face it, even beetles have a right to a home too, and good on the people with the foresight to protect this rare and helpless insect from total annihilation.

The Cromwell chafer beetle is a small flightless beetle that is the rarest and most endangered of eighteen such beetles, and this 81-hectare reserve is virtually the chafer beetle's entire habitat, with a population of between one to two thousand of the little creatures. You can walk over the reserve if you really want to, but as the beetles spend most of their time underground you are unlikely to ever see them.

Consisting of tough dry vegetation just a few centimetres high, this little reserve also protects a small fragment of the original and unusual inland sand-dune country and offers a rare glimpse into what the area around Cromwell once looked like.

 The reserve is 2 km south of Cromwell on the road to Bannockburn.

16. The Sluicings and Stewart Town

The Sluicings is an amazing area of cliffs, gulches, pinnacles, tunnels and old ruins set amid a barren landscape, and all man-made. In the late nineteenth century, technology enabled gravelly soils to be worked with high-pressure sluicing hoses that resulted in a drastic revision of the landscape. Blasted by water, the flat terrain near Bannockburn has been altered beyond recognition and has a strange appeal all on its own.

After traversing a deep gully, the track reaches a plateau and the remains of Stewart Town, which today consists only of a cottage and old apple and pear trees that still bear fruit. The tiny cottage, minus its roof, was the home of David Stewart and John Menzies, who made a small fortune by providing the water critical to the sluicing operations (the sign makes a point that both men were bachelors, so you can read into that what you will). As well as the remains of Stewart Town there are the ruins of numerous miner's huts, a blacksmith's forge and old water channels.

 Felton Road, Bannockburn 5 km north of Cromwell.

17. Highlands Motorsport Park and Museum

Ever wanted the taste of being a race car driver or experiencing some of the adrenaline of doing it without having to buy a supercar or worry about crashing it and having to fix it?

At Highlands you can do all this and more (bookings are essential).

At one end of scale you can go in a supercar like a Ferrari or a McLaren which is great on its own, but even better you get to go in it on a real racing track and go really scarily fast, driven by an experienced driver. Or you can even drive an actual racecar going fast yourself, getting tips from a professional driver at the same time.

At the other end of the scale is the museum and car collection, which just involves a leisurely stroll through a century of motoring and motorsport. The cars include older veteran models, but also more recent models in including the Aston Martin Vulcan, the only one in the Southern Hemisphere.

In between is the go-kart track, but these karts aren't slow or boring – they are actually really fast and on a great track. Its something the kids can do and it's not too expensive.

Of course, you can just sit in the café overlooking the track and watch your friends have a great time.

Highlands also runs several motorsport events throughout the year. Check the website for details.

  Corner SH 6 & Sandflat Road, Cromwell.
  Open daily 10 am to 5 pm.
  03 445 4052
  www.highlands.co.nz

18. Jackson's Orchard

Central Otago has long been famous for its fruit, especially cherries and apricots, and there are plenty of road side fruit shops to tempt visitors. Among the best is Jackson's orchards just north of Cromwell on the road to Wanaka. A large packing house surrounded by orchards has a small retail outlet at the front. Family owned, the store sells fruit picked from trees just few metres away and in addition to apricots and cherries also sells plums, nectarines, pears and peaches. Dried fruit and an exceptional range of honey are also available, and if you can't make it down to Central, you can order online. Most of the products are sourced locally. During the summer Jackson's also offers real fruit ice cream, juices and smoothies from a small kiosk out the front.

When harvest is in full swing, the packing operation is impressive to watch. There are regular daily tours of the 35 ha of orchards and in the off season (March to November) fruit pickers accommodation is available to rent.

73 Luggate-Cromwell Rd, Cromwell.

03 445 0596

www.jacksonorchard.co.nz

19. Shrek Museum

Without a doubt New Zealand's most famous sheep was Shrek, who rocketed to national and international fame in 2004. A Merino wether, living on Bendigo Station in Central Otago, Shrek cunningly avoided being rounded up for the annual shear for over six years until April 15, 2004 when he was finally brought in for shearing. Shrek was shorn live on television on April 28 by champion shearers David Fagan and Peter Casserly. The whole process took twenty minutes and the final fleece weighed a massive 27 kg (An average Merino fleece typically weighs around 4.5 kg).

From that point on, Shrek lived the life of the rich and famous, meeting with the Prime Minister in May 2004 and was even shorn on an iceberg off the Otago coast. Shrek died as a celebrity aged sixteen years on June 6, 2011.

Today the tiny township of Tarras has created a small museum dedicated to our most famous sheep and, along with numerous photos of Shrek pre and post shearing, on display are the very shears that did the job.

 Tarras township, 1 km from the junction of SH 8 and SH 8A.

20. Lindis Pass Road

Linking Central Otago to the Mackenzie basin, the Lindis Pass reaches a height of 490 m, and winds its way through classic New Zealand high country. Open, rocky and with vast swathes of tussock land, the view from the top is expansive and particularly attractive in autumn when the spare trees in the valleys turn gold, perfectly complimenting the green/gold tussock grass.

Wanaka

While not as frenetic as Queenstown, Wanaka has, in recent years, changed from a quiet lakeside backwater to a sophisticated alpine town with smart shops, luxury accommodation and modern cafés. Still, it is not hard to get away from the crowds, either on the lake or in nearby Mt Aspiring National Park.

21. Lake Wanaka Islands

Often overlooked, there are four islands within Lake Wanaka, ranging from 120 ha to just 3 ha and all are undergoing restoration. The two largest islands, both 120 ha are Mou Waho and Mou Tapu and are home to endangered Buff Weka, long extinct on the mainland.

Furthest from Wanaka, Mou Waho has a hidden glacial lake 150 m above sea level and a walk to the lake and summit (450 metres) with spectacular views will take around an hour. Once farmed and used for boat building, there are the remains of a cottage and an old stone wharf.

Mou Tapu is both pest free and, as it was never grazed, home to endangered plants and animals, as well as remnants of the original bush. There are no tracks or facilities on this island.

Tucked away in the Stevensons Arm, is Te Peka Karara (65 ha) which also hosts Buff weka and has a short walk to the summit (300m) and a pleasant beach.

The closet island to Wanaka is Ruby Island which at three hectares is also the smallest. A community planting programe is restoring the island and as it is just 1 km offshore, Ruby Island is an ideal kayak and picnic destination.

Several operators run trips to the island and the local i-site will have up to date information. Camping is available Mou Waho and Te Peka Karara.

State Highway 6, Wanaka.
03 443 7307
www.worldofdeer.com
Entrance fee.

22. That Wanaka Tree

Yes, you can fool all the people all of time. A few years ago, a lone willow tree keep popping up on social media. Photographed at sunset with a mountain backdrop and altered beyond recognition by filters, the tree looked fabulous and became an online sensation. The reality is a good deal different. Just a few metres high and sitting a little way off shore, this ordinary willow tree now attracts thousands of people. They do not linger to admire its solitary beauty in an extraordinary landscape, but rush down to the shingle shore for a minute or two to snap a selfie, then off to load it on to Instagram, Snapchat or Facebook. The frantic and constant flow of people is an extraordinary sight.

 On the lake front off the Wanaka-Mt Aspiring Road, 2 km from the town centre.

23. Glendhu Bay Motor Camp Ground

Glendhu Bay, west of Wanaka on the road to Mt Aspiring, is one of New Zealand's most iconic camping grounds. Situated right on the shores of the lake (with its own boat ramp), the camping ground has this magnificent bay all to itself. Surrounded by high peaks and strung out along the shore of the lake this is an ideal spot, whether in a tent, caravan, campervan, cabin or the new lodge. It is frequently booked out during the summer months with some families booking years in advance, but phone ahead, you never know your luck as it is a fabulous spot – too good to miss.

 Mt Aspiring Road, 10 km west of Wanaka.
 03 443 7243

24. The Paddock, Lake Hawea

Like its neighbor Wanaka, Lake Hawea was formed by a retreating glacier, and the township occupies a high bank of glacial moraine at the base of the lake with a long sweep of shingle beach. Unlike glamourous Wanaka, Hawea township is much smaller and considerably more relaxed and does not have quite the same spectacular views. What it does have is one of New Zealand's most famous gardens, The Paddock.

This is a very tough place to grow a garden. The site is exposed to wind, frequently bone dry, the soil is devoid of organic material and heavily compacted, and in winter hammered by hard frosts and occasional snow.

However, Donella and John Osborne knew what to expect as they had already managed farms in the region for twenty years before they purchased the Hawea land in 2003.

Shelter was planted to protect the garden from the fierce Nor-Westers, plants were carefully selected to cope with the demanding conditions and the most important ingredient was a good supply of water. Today the garden is an oasis of colour and texture with something to offer all year round. Bulbs thrive here and a huge range have been planted to complement other spring blossoms. Peonys love this climate, as do roses, iris, lavender and perennials. Not just about flowers, the garden has an orchard, tunnel house, berry garden and a vegetable garden. The Paddock is not just a 'nice garden' but a tribute to hard work, perseverance and working with climatic conditions.

  29 Lichen Lane, Lake Hawea.
 9.30 am to 4.30 pm Friday, Sat, Sun and Monday - best to ring first.
443 6999
0274087719

25. AJ Hackett Bungy

AJ Hackett and Henry Van Asch created the first commercial bungy site in the world in 1988 at the Kawarau Bridge near Queenstown. Today that 43 metre jump has been eclipsed by several other higher jumps, with the scariest of all being a plunge of 134 metres over the Nevis River, also just out of Queenstown. In the North Island the highest jump is 80 metres off the Mokai Bridge over the Rangitikei River. These pale in comparison to the death defying jump of 216 metres off Bloukrans Bridge in South Africa.

This is a popular tourist destination but marks New Zealand's pioneering contribution to the world of adventure sport.

  AJ Hackett Bungy.

State Highway 6, Gibbston Valley, Queenstown.
0800 286 4958
www.bungy.co.nz

26. Edith Cavell Bridge

Accused of treason for helping Allied soldiers escape German occupied Belgium, British nurse Edith Cavell was executed by firing squad on October 12, 1915. Her death sparked international outrage and her courage and bravery became legendary. Memorials in her honour were erected throughout the British Empire, though the naming of a bridge in New Zealand took a more circuitous route.

Designed by Frederick Furkert and built of steel and concrete, the single lane bridge over the Shotover River considerably improved travel in the area. Jack Clark, an old miner who lived near the bridge, decided that the bridge should be named after nurse Edith Cavell, although she had no connection with New Zealand let alone Central Otago. The name was not popular with officials, but Clark took matters into his own hands and painted 'The Edith Cavell Bridge' on a sign and on the bridge itself and eventually the officials gave in and the name stuck. Today the Edith Cavell Bridge is recognized as a Category One Heritage Structure.

 Arthurs Point, Shotover Gorge on the Queenstown to Arrowtown Road.

27. Oxenbridge Tunnel

This short walk along the Shotover River leads to a lookout point above the rugged gorge and the Oxenbridge Tunnel. Between 1906 and 1910, the Oxenbridge brothers decided to build a tunnel to divert the Shotover River and thereby make a fortune from gold in the river bed. Progress was slow and very costly and when the four metre square tunnel was complete, the entrance up river was a metre too high and only half river water flowed through the tunnel. Despite all their efforts the scheme was a disappointment as only a small amount of gold was ever recovered. Today this is a good perch from which to watch jets boats on the river below. Spot, too, the rusting steam engine strangely marooned on a rock in the middle of the river.

 The track begins at a small carpark at the end of Kerry Drive. If walking up from the town start at Belfast Street and add another 30 minutes to your walk time.

28. The Road to Skippers

This is the place to test your nerves, and it's definitely not a drive for the less confident motorist. One of New Zealand's legendary roads, the road to Skippers has hardly changed since it was built in the 1860s to service the gold-mining settlements along the Shotover River.

Unsealed and very narrow, the road is more suited to four-wheel drives or at least vehicles with a reasonably high wheelbase. Not for the faint-hearted, there are huge drops into the Shotover River and the road also requires considerable backing skills if another vehicle happens to be coming the other way, as long stretches are only one-way. The scenery, though, is well worth it. Winding high above the dry rocky landscape, the road more or less follows the Shotover River, and with very few trees the views are endless.

All that remains of the Long Gully Pub, built in 1863 and burnt down in 1951, is the fireplace and chimneys, while at the end of the road is a camping ground and the restored nineteenth-century stone schoolhouse. The wooden Mt Aurum homestead was destroyed by fire in 2018.

The historic Skippers suspension bridge was built in 1901, while an even older bridge over the Shotover was built in 1864 and is now used for bungy jumps. If you don't want to drive, several operators run 4WD tours along the road.

📍 The road to Skippers is north of Queenstown and is a continuation of the road to the Coronet Peak ski field.

29. Queenstown Hill/Te Tapunui

Rising steeply behind this bustling tourist town, the quiet summit of Queenstown Hill affords a spectacular view of Lake Wakatipu and the surrounding mountains.

A time long ago, the area now occupied by the lake was the favoured resting place of an ogre, sometimes called Kopuwai. All was well until the ogre kidnapped the wife of a local Maori chief. Unable to tackle the giant ogre, the chief bided his time until the ogre went to sleep between the mountains. Seizing his chance, the chief rescued his wife and, to prevent revenge, he heaped wood over the giant and burnt him to death. The giant hole left by the ogre filled with water, creating the lake; and all that remains of the ogre is his beating heart, which still causes the lake to mysteriously rise and fall.

This track is a solid uphill slog. The initial loop section is known as the Time Walk. Beginning through a beautiful wrought-iron gate, a series of illustrated panels takes the walker from the past to the present and finally the future, represented at the top by Caroline Robinson's simple sculpture *Basket of Dreams*. To follow the panels in the correct sequence, turn right at the junction where the track becomes a loop. This direction is also the gentler grade to the top.

Most of the walk is through pine and Douglas fir, with the occasional view glimpsed through the branches. However, near the top the vegetation is open, and a grand view of the lake, mountains and town is laid out before you. At the small pond on top of the ridge, veer left to the *Basket of Dreams* and the track downhill; or, if you are feeling energetic having got this far, the track to the right will take you to the top of Queenstown Hill (907 m), which is just fifteen minutes' walk away.

This is a steep walk that climbs up 500 metres from the carpark to the top and will take two to three hours. It is an excellent track so take your time and the rewards are fantastic views over the lake and town.

- 📍 The track begins at a small carpark at the end of Kerry Drive.
- 🕒 If walking up from the town start at Belfast Street and add another 30 minutes to your walk time.

30. Moke Lake

Just a few kilometres from Queenstown, Moke Lake is a small alpine tarn in the heart of the working high country Closeburn Station, and feels a million miles away from the cool bars and swish hotels of Queenstown. Surrounded by steep tussock clad hills, the road to the lake is narrow and gravel, and several short sections are one way only (a good way to improve your backing skills). At the end of the road is a very popular but basic camping ground and the start of the easy two-hour return walk to Lake Despair.

- 📍 From Queenstown drive 14 km on the road to Glenorcy, then turn right into Moke Lake Road and drive 7 km to the end of the road at the camping ground.

31. Little Paradise Lodge, Mt Creighton, Glenorchy

Tucked away above the road to Glenorchy is an extraordinary garden and lodge, the handiwork of Swiss immigrant Thomas Schneider and his Philippino wife Christy. Eclectic is an understatement, and rustic and quirky don't do justice to the detail and precision gone into this creating the unique Little Paradise Lodge.

Using natural materials, particularly stone and wood, Thomas has individually crafted each room so that the wood gleams and the stone comes to life. Murals adorn the walls, toilet cisterns become fish tanks, everywhere there are details that constantly surprise and never fail to delight.

The gardens are a rambling combination of native and exotic plants with little time for straight lines and formality. Thousands of daffodils light up the garden in spring and huge Himalayan lilies reach to the clear blue skies during the summer. Small ponds are home to native eels and trout hatcheries while the fruit trees and flowering shrubs attract birds and house bees.

Lying directly on the 45th parallel, it is precisely halfway between the equator and the South Pole.

Accommodation varies and includes shared rooms, ensuites and a separate cottage.

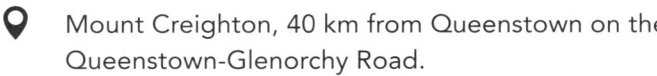

- Mount Creighton, 40 km from Queenstown on the Queenstown-Glenorchy Road.
- 03 442 6196
- www.littleparadise.co.nz
- Entry fee.

32. Glenorchy, the Dart Valley and a Lost Railway Shed.

The old adage that 'it is better to travel than to arrive' very much applies to Glenorchy. While the small village of Glenorchy isn't up to much, the trip along the lake from Queenstown has magnificent vistas both of the mountains across the lake and up the Dart River into the heart of Fiordland. There are several excellent walks along the road from Queenstown and further up the Dart River Valley, including access to the famous Routeburn and Caples and Greenstone Tracks. The area is also notable as yet another *Lord of the Rings* location and jet boating on the

Dart is famous for both the thrill and the scenic backdrop. This road also leads to the southern access point of the Mt Aspiring National Park.

For railway buffs, the village does have the curious attraction of an old red railway goods shed, though no railway ever reached Glenorchy. The shed is a reminder of the era when transport on the lake was once part of the New Zealand Railways network and Glenorchy was linked by boat to Queenstown and the railway head at Kingston at the southern end of Lake Whakatipu.

In summer this road, and especially the roads west of Glenorchy, have become busy with visitors heading up to Paradise seeking out *Lord of the Rings* locations and for the compulsory Instantgram snap shot in front of the Paradise sign. A long section of the road beyond Glenorchy to Paradise is gravel, narrow and extremely dusty in summer. In the off-season it is magical, but whatever the season don't forget your sandfly repellant.

33. Central Otago Vineyards

When the first vineyard was established in the Gibbston Valley the venture was treated with much scepticism, but now Central Otago is producing some of New Zealand's best wines and has, without a doubt, some of the most scenic vineyards in the country. In addition to the stark and rugged terrain, the weather is by New Zealand standards extreme: hot and dry in the summer, very cold in winter. While pinot noir is the area's signature wine, Central Otago also produces some award-winning white wines including chardonnay, pinot gris and riesling. The main areas for wine production are around Cornwell and the Gibbston Valley in the Kawarau Gorge.

Chard Farm Winery

The setting for this vineyard is spectacular with the grapes planted to the very edge of the wild Kawarau River gorge and steep rocky hills creating a towering backdrop to the French-style winery. The narrow road is a trip in itself and is like a mini 'Road to Skippers' and was, during the nineteenth century, the main road through the gorge. It does have an advantage in that the road is so narrow that tour buses can't fit through! Like other Central Otago vineyards, Chard Farm offers chardonnay and riesling, in addition to its award-winning pinot noir.

- 📍 Chard Farm Road, off SH 6, Gibbston.
- 🕐 Cellar door open Monday to Friday 10 am to 5 pm, Saturday and Sunday 11 am to 5 pm.
- 📞 03 441 8452
- 🌐 www.chardfarm.co.nz

Gibbston Valley Wines

Gibbston Valley Wines were the pioneer vineyard of the area with plantings as early as 1981. Their first commercial wine bottled in 1987 and their pinot noir has over the years won numerous awards. Today the range is considerably more extensive and includes chardonnay, pinot gris, sauvignon blanc, riesling, gewürztraminer and pinot blanc. In addition to wine tasting, Gibbston Valley has a superb café in a garden setting and right next door is the Gibbston Valley Cheese Company which produces boutique varieties from both cow's and sheep's milk using traditional methods.

- 📍 SH 6, Gibbston.
- 🕐 Cellar door open 10 am to 5 pm.
- 📞 03 442 6910
- 🌐 www.gibbstonvalley.co.nz

Rippon Vineyard and Winery, Wanaka

One of the country's most photographed wineries, Rippon Vineyard is located on a broad slope just above Lake Wanaka. Famous for its vistas of rows of grapes leading down to the lake, Rippon is especially attractive in autumn when the yellowing leaves of the vines contrast with the bright blue of the lake. The vineyard is an easy walk along the lake from central Wanaka and now has a restaurant high above the vineyards with spectacular views.

One of the earliest vineyards in Central Otago, the DSIR first started experimental plantings here in 1975, and by 1981 the vineyard was already extensively planted. Today Rippon works on biodynamic farming principles with no irrigation and while pinot noir is the signature wine, other varietals include riesling, sauvignon blanc, gewürztraminer and osteiner.

 5 km west of Wanaka on the Mt Aspiring Road.
 Cellar door open daily 11 am to 5 pm.
 03 443 8084
www.rippon.co.nz

The Wooing Tree Winery, Cromwell.

Specialising in chardonnay, pinot noir, rosé, and blondie (made from pinot noir), The Wooing Tree Winery takes its name from solitary and rather ordinary pine tree at the back of the vineyard overlooking long rows of grape vines. No one knows how old the tree is but it is said to date back to the 1920s and for as long as anyone can remember, this is the tree where local sweethearts met, far away from prying eyes. Solid and well anchored in the sandy soil, the tree is able to withstand the fierce winds and storms the sweep down from the mountains, displaying some of the very ingredients that love needs to survive the tempest of life.

One of many such pine trees dotting the open landscape around Cromwell, the tree was part of block sold for vineyards and, unaware of the tree's importance, the new owners gave the go-ahead to clear the land of trees prior to planting grapes. About to lose the very tree dear to their hearts, locals went into action to save the tree. Out came stories of romance, marriage proposals and even conceptions, all linked to this one old pine tree. The new owners, impressed with tales of love and passion, not only saved the tree, but went one step further and named their new vineyard The Wooing Tree.

Today the tree remains a favoured spot for lover's trysts and marriage proposals and the winery is a popular venue for weddings held under the wide spreading branches of the tree of love.

The tree is in the middle of a working vineyard and you first need to ask permission at the tasting room/café to visit the tree.

- 64 Shortcut Road, Cromwell.
- Open daily August to April 10 am to 5 pm. May to July 11 am to 4 pm.
- 03 445 4142
- www.wooingtree.co.nz

DUNEDIN AND THE OTAGO PENINSULA

1. New Zealand's Tallest Tree
2. Mt Cargill/ Kapukataumahaka
3. Aramoana Beach and Breakwater
4. Port Chalmers
5. Careys Bay Hotel
6. Lady Thorne Dell
7. Signal Hill
8. Ross Creek Reservoir
9. Dunedin Botanic Gardens
10. University of Otago
11. Dunedin Museum of Natural Mystery
12. Olveston
13. Trees of Knox Church
14. The Savoy Tearooms/ Etrusco
15. Dunedin Public Art Gallery and Dunedin Street Art
16. New Zealand Sports Hall of Fame
17. Otago Settlers Museum
18. Historic Dunedin
19. Cheese Rolls
20. Dunedin Gasworks Museum
21. St Clair Hot Salt Water Pool
22. Tunnel Beach
23. Glenfalloch Woodland Garden
24. Sandymount Walks
25. The Pyramids and Victory Beach – Okia Reserve
26. Otakau Marae

1. New Zealand's Tallest Tree

For those who take the Australia/New Zealand rivalry to heart, this is going to be hard to take. Not only do they trash us at sport, but also the tallest tree in New Zealand is a blimmin' Aussie. This gum tree, *Eucalpytus regans*, towers more than 30 metres higher than the revered kauri Tane Mahuta (51 m) and 18 metres taller than our tallest tree, the kahikatea (66.5 m). Reaching 83 metres, the tree is part of a large grove of gums that were self-sown after a fire in 1900, with the ash from the fire providing a fertile base to give the seedlings a good start in life. The grove is surrounded by native bush and the area is now protected as part of the 300 ha Orokonui Ecosanctaury just north of Dunedin City. The walk to the tree takes around one hour return.

- 📍 The entrance to the sanctuary on Blueskin Road is well marked from SH 1 at Waitati, and from Dunedin via Port Chalmers or off the Mount Cargill Road.
- $ Entrance fee

2. Mt Cargill/Kapukataumahaka

Frequently mist-shrouded, the heights of this 676 m peak offer huge 360-degree views north and south, with a cairn indicating all the key geographical features. The summit is very exposed and both the vegetation and climate are definitely subalpine. If the day dawns cloudy and wet, don't bother with this trip: you will not see a thing. If the day dawns fine, make this your priority.

Mount Cargill is known in Maori as Kapukataumahaka and is said to represent (depending on the version) the body of a warrior or of a princess, with Buttars Peak the head and Mt Cargill the body.

You can easily drive to the top of Mt Cargill, but the track through regenerating bush and past the Organ Pipes is much more rewarding. All the hard climbing on this walk is in the first fifteen minutes, as the track goes solidly uphill with quite a few steps in this first section before it levels off. From there it is a surprisingly easy walk to Mt Cargill, well within the capabilities of anyone with reasonable fitness, and takes just two hours return.

 Take Pine Hill Road (off SH 1) to Cowans Road which leads to the top.

For the walking track follow the North Road in the North East Valley until it eventually morphs into Mt Cargill Road, a distance of 8 km. The car park is 3 km on left, but there is very limited parking space.

3. Aramoana Beach and Breakwater

Situated at the entrance to Otago Harbour, opposite Taiaroa Head, Aramoana is a natural sand spit that has built up over millennia to almost enclose the harbour and protect the shallow waters from the open sea. The beautiful white sandy beach is split by the long breakwater that was primarily constructed to stop the channel silting up. This is a great place for a stroll, especially when a heavy swell rolls in from the east, or to watch ships coming and going from the harbour. Take binoculars and you might spot albatross in flight from the colony just opposite on Taiaroa Head, and fur seals and blue penguins are not uncommon here.

Just inside the breakwater, a track and boardwalk leads through the extensive tidal salt marshes which are home to numerous wading birds, including godwits in the summer months. The beaches either side of the breakwater are ideal for that leisurely stroll and, for those in the mood for something more demanding, a three-hour return hike to Heyward Point with fantastic coastal and harbour views is recommended. This track begins to the left when coming into Aramoana.

The settlement itself consists mainly of old-fashioned cribs sheltering behind the dunes, and fortunately plans to build an aluminium smelter here in the 1970s came to nothing, preserving a particularly attractive spot for the enjoyment of future generations.

For many New Zealanders the name Aramoana is synonymous with the one of New Zealand's worst murders, but this association does a great disservice to what is a very attractive area. On November 13 1990, loner David Gray went on a rampage through the small seaside settlement of Aramoana after an argument with a neighbour. Armed with a semi-automatic rifle he indiscriminately killed thirteen people including the first police officer on the scene, Stewart Guthrie. Finally trapped in a house, Gray himself was shot by the police when he came out of the house firing from the hip. A further four people were wounded. Three of the dead were children, as were two of the wounded.

📍 10 km from Port Chalmers continuing east along the Otago Harbour to the very end of Aramoana road.

4. Port Chalmers

While Dunedin itself lies at the head of Otago Harbour, the harbour is too shallow and narrow for substantial shipping, and from the early days Port Chalmers was developed as the deep-water port for the city. New Zealand's third-oldest town (founded in 1844), Port Chalmers has many fine stone buildings, most of them constructed between 1874 and 1880. Stonemasons from the Isle of Portland were employed to build the dry dock in 1872, then the biggest in the country, and when that was completed sought other work locally. Historic buildings in the town include the Port Stables (1867), National Bank (1877), The Municipal Buildings (1889), Iona Church (1883), and Holy Trinity Church (1874). It was from Port Chalmers that New Zealand's first cargo of frozen sheep meat left for Britain on the clipper *Dunedin* in 1882.

The small Port Chalmers Museum is jam-packed with fascinating objects and feels more like a smart antique shop than a museum. No fancy lighting or interactive display for bored kids here. Strong on maritime history, the Painting Room has a huge canvas of nineteenth-century Port

Chalmers, and there is a massive old diver's suit along with cannons from the perfectly named pirate ship *The Don Juan* which was built in 1857, and the remains of which are still visible at low tide at Deborah Bay. The stone building was originally the post office, opened in 1877 (check the website for details www.portmuseum.org.nz).

Yet another pirate ship, the *Cincinnati* supplied the mast that was erected at Observation Point or Flagstaff Lookout in 1864 and used to carry signal flags and lamps to guide ships to the port. The hill is a great spot to watch the busy wharves just below.

 14 km from central Dunedin on SH 88.

5. Careys Bay Hotel

While the Careys Bay Hotel is popular with locals, most visitors don't make the short trip out to Port Chalmers and miss one of this region's most pleasant spots. Constructed of local bluestone, this pub was built in 1874 at Careys Bay, just out of Port Chalmers itself, and today looks out over the local fishing fleet. Immaculately restored, walking into the hotel is like stepping back in time to the nineteenth century (or at least the very best of the nineteenth century). Warm wood panelling, original sash windows, a timber staircase and beautiful stonework over 125 years old meld together to create one of New Zealand's best pub experiences. But the hotel is not all about history. Careys Bay Hotel also has an impressive collection of Ralph Hotere paintings, who is without doubt one of New Zealand's leading contemporary artists. The pub also serves very good food in the dining room and the attractive courtyard.

 17 Macandrew Rd, Careys Bay.
 03 472 8022
 www.careysbayhotel.co.nz

6. Lady Thorn Dell

Tucked away above Port Chalmers is an old quarry that has been turned into a small garden. A quarry turned garden isn't that unusual in itself, but this is no ordinary place as this is the quarry that supplied the distinctive bluestone for some of the city's most important historic buildings. Named after Lady Thorn, a former Port Chalmer's mayoress, the garden has been developed since 1998 by the local Lions Club and features a range of shrubs, small trees and spring flowering bulbs. However, it is the springtime rhododendrons that really steal the show from mid-October to mid-December. On the quarry rim is a viewing platform over the town that includes historical photos taken from the same point. The names on the quarry face are not the work of graffiti artists or fans of some obscure sports teams but the work of sailors who scaled the steep cliffs of the quarry to boldly paint the name of their visiting ship.

Parking is very limited, but it is just a short, but steep climb up from the town.

 Church Street, Port Chalmers.

7. Signal Hill

The Cargill Lookout on Signal Hill, to the north of the city, has fine views over Otago Harbour and the central business district. Dunedin, however, is a city of views and what makes this viewpoint special is the massive New Zealand Centennial monument. It is two chunky Tolkienesque statues: one of a woman holding a skein of wool, entitled 'The Thread of Life'; the other of man with a book, called 'History'. Designed by FW Sturrock and Frederick Staub, the bronze figures were originally planned to be unveiled for the centenary of the signing of the Treaty of Waitangi in 1940, but the outbreak of WWII delayed the project until the 1950s. Commemorating the connection between Scotland and Otago, the monument also incorporates a large stone from Edinburgh.

📍 End of Signal Hill Road, Opoho.

8. Ross Creek Reservoir

Tucked away off the Leith Valley, Ross Creek Reservoir is recognised as an outstanding engineering achievement by IPENZ (Institute of Professional Engineers New Zealand). The earth dam was built in 1867 to provide water to a town rapidly expanding with the influx of wealth from the gold rushes further inland, and today the reservoir is the oldest still in existence in New Zealand and is still part of the city's water system.

A short walk from the road through a mixture of introduced and native trees (including some very large native tree fuchsias), the original bluestone walls still line the dam, though it is the old valve tower that is the highlight. The tower was built at the same time as the dam in 1867 and the simple, elegant structure with its curved roof is distinctively Victorian.

📍 The track to reservoir starts just over the bridge on Rockside Road near the intersection with Malvern Road, North Dunedin.

9. Dunedin Botanic Gardens

Established in 1863 on the site where the university now stands, new gardens were laid out on this site in 1868. The gardens naturally fall into two parts: the original lower gardens are flat and are very Victorian in layout; while the upper section across the Water of Leith is quite different with steep terrain, and the plantings – featuring the larger tree and shrub collections – far less formal. There are three highlights within the gardens worth seeking out.

The first highlight is the stunning perennial herbaceous borders. Much loved in traditional English gardening, herbaceous borders do not thrive in the generally warmer New Zealand climate. Here in Dunedin, however, with its cool winter and mild summer temperatures, the herbaceous border walk is the best in the country. One side of the walk is a long perennial border, while the other side is a series of short borders arranged in blue, red, white and yellow. The borders are at their peak between December and February.

Number two on the list is the ornate Wolfe Haven Fountain. Built in 1898, the fountain originally stood in the Queen's Gardens by the railway station. During the New Zealand and South Seas Exhibition held in Dunedin in 1925, the fountain graced the foyer of the Grand Court, after which is was moved yet again – this time to the Botanic Gardens where it has finally stayed put. The cast-iron fountain comprises three tiers, with the traditional theme of cherubs and fish topped by a heron spouting water. The setting is further enhanced by a formal garden of box hedging and topiary.

Number three is royal oak tree planted in June 1863, to much local fanfare, to commemorate the wedding of Prince Albert to the Danish princess Alexandra earlier that year. However, the gardens weren't established here until 1868 so how could this tree have been planted on this spot five years earlier? The answer to this conundrum is that the tree was originally planted on the university site and, when the gardens were relocated, the oak tree was dug up and moved to the new gardens where to this day, while showing its age, it is well cared for.

 Corner Great King and Opoho Streets.

10. University of Otago

With a student population of 20,000 in a city of 130,000 residents, Dunedin is more influenced by its students than any other university city in New Zealand. The University of Otago, established in 1869, is New Zealand's oldest university. The complex of stone buildings was designed in the Gothic Revival style by Maxwell Bury and completed in 1878, though the clock tower was without an actual clock until 1930. Other buildings that followed took their lead from the style of the first building, creating a unified look that is unlike any other New Zealand university. Well worth a leisurely stroll through the campus.

📍 Union Place, off Cumberland Street (SH 1).

11. Dunedin Museum of Natural Mystery

Most boys at some point of their young lives have a little cache of found treasures: favourite stones, shells, a broken knife and very likely the skeletal skull of a bird or rat. The collection of Bruce Mahalski takes this to a whole new level. While the Museum of Natural Mystery is more than just animal skulls, they do dominate the collection. Meticulously displayed, row after row of bleached skulls hang in a very orderly fashion from the walls of several rooms. The result is neither macabre nor ghoulish, but it is bizarre and at the same time surprisingly intriguing and even mesmerising.

Dispersed among the skulls are other curiosities, some with natural history flavours, while others have little or no connection with the main collection of skulls. Most intriguing is a Lionel Terry painting from 1927 when Terry was incarcerated at Seacliff Lunatic Asylum after killing Chinese immigrant, Mr. Joe Kum Yung, in Wellington in 1905.

📍 For opening hours check the website.
61 Royal Terrace, Dunedin.
🌐 www.royaldunedinmuseum.com
$ Entrance fee.

12. Olveston

Often overlooked by visitors to Dunedin interested in a trip to the more dramatic Larnach Castle, Olveston is without a doubt one of the best 'old house' experiences in the country. In most old homes the furniture has long since disappeared, but what makes Olveston so special is that it is crammed full of the original furniture and ornaments with very little changed since the house was first built.

Completed in 1906, the house was commissioned by David Theomin, a Jewish immigrant who developed a very successful music business in Dunedin in the latter half of the nineteenth century. Designed by London architect Sir Ernest George, no expense was spared in the construction and the house included every modern convenience from a central heating system and telephone, through to a shower and heated towel rail in the bathroom. Unfortunately for the family the only son, Edward, died at an early age and the only daughter, Dorothy, died childless in 1966. She left the house to Dunedin City which, at the time, was not particularly thrilled to receive such a cumbersome gift, although today it is recognised as a local treasure.

So little has been altered in the house over the last 100 years that it appears the Theomins have just gone out for the day and are due back any moment. The kitchen contains complete dinner sets (all ready for serving); personal ornaments still sit on the bedroom dressing tables; while the only thing missing from the billiard room is the cigar smoke. All tours of the house are guided which adds immensely to the experience, so if your time is in Dunedin is short put a visit to this magnificent house at the top of your list.

 42 Royal Terrace, Dunedin.
 Open daily, check the website or phone for tour times.
 03 477 3320
 www.olverston.co.nz
 Entrance fee.

13. Trees of Knox Church

Despite its prominent position astride busy George Street, the historic Knox Church (built in 1876) is often overlooked by visitors to Dunedin in favour of the elegant First Church near the Octagon. In the grounds of the church are several fine old trees that once graced the gardens of the original manse that was demolished in 1977. Behind the church is a spectacular 20-metre high copper beech planted in 1898, and situated in front of the building is a weeping ash, one of the country's most photogenic trees. A southern rata planted in 1880 flourishes in the old garden and although only 10 metres tall is perfectly formed.

 Corner of George and Pitt Street.

14. The Savoy Tearooms/Etrusco

In their day, the Savoy Tearooms were the epitome of the great English tearooms. Located on the first floor of the Haynes Building in Princes Street, the Savoy was the place for high teas, lunchtime dinners, and those special occasions. This is where you came for bone china and Victoria sponge, which were eventually overtaken in the 1970s – the era of pottery mugs and muffins – but the tearooms limped on until they finally closed in 1989. Standing empty for some time before being resurrected as a restaurant, today it is half the size of the originally Savoy which at one time had reception rooms next door.

In the early 1990s Federico and Meegan Gianone arrived with two small sons in Dunedin and took a gamble on the old Savoy. Renaming it the Etrusco At The Savoy, they ensured all the features that made the Savoy so attractive and elegant have not only survived but are also loving valued. The magnificent plaster ceilings are all original, along with the oak panelling, light fittings, faux marble pillars and even most of the furniture. All the fabulous Edwardian leadlight windows, each with three-coloured heraldic shields, have survived intact and you need to come early if you want a seat by the windows. More recently the original wooden floors have been restored, complete with thousands of tiny indentations made by generations of elegant high heels clicking across the surface. In winter the old fireplace blazes with both real and remembered warmth.

Twenty years on it is still a family business with sons Rion and Zane actively involved in this lively Italian pizzeria and spaghetteria and the mixed clientele, moderate prices and welcoming staff make this an ideal place for dinner out when you are in Dunedin.

  8A Moray Place, Dunedin.
  www.etrusco.co.nz
  03 477 3737

15. Dunedin Public Art Gallery and Dunedin Street Art

Formerly the old DIC department store, this immensely stylish art gallery was opened in 1996 and is big enough to be interesting, yet small enough to be welcoming. The gallery itself holds a wide collection of New Zealand and European art, and in recent years has attracted some exceptional international art exhibitions to Dunedin. There is a permanent exhibition room for Dunedin-born artist Frances Hodgkins (1869–1947), internationally recognised as one of New Zealand's most significant Neo-Romantic painters of the 1930s and 40s.

Dunedin is also recognised as having one of the country's best collections of street art, most which can be found in a concentrated area south of the Octagon. For an easy guide and map go to the street art website dunedinstreetart.co.nz

  30 The Octagon.
  Open daily 10 am to 5 pm. Closed Christmas Day and Good Friday.
  www.dunedin.art.museum
$ Koha/donation.

16. New Zealand Sports Hall of Fame

The Hall of Fame is dedicated to New Zealand's greatest sports performers and is crammed full of the most amazing sports memorabilia, guaranteed to delight and surprise sports and non-sports fans alike. Covering over thirty different sports, the displays include New Zealand's first Olympic medal won by boxer Ted Morgan at the 1928 Amsterdam games; jockey Bill Skelton's riding kit; and a reconstructed long-jump pit showing Yvette Williams' amazing jump at the Helsinki games in 1952.

 Dunedin Railway Station, Anzac Avenue.
 Open daily 10 am to 4 pm. Closed Christmas Day.
 www.nzhalloffame.co.nz
$ Entrance fee.

17. Otago Settlers Museum

This collection began in 1898 when the Otago Settlers Association began accumulating documents and portraits for the fiftieth anniversary of the founding of Dunedin city. In 1908 the first gallery opened and featured hundreds of portraits, mainly of Scottish pioneers. The cumulative effect is both intimidating and spellbinding. Fierce, staunch faces peer down at you and you immediately feel compelled to be quiet and well behaved. 'What have you done with our hard work?' these faces ask. This experience must be doubly daunting if you are in fact descended from any of these people. Much of this fierce countenance comes from the photography methods of the time. Subjects had to sit very still for a long time so holding a blank unsmiling face was much easier than holding a cheeky grin for several minutes. Photography was rare, so a formal portrait was a serious occasion that entailed best Sunday clothes and grave face. No doubt these people laughed, danced, sang and joked, but certainly not on this occasion.

Today the museum has a much broader brief and includes extensive displays on Maori and Chinese histories, as well as the social and economic background of Otago province. The museum retains its original Edwardian galleries, and is linked to the old art deco NZR Transport Building which appropriately holds the transport collection.

- 31 Queens Gardens.
- Open daily 10 am to 5 pm. Closed Christmas Day and Good Friday.
- www.toituosm.com
- Entrance fee.

18. Historic Dunedin

Very much the boom-town during the second half of the nineteenth century on the back of Central Otago gold, growth in Dunedin in the twentieth century has been far more modest and has meant that the city has retained many of its fine Victorian buildings. Most of the historic buildings are clustered around the Octagon and along Princes Street, once the heart of the business district. All are within easy walking distance of the central city, and the i-SITE in the Octogon has brochures for two historic walks. Both are 2 km in length and take about one hour each.

Four buildings worth seeking out in their own right are as follows:

Crown Milling Company (Manor Place) is one of New Zealand's oldest industrial buildings. This substantial flour mill was originally built in 1867, with the fifth floor added in the 1890s, and is now apartments.

Dunedin Prison (Lower High Street) was built of brick in 1896 (closed in 2007), with the design heavily influenced by the New Scotland Yard building in London. The prison offers tours on Saturday morning.

New Zealand Rail Road Services (Cumberland Street). Now part of the Otago Settlers Museum, this building is a substantial art deco structure (built 1939) and rare in mainly Victorian Dunedin.

St Joseph's Roman Catholic Cathedral (Corner Rattray and Smith Streets) is tucked above the city away from the Anglican Cathedral and Presbyterian First Church. In contrast to his more Romanesque-style churches (Invercargill, Christchurch, Waimate), renowned church architect

FW Petre designed this church in the Gothic Revival style. Built of bluestone, the church was opened in 1886.

19. Cheese Rolls

Northerners (in this case everyone living north of the Waitaki River) are baffled by the enthusiasm for cheese rolls in this area. New Zealand has very few distinctive regional foods, but the humble cheese roll is one of these. Mostly confined to Otago and Southland, the cheese roll is pretty much as it sounds – cheese rolled up in a slice of bread and toasted until the cheese starts to melt. Affectionately known as 'Southland sushi', unfortunately the cheese roll is usually a sorry affair. Generally prepared and popped in a warmer along with sausage rolls and pies, most cheese rolls dry out, ending up greasy and tasteless.

All that said, searching out a good, freshly made cheese roll is worthwhile, and for years the café at Mega Mitre 10 is a local favourite – so much so that the place is usually packed, especially on weekends.

And the secret to a great cheese roll? Well it's not too complicated: good quality ingredients and the rolls freshly toasted to order.

At the Colombus Café the rolls are made with extra-long multi-grain bread, which means not only tastier bread, but more layers per roll as well. Sprinkled generously with grated cheese, the rolls are then topped with chopped red and spring onions along with secret ingredients. Finally the roll is toasted with a knob of butter to create an outstanding tasty treat.

📍 Colombus Café, Mega Mitre 10.
350 Andersons Bay Road, South Dunedin.

20. Dunedin Gasworks Museum

Opened in 1863, these gasworks were the first in New Zealand to produce coal gas. Located in South Dunedin, this was also a rapidly growing industrial area at the time, supplying goods to the goldfields in Central Otago and the boom town of Dunedin. After 124 years of production, the gasworks finally closed in 1987. The complex is surprising large and the remaining buildings are largely Edwardian, though the 24-metre-high boiler-house chimney is believed to date back to the 1880s. One of only three such museums in the world, the highlight is the working stationary steam engine that at one time pumped coal gas to Dunedin households and even now is driven by steam.

 20 Braemar Street, South Dunedin.
 Open every Sunday, 12 noon to 4 pm.
 www.gasworksmuseum.org.nz
$ Entrance fee.

21. St Clair Hot Salt Water Pool

Saltwater pools were once common in coastal cities and towns. They were an economical way to provide a swimming facility by merely building a simple concrete pool that was filled by the high tide. Today only two saltwater pools survive, Parnell in Auckland and St Clair in Dunedin. St Clair and St Kilda are two magnificent sandy beaches on the south coast of Dunedin and have been popular swimming spots for locals for many years. With nothing between them and the Antarctic, the beaches are often exposed to dramatic seas, and at the rocky southern end of St Clair beach the saltwater pool cops its share of wild water. The site is spectacular and that is what makes this pool so special. Located on a rocky shelf, the pool is open to the ocean on two sides. To the east is the long sweep of shoreline, popular with surfers who zip past the pool just metres away. To the south is the Southern Ocean, pounded by high seas that occasionally break over the protecting walls, sometimes even closing the pool.

A pool was first built in 1884 and has gradually developed over the years – at one stage in the 1940s it even included a hydrotherapy clinic. Thankfully, heated since the early 1960s, St Clair was thoroughly renovated in 2003. St Clair Pool today is a modern swimming facility particularly popular with those of mature years keeping fit, and it is claimed that some older local folk walk down to the pool early in the morning still clad in their pjs and dressing gown. A small café, part of the pool complex, offers good coffee, wraps, cake, the ubiquitous cheese rolls and an exceptional view.

📍 The Esplanade, St Claire.
🕐 Open 1 October to 31 March. Weekdays 6 am to 7 pm, weekends 8 am to 7 pm.
$ Entrance fee.

22. Tunnel Beach

The Otago coast is not short of dramatic scenery, but Tunnel Beach is a standout. Accessed by a short walk of around one hour return over farmland, Tunnel Beach is a magnificent seascape of dramatic cliffs, a boulder beach cove and a natural sea arch. From the top of the arch there are marvellous views south along the coast, and in wild weather waves pound the rocks beneath – the greater the swell, the more impressive the wave action. From the top of the arch a low tunnel with shallow steps leads down to a cove, sometimes sandy, sometimes bouldered, depending on the action of the tides and weather.

This tunnel was constructed by John Cargill, son of the prominent settler William Cargill, as private access to the beach so his daughters could swim away from the prying eyes at the public St Clair's beach. The tunnel turned out to be a big mistake for Mr Cargill, as unfortunately one of the girls drowned here. Needless to say, the sea here is not safe for swimming. It is a bit of a mission to find Tunnel Beach and you will need a car.

📍 Follow the 'Southern Scenic' route south of Dunedin, and from Blackhead Road turn left into Tunnel Beach Road.

Otago Peninsula

An old volcano, the peninsula has character all of its own and no visit to Dunedin would be complete without touring here. On the north side the road follows the coast, weaving in and out of small bays with colourful boat sheds, ideal for sailing, swimming and windsurfing. Another road follows the high ridges of this rugged peninsula with spectacular views in every direction. An excellent alternative to driving is to take a harbour boat trip on either the *Monarch* (www.wildlife.co.nz) or Port to Port (www.porttoport.co.nz), both of which offer a variety of daily tours. *www.otago-peninsula.co.nz*

23. Glenfalloch Woodland Garden

Glenfalloch, meaning 'hidden valley' in Gaelic, was established by George Russell in 1871 and was accessible, at the time, only by sea. The homestead, constructed of kauri and Baltic pine, still survives in the garden where some of the trees date from 1872. Over the years extensive and diverse tree planting continued, and in 1917 Glenfalloch was sold to Philip Barling who, over the next forty years, set about creating an idyllic English garden. Philip's son, John, inherited the garden in 1956 and planted the rhododendrons and azaleas. Many of the plants in the garden are over 100 years old.

Native trees are not forgotten and beyond the formal plantings, the gardens narrow into a steep bushclad gully, the focus of which is a 1000 year old matai tree.

The gardens are especially appealing in summer (the café is open as well) but worth visiting all year round.

- 430 Portobello Road.
- Gardens are open daily 8am to dusk.
  The restaurant is open Thursday to Sunday 11 am to 3 pm.
- www.glenfalloch.co.nz

24. Sandymount Walks

The Otago Peninsula is well endowed with walks of varying length, and three of the best short walks are from Sandymount on the central southern side of the peninsula.

From Sandymount, appropriately named as it is a sand dune high on a hill, the walks begin through an atmospheric avenue of dark macrocarpa trees and emerge into bright light and tussock grass by a classic New Zealand woolshed rustic and red in colour. From here the easy walk leads to The Chasm where dramatic cliffs fall away into the wild Southern Ocean. There are spectacular views both north and south and below to Hoopers Inlet and Allans Beach. Beyond The Chasm the walk continues to Lovers Leap with more spectacular views. You can continue this as a loop walk over the low summit of Sandymount, but the views, obscured by tall flax, are minimal. Back at the carpark there is a slightly longer walk to Sandfly Bay where there is a hide for penguin watching, though this walk can be shortened considerably by driving to the bay via Ridge Road. Sandfly Bay takes its name not from the pesky insect, but from the sand driven far uphill by the ferocious winter winds.

📍 Sandymount Road is off Highcliff Road, which runs along the ridge of the peninsula.

25. The Pyramids and Victory Beach – Okia Reserve

In the third century BC Egyptian colonists arrived on the ship the *Victory* and established a settlement on the Otago Peninsula. While the colony died out, they left behind two pyramids marking the graves of the 'Pacific Pharaohs' . . . Okay, so imagination is not such a bad thing, and the walk from the road to Victory Beach passes between two pyramids that will spark plenty of flights of fancy.

The two small hills called 'the Pyramids' are actually volcanic in origin – a testament to the peninsula's fiery birth. A careful look at the seaward side of the smaller pyramid shows the volcanic basalt columns which are precise in their geometric structure (similar to the Organ Pipes on Mt Cargill). There is also a short scramble to the top of the smaller pyramid for a view over the dune country.

The Pyramids are located in the Okia Reserve, a mixture of wetland and dune country that lies behind Victory Beach, itself a beautiful isolated sweep of white sand and home to sea lions, fur seals and blue and yellow-eyed penguins. Take care in the scrub-covered dunes behind the beach, as the easily camouflaged Hooker's sea lions that rest there can be quite aggressive if disturbed. Penguins also nest in the dunes, so respect their space.

The beach takes its name from the ship *Victory* that foundered on its shores while under the command of a proverbial drunken sailor, though very little remains of the wreck. The beach is totally undeveloped, open to the Southern Ocean, and is about as close as you can possibly get to pristine on the peninsula.

 Just beyond Portobello village, turn right into Weir Road and follow it to the end. It is a gravel road but in reasonable condition.

26. Otakau Marae

The name Otago is a European corruption of the Maori word Otakau, meaning 'the place of red ochre'. This peninsula suited the needs of early Maori, and the pre-European population was estimated to be well over 3000 people, though overall the Maori population in the cooler southern climate was relatively small. The warm, north-facing bay favoured the growing of crops, the sheltered harbour was ideal for safe fishing, the forests were home to numerous birds, and the large tidal estuaries offered easy access to shellfish beds.

Taiaroa Head was the location of the main pa on the peninsula and was named after famous fighting chief Te Matenga Taiaroa, who stopped Te Rauparaha's invasion of Ngai Tahu land in the 1830s. A fort built in the nineteenth century obliterated all signs of the old pa, and very few traces of Maori occupation can be found around the harbour.

Early relationships between Maori and Pakeha were mainly mutually beneficial and intermarriage was common but, as the number of settlers increased, Maori were gradually marginalised and disadvantaged.

Otakau, always a major settlement, is today one of the few surviving marae in Otago. The existing complex was built in 1940 and opened by the then Prime Minister, Peter Fraser. Set on a small rise and consisting of the wharenui *Tamatea* and a small Maori church, the buildings at first glance appear fairly typical of any marae in the country, though the wharenui has an unusually high gable and very shallow porch. But take a closer look. At a distance, the buildings appear to be constructed of stucco with traditional wooden carvings, but on closer inspection all the 'carvings' – and in fact the whole building – is made entirely of concrete. Maori were adept at adapting European technology for marae buildings while at the same time retaining key traditional elements. One of the most enduring arts has been carving, and the use of concrete at Otakau instead of wood is very radical if not totally unique.

While visitors are welcome, this is not a tourist attraction so please be respectable. Do not visit if there is a function or gathering.

- Harrington Point Road.
- Koha/donation.

SOUTH OTAGO AND THE CATLINS

1. Sinclair Wetlands/Te Nohoaka o Tukiauau
2. Benhar Pottery
3. Bull Creek
4. Clutha Punt - Tuapeka Mouth
5. Lawrence and Gabriel's Gully
6. Whale Fossil Lookout
7. Nugget Point
8. Tunnel Hill
9. Jacks Blowhole
10. Cannibal Bay
11. The Dolphin at Pounawea
12. Traills Tractor
13. Niagara Falls and Waikawa
14. Curious Curio Bay
15. Slope Point
16. Waipapa Point

1. Sinclair Wetlands/Te Nohoaka o Tukiauau

While there is no longer any doubt of the importance of wetlands to the environment, more often than not they are not exactly the most exciting places to visit. By their very nature they are damp, muddy, flat, and it is often hard to see anything. In winter they flood and in summer they dry out and smell bad. Even the old name 'swamp' at least had an air of mystery and intrigue. The Sinclair Wetlands, however, are fortunate in having two small islands linked by a high causeway that not only allows the visitor to walk deep into the wetland itself but also provides excellent views over the entire reserve. These wetlands are also testament to the vision of one man – Horrie Sinclair. Horrie (Horace) purchased the land in 1960 and allowed it to revert back to its original state, thus saving one of the countries most important wetlands. Now covering 315 hectares, and together with the adjoining lakes Waihola and Waipori, these wetlands are all that remain of the huge swamp that covered most of the Taieri Plain, which has long since been drained for farmland. In addition to the forty bird species that breed here, another forty-five bird species have been recorded in the wetland. There is limited freedom camping, both powered and non-powered.

854 Berwick Claredon Road, South Taireri.
This road runs west of lakes Waihola and Waipori just off SH 1 south of Mosgiel.

03 486 2654

www.tenohoaka.org.nz
$ Koha/Donation.

2. Benhar Pottery

Once known as 'the Staffordshire of the South', the area around Millton was previously the centre of a major pottery industry rather than a prison. Using local clay, most kilns produced brick, pipes and practical pottery such as toilets and hand basins, but some also produced domestic ware of varying quality. Located south of Milton, and almost at Balclutha, Benhar was one of New Zealand's earliest and most important commercial potteries. During its long history from the 1890s until the 1970s, the pottery produced bricks, pipes, ceramic toilets and (in the 1920s and 1930s) tableware, which is now very rare and very collectable. Unfortunately, today the pottery at Benhar is derelict, but intact, with its beautifully built brick kilns and towering chimney still dominating the landscape. The small village still retains the brick worker's cottages and 'Lesmahagow' – the grand Edwardian home of the McSkimming family who owned the pottery (now a bed and breakfast).

📍 Benhar is 2 km off SH 1, 3 km north of Balclutha.

3. Bull Creek

Lying east of Milton on the South Otago coast, Bull Creek is a small settlement of cribs huddled near the mouth of a substantial stream. The stream cuts deeply through the rolling coastal hills and a significant stretch of the creek near the sea is flanked by attractive native bush, home to native birds and in particular the bellbird. A walkway along the creek through the bush is an easy stroll, and there are several popular swimming holes sheltered from the coastal wind with warmer and safer water than the sea. Unlike the long stretches of sandy beach north and south, the coast around Bull Creek is rocky with small sandy coves suitable for swimming if you can brave the water temperature. These picturesque coves are further enhanced by unusual sand, which consists of coarse golden sand overlying finer white sand creating a beachscape that is especially appealing. The cluster of seaside cribs are mostly of the older homebuilt variety that together with bush and the coves create a bucolic seaside settlement rarely found on the New Zealand coast.

📍 Bull Creek is 26 km east of Milton off SH 1.

4. Clutha Punt - Tuapeka Mouth

Tuapeka Mouth was the closest point on the Clutha River to the lucrative goldfields just to the north. The river at this point was too wide and swift-flowing to build a bridge, and punts was used to move both people and vehicles across. Punts and ferries were a regular feature on New Zealand rivers, but today few ferries remain and this punt is said to be the only one left in the Southern Hemisphere. Operating since 1896, this unique craft uses the prow of the punt and large rudders to direct the flow of the current to self-propel the punt across the river on overhead wires. The punt was part of a network of transport that offered a regular shipping service between Tupeka Mouth and Balclutha (Clutha is the ancient Gaelic name of the Clyde River in Scotland).

- From SH 8 at Lawrence take the Tuapeka West Road and drive 24 km to Tuapeka Mouth.
- The punt only operates daily 8 am to 10 am and 4 pm to 6 pm (3 pm to 5 pm in winter) so time your trip accordingly.

5. Lawrence and Gabriel's Gully

Once a prosperous gold town, Lawrence in 1862 had a population of 11,000 (Dunedin at the time had a population of 6000) and was then known as The Junction, as the town was located on the junction of the Tuapeka and Wetherstons streams. Now a popular stopping point on the road between Central Otago and Dunedin, the town still retains numerous historic buildings ranging from the grand Bank of New Zealand (now a café) through to the more modest Athenaeum (combination library and educational facility) and the Chinese Joss House (now a private home). Lawrence was also the home of J Wood who composed the national anthem 'God Defend New Zealand', first played in Dunedin on Christmas Day 1876 (Thomas Bracken wrote the words). A walking map of the historic buildings is available from the Information Centre in the main street, which also houses the local museum with displays of mining equipment, the history of the Chinese mining community and a reconstruction of the interior of a tiny miner's cottage.

Lawrence owed its prosperity to Gabriel's Gully, just 4 km away and the site of New Zealand's first major goldrush after Tasmanian prospector Gabriel Read discovered gold here in May 1861. By September that year over 6000 miners had set up camp in the Gully looking to make their fortune and while the easy alluvial gold was quickly exhausted, other discoveries were made nearby, including at Blue Spur, Waitahuna, Munro's Gully and Adams. The overall area was known as the Tuapeka Goldfields. A popular folk song of the time had as its chorus, 'Bright fine gold, Bright fine gold, One a pecker, Tuapeka, Bright red gold'.

Today not much remains of the bustling gold field and a loop walk of around ninety minutes takes the visitor through the most important sites interspersed with excellent information boards. There is an attractive picnic area by a pond another 250 m further on from the beginning of the walk.

6. Whale Fossil Lookout

Just west of Milburn and protected by a small shed, is a collection of fossils dating back 25 million years, all discovered in the local Milburn Quarry. The most significant is a whale fossil, but there are also dolphins and shellfish. A bonus is the great view over the Tokomairiro Plain.

 From SH 1, 7 km north of Milton, turn into Limeworks Road and then in Jensen Road. The fossils are to the right, a total distance of 4 km from SH 1

The Catlins

For years the southeastern corner of the South Island was very much a remote destination, but recently it has become one of the more popular driving trips in the country. Fortunately it does not yet attract bus tourist trade. It is good sealed road, with facilities and accommodation both at Balclutha and Owaka, and especially appealing is that most of sights along this road are just a short side trip off SH 92.

However, before Southlanders object to this region appearing in the South Otago section, the Catlins only appear in this part of the book because most visitors travel here in a southward direction and the last entries in this section (ordered from north to south) are part of Southland and not Otago.

7. Nugget Point

Wild and windswept Nugget Point is named after the group of jagged rocks just offshore, and this track leads out to the most spectacular views both north and south along the coast. The historic lighthouse on the point was built in 1870 when Port Molyneux, just to the north, was an important port and the rugged Catlins coast took a high toll on shipping.

Just before the lighthouse a steep track leads down to Roaring Bay (ten minutes one way) where there is a hide to watch both blue and yellow-eyed penguins which come ashore to nest late in the day. On the rocks below the point is a unique seal contain, as this is the only location in New Zealand where elephant seals, fur seals and Hooker's sea lions share the same colony. The seals are hard to see because the track is 130 m above the sea and the animals blend easily with the colour of the rocks. Binoculars are very useful. The walk takes around thirty minutes return and the track is largely flat and well formed.

> ◉ From Balclutha drive to Port Molyneux and then on to Kaka Point and follow the unsealed coast road for 8 km to Nugget Point.

8. Tunnel Hill

Constructed with pick and shovel, this 250-metre-long rail tunnel on the Catlins branch line was opened in 1895 and closed in 1971. A light is useful, and for those interested in railway history an old railway station and goods shed still stand at Maclennan further to the south.

 5 km north of Owaka on SH 92

9. Jacks Blowhole

Both Jacks Bay and Jacks Blowhole are named after Tuhawaiki, better known to Pakeha as 'Bloody Jack'. The name has nothing to do with bloodthirstiness, but rather Tuhawaiki's fondness for using 'bloody' as a swear word.

Tuhawaiki was a great Ngai Tahu warrior who played a key role in the defeat of Te Rauparaha near Cape Campbell in 1831. Again in 1835, with Taiaroa, he pushed back Ngati Toa forces led by the rangatira Te Puoho in the South Island, and finally defeated Te Puoho near Mataura in 1836, after Ngati Toa had launched a surprise attack on Central Otago by sweeping unsuspected down the West Coast and through the Haast Pass.

In April 1840 he signed the Treaty of Waitangi on board the *HMS Herald* at Ruapuke Island in Foveaux Strait, and later travelled to Wellington in his own ship the *Perseverance* to meet the Governor. Known for his shrewdness, natural intelligence and vast knowledge, Tuhawaiki was also fond of being grand and had a special liking for dressing in splendid military uniforms. When he signed the deed of sale for the Otago Block, he called himself the 'King of Bluff'.

Nearby Tuhawaiki Island is also named after Jack and relates to the following story. When Te Rauparaha trapped Tuhawaiki and his men on False Island to the north of Owaka River mouth, Tuhawaiki escaped by swimming to the island that now bears his name. In 1844 Tuhawaiki drowned when his ship hit rocks south of Timaru at a location now known as Tuhawaiki Point.

Real Kiwi cribs snuggle along the shore of this beautiful beach dominated by the cliffs of Catlins Heads. From the southern end of the beach an easy track across private farmland leads to the dramatic Jacks Blowhole, which you will hear before you see. Over 200 metres from the sea, the hole is 55 metres deep, and the boom of the blowhole at high tide is especially impressive. A track goes around the blowhole with two lookouts enabling a good view of the crashing waves below. The blowhole is also known to Maori as Opito or 'the navel'.

From the track are excellent views of Jacks Beach and the walk takes about one hour return.

> Turn off SH 92 at Owaka and drive towards Pounawea.
> After 2 km turn right into Jacks Bay Road and drive the 8 km to the end of the road. The track begins at the southern end of the beach.

10. Cannibal Bay

Cannibal Bay, a magnificent sweep of deserted beach, is just one of several beautiful beaches in the Catlins area, though unfortunately the water is pretty cold even in summer. The cool water does not deter the handy band of board riders that make the pilgrimage to one of New Zealand's best surf beaches. Cannibal Bay, like other Catlins beaches is also home to sea lions that are fairly common along this coast and while sea lions may appear awkward, they can be very aggressive and move surprisingly fast, so it is best to keep a good distance. If surfing is not for you, then a half hour walk south along the beach will take you to False Islet and Surat Bay on Catlins River estuary.

> From Owaka drive 4 km north on the Owaka Highway and turn right into Cannibal Bay Road and drive 11 km to the end of the road.

11. The Dolphin at Pounawea

No, this is not a southern version of Opo or Moko, but a device to assist ships navigate narrow rivers. In the middle of the estuary of the Catlins River at Pounawea is a simple wooden structure built in 1882 (costing just 25 pounds!) and is in reality a very fancy and very strong post. All boats had to do was to tie up to dolphin and then allow the force of the turning tide to swing the boat around in the confines of the narrow estuary channel. While once very commonplace, the fact that they were usually cheaply constructed out of wood has meant that very few dolphins survive today.

 Pounawea is 3 km east of Owaka and the dolphin is located just off shore on the waterfront at Pounawea just by the camping ground.

12. Traills Tractor

The original 'pushme, pullyou', the Traills tractor is a hybrid beast that is both train and tractor. A Fordson tractor was adapted by the Traill brothers to run on rails and could either push or pull log-laden carriages from the bush to the mill. The tractor is a survivor from the heyday of timber milling in the Catlins area that continued well into the twentieth century, though fortunately large stretches of native bush remain. Located on the site of the old Cook's Sawmill, the tractor is now restored and protected from the weather.

 The tractor is a five-minute walk from SH 92 just south of the Fleming River Bridge, south of Papatowai.

13. Niagara Falls and Waikawa

It's good to have a sense of humour, and these falls are so tiny that an early surveyor named them after the more impressive Niagara Falls in North America that he had recently visited. No more than half a metre high – if that – the Niagara Falls are located on the Waikawa River on the way to Curio Bay, just north of the township of Waikawa.

This town, originally a whaling station, is almost as tiny as the falls themselves and has a small local museum in the old school packed with historic photographs, old Maori adzes, moa bones and local memorabilia. One curious exhibit is an embroidery made by local man Herbert Campbell while a POW during WWI. Whatever your thoughts on this as an appropriate pastime for a soldier, to his credit he made a very good job of it with incredibly neat and precise stitching. Nearby Porpoise Bay is home to rare Hector's dolphins (which are less than half the size of the more common bottlenose dolphin).

   7 km north of Waikawa in Eastern Southland (Catlins Road).

14. Curious Curio Bay

Fossilisation occurs when silica replaces the wood of trees creating an exceptionally hard stone. Subsequently, when the surrounding softer rock is worn away by actions of wave erosion, the entire shape of these ancient trees is exposed. Curio Bay in Southland is recognised as one of the best-preserved examples of fossilised forest in the world, and a glimpse into the Jurassic period.

Stumps, tree trunks, branches and logs are all easily discernible in the wide rock shelf. These ancient forests stood over 180 million years ago and include the ancestors of modern kauri and Norfolk pine as well as numerous subtropical ferns and cycads. Indications are that at least four separate forests were destroyed over a period of 20,000 years by a series of cataclysmic events such as volcanic eruption and massive landslides.

The exposed fossils at Curio Bay appear to be just part of a much greater fossil bed as similar fossils have been found at Waikawa Bay. The fossils are only exposed at low tide.

📍 12 km off the Chaslands Highway from the Waikawa turn-off. Tumu Toka is a new interactive centre detailing the geological background to the fossils.

$ Entrance fee.

15. Slope Point

Standing on Slope Point you really do wonder why you came. Bleak, and so windswept that even the grass can't stand up straight, Slope Point's sole claim to fame is that, at 46.4 degrees south, it is the most southerly point of the South Island – just a tad further south than Bluff. Just before you get there, check out the macrocarpa trees on the right – it's so windy that they have no greenery on their south side and only grow to the height of a hedge (at least the wind saves on hedge trimming).

The point is a cold twenty minute walk from the end of a gravel road, and is marked by a post pointing to various distance spots around the world. The trick is to walk as fast as possible, dressed as warmly as possible, spend the least time possible, take a photo as quickly as possible, and then hurry back to your car, laughing like a drain at how idiotic you were to come all this way to see bugger all and freeze your bum off at the same time. But let's face it, a good laugh is worth the trip – though remember that it's closed for lambing from 1 September to 1 November.

📍 Slope Point Road, 6 km south of Haldane.

16. Waipapa Point

First, if you are driving 5 km south of Otara in Auckland you are way off track, as this Otara is well and truly in Eastern Southland. This surprisingly attractive spot on a rather inhospitable coastline is dominated by the historic lighthouse built in 1884 – the last wooden lighthouse to be built in the country.

The light was erected in response to New Zealand's worst shipping disaster which occurred in the early hours of 29 April 1881 when the *Tararua*, sailing from Dunedin to Bluff, struck the Otara Reef just to the north of Waipapa Point. Although the weather was fair, the seas became rough on the incoming tide and several lifeboats were swamped as soon as they were launched. Eventually the ship broke in two, and despite being clearly visible from shore, few survived the wild surf. Many of the 131 who perished are buried in the '*Tararua* Acre' just to the east of the point. The beach below the lighthouse is often frequented by sea lions.

📍 5 km south of Otara, Eastern Southland.

SOUTHLAND

1. Waikaia Bottle House and Switzers Museum
2. Croydon Aviation Heritage Centre
3. Eastern Southland Gallery
4. Fleming's Creamoata Mill
5. Hokonui Moonshine Museum
6. Gore Gardens and Aviaries
7. Minnie Dean's Grave, Old Winton Cemetery
8. Sweetbreads, Top End Takeaways, Winton
9. Forest Hill and Tussock Creek Reserves, Central Southland
10. The Stumpery, Queen's Garden, Invercargill
11. The Queen's Chair, Grand Hotel, Invercargill
12. E Hayes and Sons Ltd
13. The White House and The Greenroofs
14. Two Churches and Temple
15. Bluff
16. Riverton
17. Cosy Nook/Mullet Bay
18. Otautau War Memorial
19. Monkey Island/ Te Puka o Takitimu
20. Clifden Suspension Bridge
21. Lake Hauroko and the 1000-year-old Totara
22. Lake Monowai
23. Mossburn
24. Gunn's Camp
25. Lake Marian and the Marian Falls
26. Hollyford Airstrip
27. Humboldt Falls
28. Cook's Globe, Rakiura Museum
29. Kiwi Watching

1. Waikaia Bottle House and Switzers Museum

In the mid-80s a group of semi-retired farmers on a trip to Queensland were enormously impressed by the Ginger Bottle House and enthusiastically decided a bottle house was just the thing for Waikaia (somehow one feels that a lot of drink was involved). Returning home with their enthusiasm undiminished, they set about scouring the district for suitable bottles. Not any old bottle mind you – they needed green wine bottles with a hollow base – and they needed a lot of them. Queenstown, full of tourists consuming large quantities of wine over dinner tipped the balance and finally when 20,000 bottles were collected it was time to build. Southland farmers are very much do-it-yourself folk and away they went. This time their skills didn't match their enthusiasm, and the poor-quality mortar and application to match meant the whole structure had to pulled down and all 20,000 bottles cleaned. Unskilled they might have been, but they were not daunted (although on the second attempt they did enlist the help of skilled bricklayer).

Over thirty years later, the Waikaia bottle house can now lay claim to be the only bottle house in the Southern Hemisphere: their inspiration in Queensland has long since been demolished. The construction may sound a bit 'down on the farm', but the building is surprisingly lovely. On a bright day the heavy green glass diffuses the sunshine and the interior is lit with a beautiful ethereal glow. A simple spiral staircase winds to the top of the bottle structure.

Today the bottle house is part of a smart new museum complex detailing the history of the old gold mining settlement originally named Switzers. Once a rowdy goldmining town, the last mine, King Solomon's mine, closed in 1937 and the railway stopped running in 1959. The pride of the new museum is, of course, more bottles – this time 2800 old vintage bottles left over from the days when Waikaia was more famous for its dance halls and pubs. For a small community of less than 1500 people, it really knows that size doesn't matter when it comes to getting the job done.

   39 Blaydon Street, Waikaia.
    Open Summer - Labour Weekend to Easter 11am to 4 pm.

Winter - Easter to Labour Weekend Saturday & Sunday 1 pm to 3 pm.
020 4121 0180
Entrance fee.

2. Croydon Aviation Heritage Centre

Kiwi ingenuity is a constant source of surprise. At Mandeville, just west of Gore, the Croydon Aircraft Company has successfully based an international business restoring biplanes and, in particular, the de Havilland Tiger Moth. Now fancy that! It is an appropriate home for such an enterprise, as an airfield has existed here since the 1920s. Today you can take a flight in a vintage aircraft and see restoration projects underway (by prior arrangement only, 03 208 9755).

The small museum, The Croydon Aviation Heritage Centre is unusual in that all the aircraft on display are operational. Most of the aircraft are from the 1920s and 30s. Of particular importance is the de Havilland Fox Moth, New Zealand's first registered commercial aircraft and the de Havilland Dragonfly, one of only two operational planes of this type in the world.

Right alongside the grass runway is an appealing café, Miss Cocoa Coffee, which was originally the Railway Hotel and was the closest pub to Gore when that town was 'dry' in the early years of the twentieth century. Currently plans are underway to restore one kilometre of track for steam engines.

Mandeville, 17 km north west of Gore on SH 94.
03 208 9755
www.croydonaircraft.co.nz
Entrance fee to Heritage Centre.

New Regent Street, Christchurch.
(Christchurch City and the Banks Peninsula #3)

185 Empty White Chairs, Christchurch. (Christchurch City and the Banks Peninsula #6)

Ohinetahi Garden, Teddington Bay. (Christchurch City and the Banks Peninsula #26)

Allandale Gaol. (Christchurch City and the Banks Peninsula #27)

French Peak Winery. (Christchurch City and the Banks Peninsula #29)

Okains Bay Museum, Okains Bay. (Christchurch City and the Banks Peninsula #32)

The Madeira Hotel, German and Portuguese Akaroa. (Christchurch City and the Banks Peninsula #33)

Temuka Pottery, Temuka. (South Canterbury/Mackenzie Country #6)

The Empress Flour Mill, Waimate. (South Canterbury/Mackenzie Country #25)

Waimate Silo Murals, Waimate. (South Canterbury/Mackenzie Country #25)

Ted's Bottle, Waihao Forks Hotel. (South Canterbury/Mackenzie Country #27)

Nicol's Forge, Duntroon. (North Otago #3)

Danseys Pass. (North Otago #6)

Above: Historic Oamaru, Steam Punk Museum. (North Otago #7)

Criterion Hotel, Oamaru.
(North Otago #8)

Totara Estate and Clarks Mill.
(North Otago #12)

Hayes Engineering Works, Oturehua. (Central Otago #5)

Flat Top Hill and Butchers Dam. (Central Otago #9)

That Wanaka Tree, Wanaka. (Central Otago #22)

Oxenbridge Tunnel, Shotover River. (Central Otago #27)

Museum of Natural Mystery, Dunedin. (Dunedin and the Otago Peninsula #11)

Cheese roll. (Dunedin and the Otago Peninsula #19)

Lover's Leap, Sandymount Walks. (Dunedin and the Otago Peninsula #24)

Left: Otakau Marae. (Dunedin and the Otago Peninsula #26)

Bottom: Benhar Pottery, (South Otago and the Catlins #2)

Cannibal Bay. (South Otago and the Catlins #10)

Traills Tractor. (South Otago and the Catlins #12)

Minnie Dean's Grave, Old Winton Cemetery. (Southland #7)

Sweetbreads, Top End Takeaways, Winton. (Southland #8)

The Stumpery, Queen's Garden, Invercargill. (Southland #10)

E Hayes and Sons Ltd, Invercargill. (Southland #12)

Masonic Lodge, Invecargill. (Southland #14)

Left: St Mary's, Invercargill. (Southland #14)

Bottom: Lake Hauroko. (Southland #21)

3. Eastern Southland Gallery

What do you call a moron from Gore? A Goron! Okay, a bad joke, but it accurately reflects the opinion held by many about Gore – albeit clearly an opinion held by those who haven't been to Gore lately. Apart from trout fishing, the Hokonui Moonshine Festival, a glorious public garden, Hokonui Fashion Awards, Croydon Aircraft Company – and not to mention good coffee and food – Gore has one of the finest art galleries in the country. Nicknamed the 'Goreggenheim', the gallery received a major boost with the gift of a collection from John Money, an ex-New Zealander now living in Baltimore. Along with the art collection, money was also made available to redevelop the 1910 historic Carnegie Library into a modern art gallery.

The Eastern Southland Gallery now holds fine collections by New Zealand artists such as Ralph Hotere, Rita Angus, and Theo Schoon, and in fact holds over fifty pieces by Hotere – making this the largest collection of his works in New Zealand. However, what takes the visitor totally by surprise is the amazing collection of African art, the likes of which you are unlikely to see elsewhere in New Zealand. Mainly from the Bambarra, Dogon and Baga regions of West Africa, these carvings feel surprisingly contemporary and their size alone makes them impressive.

- Hokonui Drive, opposite the information centre
- Open Monday to Friday 10 am to 4.30 pm, weekends and public holidays 1 pm to 4 pm.
- 03 208 9907
- www.esgallery.co.nz
- Koha/donation.

4. Fleming's Creamoata Mill

You either hated or loved 'Sergeant Dan, the Creamoata Man'. You hated him if you HAD to eat your Creamoata porridge, or loved him if your idea of the perfect breakfast was rolled oats with brown sugar and cream. Dominating the centre of Gore is the old Creamoata Mill, complete with a huge 'Sergeant Dan' painted down the side of the building.

The iconic 'Creamoata Man' was an advertising device from the 1920s designed to promote Creamoata porridge made from locally grown oats. The main building was constructed in 1892, while the 30-metre chimney dates from 1912 and is classified Category 1 by the Historic Places Trust. There is a Creamota exhibition at the Croydon Aviation Heritage Centre.

📍 Gorton Street, Gore, in the middle of Gore – and if you can't find it you need glasses!

5. Hokonui Moonshine Museum

With the advent of prohibition in 1900, locals set up illegal stills in the nearby bush-cloaked Hokonui Hills, and over fifty years (and thirty arrests) produced what was regarded as the best bush whisky in the country. In particular the McRae family, originally a clan from the Scottish Highlands who settled in the district in the 1870s, managed to dodge the law, producing a fine dram for over eighty years. The Hokonui Moonshine Museum tells this story, among others, but what makes this place hugely appealing is that it is both informative and entertaining in a way most museums seldom achieve.

Here you will find a recreation of an illegal bush still, as well as the story of the people behind the stills and the law enforcers who set out to catch them. The history of the temperance movement is also outlined, and its strong connection with the early politicisation of women. At one point in the museum, visitors have to choose between the bar and Temperance Hall – although those who choose the bar eventually find themselves back in the hall. Whisky from the original McRae recipe is now produced legally and is for sale at the information centre, along with Hokonui whisky chocolates.

On the last weekend in February, Gore is packed as locals turn out for the Hokonui Moonshine Festival, a celebration of food, music, and of course the famous Hokonui whisky. You can even hire out the pre-prohibition bar for a private function. Miss Gore and you will miss one of the best museum experiences in the country.

📍 16 Hokonui Drive, SH 98.
The Moonshine Museum, Gore Heritage Centre and Information Office are all in the same building.
🌐 www.goredc.govt.nz
$ Entrance fee to Moonshine Museum.

6. Gore Gardens and Aviaries

One of the essentials of any colonial town of note were public gardens. Public gardens were more than a place to relax and enjoy quiet contemplation among the roses and English trees. Gardens were a place to meet friends, especially on late Sunday afternoon. After church, a large roast dinner, a pleasant nap and still dressed in Sunday best, locals came to socialise and be entertained in the public gardens. Along with formal plantings and shady trees, gardens frequently included bird aviaries, a pond or fountain and most importantly a band rotunda where the local brass band performed popular tunes of the day.

Set aside as a reserve in 1874, the gardens were finally established in 1906 by David Tannock, who had previously worked as a horticulturalist at the Dunedin Botanic Gardens. Just as popular now as they were when they opened, the gardens host the Gore Rhododendron Festival in October, and the Christmas in the Park concert in December.

📍 11 Fairfield Street, Gore.

7. Minnie Dean's Grave, Old Winton Cemetery

Baby farming was not an unusual occupation in the nineteenth century, though the term was usually an insult, as baby farmers – particularly in the UK – frequently ended up in court for neglecting and even murdering their charges. However, in a time when unmarried mothers or poor parents had a great deal of difficulty caring for their children, paying baby farmers was often the only option.

Born in Scotland in 1844, Minnie (Wilhelmina) Dean arrived in Invercargill in the 1860s with two small children, and in 1872 married farmer Charles Dean and moved to Etal Creek. Farming at the time was difficult, so Minnie took in children to supplement the family income, caring for up to nine children at any one time. Infant death was common at the time and Minnie had already come to the attention of authorities when several children in her care died, though at the time she was cleared by the coroner of any wrong doing.

In 1895 Dean boarded a train in Winton carrying a baby and a hatbox, but was seen by a guard leaving the train in Lumsden with only the hatbox, which guard said was surprising heavy. With suspicions aroused, Dean was unable to produce the child recently placed in her care and when her garden was dug up three bodies were found: one of which had died from suffocation, one from an overdose of laudanum and the death of the third child was unknown.

Charged with murder, Minnie Dean was found guilty and hanged in Invercargill on 12 August 1895 – the only woman to receive the death penalty in New Zealand.

The following year legislation known as the Infant Protection Act was passed to improve children welfare. For many years her grave in the Winton cemetery was unmarked, until in January 2009 when a headstone was placed on the graves of Minnie and her husband by their descendants.

From the main gate, walk straight to the back of the cemetery where to the left is a flat gravestone marked Charles Dean and Wilhelmina McCulloch.

 Old Winton Cemetery, SH 6, 1 km north of Winton.

8. Sweetbreads, Top End Takeaways, Winton

If eating offal is not for you, stop reading now. Probably the most badly named food on offer, sweetbreads are neither sweet nor bread, but organs from the thymus gland and pancreas, and in New Zealand they are nearly always from lambs. Once popular meat sweetbreads, like most offal, have fallen way out of culinary fashion – which is a great shame as they are delicious. If you are passing through Winton and have a taste for the adventurous, now is the time to stop and try sweetbreads.

At Top End Takeaways it is one of the most popular items on the menu. They only use lamb 'throat' sweetbreads, which are then dipped in a seasoned crumb mix and deep-fried. Along with the more conventional burgers and fish and chips (try the Winton Stopover Burger), Top End Takeaways also offers two other New Zealand delicacies: Paua Patties and Bluff oysters.

 296 Great North Road, Winton.
 03 236 8296

9. Forest Hill and Tussock Creek Reserves, Central Southland

Heddon Bush, Ryal Bush, Gummies Bush, Centre Bush, Spar Bush, Mabel Bush, Grove Bush, Wreys Bush, Otaitai Bush, Wrights Bush and Myross Bush are all Southland names that refer to the vast forests that once covered the Central Southland plain. Today there is hardly a stick of native bush left standing.

These two adjoining reserves, just southwest of Winton, contain the only native bush left in Central Southland, and even this was milled for the larger trees. The contrast between the dense bush, the open farmland of the plains, and the stark grassy hills could not be greater. However, this bush contains a surprising number of native birds, a giant rata tree, huge native tree fuchsias, a cave complete with cave wetas and a good lookout point over the plain.

The track from the Tussock Hill end of the reserve is one of the most beautifully graded bush tracks in the country and can only have been built by someone with roading experience rather than the local scouts on the weekend! It is so gradual and so well graded that you hardly know you are walking uphill. If you're looking for a bush walk to stretch your legs, this is a pretty good option in Southland.

📍 There are two entrances to the reserve off SH 6, 5 km south of Winton.

10. The Stumpery, Queen's Garden, Invercargill

Covering 200 ha, the Queen's Gardens were originally established in 1857. Formal planting began in 1872 and today the gardens are one of New Zealand's finest public parks. However tucked away in a corner not far from the main entrance is the unusual and intriguing Stumpery. Created by local artist Frank Wells, the concept of a Stumpery is not new, originating in Victorian Britain as a way to utilise woodland areas damaged by storms. Here in Invercargill damaged trees, old railway sleepers and ancient roots from peat bogs have been transformed into myriad strange shapes combined with the practical – like a nice bench for a comfy sit down. This twisted fantasy world feels like an ancient Druid place of worship and, while it's a great place to visit during the day, it would be very creepy at night.

📍 The Stumpery is to the right off the main entrance off Gala Street.
Queen's Gardens, Gala Street, Invercargill.

11. The Queen's Chair, Grand Hotel, Invercargill

The Grand Hotel opened in 1913 and quickly became the leading hotel in the city. Constructed after the city went dry, The Grand gained its reputation on excellent food, stylish function rooms and modern accommodation. It was therefore no surprise the hotel hosted the Queen and Prince Philip on their tour of Southland in 1954. Undergoing continual restoration, enormous reception rooms on the first floor are especially impressive and, although not in the best condition, feature intricate plaster ceilings, massive ornate mirrors and period fireplaces (the Grand is a Category 2 Historic Place).

Holding pride of place are two ornate chairs in a small corner lounge – one for the Queen and another for Prince Philip. What makes the chairs so special is that this is where Queen Elizabeth broadcast her farewell speech over the radio on 29 January 1954 before departing from Bluff the following morning.

76 Dee Street, Invercargill.
022 123 4276

12. E Hayes and Sons Ltd

Engineering runs in this family's blood. Ernest Hayes set up his workshop in Oturehua in 1895 (see the entry in Central Otago) and in 1932 his son Irving set up a branch in Invercargill, E. Hayes and Sons. Expanding over the years, by 1956 the store covered an entire city block. Not stopping there, in 2009 the store grew even bigger, adding giftware, kitchen goods and automotive products. Still in the family, the current Managing Director Neville Hayes now has his daughter and son involved in the business. Operating under the Hammer Hardware and Tradezone Industrial brands, the store is famous for its '100 Metre Tool Wall', boasting that it has every tool you will ever need.

All that is impressive, but that's far from the end of it. With a passion for engineering, the Hayes family also have a passion for collecting, and scattered throughout the store are well-presented displays of classic cars, vintage motorbikes, early machinery, old pumps and engines and even the company's original delivery van. The Hayes family also had a close connection with that other famous Invercargill son Bert Munro, and taking pride of place in the store is the legendary record-breaking motorcycle, 'The World's Fastest Indian'.

So, whether it's a skill saw, a dinner set, or a peek at a world-famous motorbike, this is the store for you.

 168 Dee Street, Invercargill.
 03 218 2059
 www.ehayes.co.nz

13. The White House and The Greenroofs

In 1905 the Invercargill and Mataura electorates voted by a narrow margin to go 'dry' while central and western Southland (including Bluff) stayed 'wet'. For two country hotels – The Wallacetown Hotel and the Junction Hotel, both just north of the city – this decision was a bonanza as they were the nearest watering holes for Invercargill folk fond of a drop. Legend has it that local taxis made more money from running alcohol into the city than from passengers.

In the early twenties, the two hotels fell foul of the Licensing Commission when the Junction Hotel (at Lorneville) changed its name to the Wallacetown Junction Hotel. The hotels were just 5 km apart and in 1922, to sort out the confusion, the Commission stepped in and renamed them. The Wallacetown Hotel became Greenroofs Hotel, and the Wallacetown Junction Hotel became the White House Hotel, after their respective colour schemes.

Today the White House Hotel still retains its name and is still white, while Greenroofs has only recently reverted back to the Wallacetown Tavern, but still has its distinct green roofs.

14. Two Churches and Temple

Invercargill is clearly a place to show off and these three grand buildings, all Category One historic buildings, are clearly a case in point.

In strongly Presbyterian Invercargill, it comes as a surprise that the most imposing church in the city is not Protestant but Catholic. Designed by renowned church architect FW Petre and built in 1905, the dome of St Mary's dominates the city's skyline. Perhaps the local Catholics felt they needed to make a bold statement about their presence in the town as the building, while tall, has a very modest ground floor plan more accurately reflecting the true size of the Catholic congregation.

Just a few metres down the road is the spectacular Masonic Lodge, opened in 1926 and undoubtably the finest Masonic building in the country. Elevated above the street, a flight of wide steps leads up to the portico of fluted Doric columns, a splendid example of the 1920 Greek rival architecture. The Doric theme continues inside the building, which is crowned by a dome.

Not to be outdone, the First Presbyterian Church is also a striking building. Constructed in brick and opening in 1915 it replaced an older wooden church, which was Invercargill's largest wooden building. It was architect John Mair's first major commission and remains his best-known building. Widely criticised at the time for being 'garishly modern' and even worse 'too Catholic', the striking Romanesque and Byzantine lines of this church still look stylish today.

St Mary's Basilica, 65 Tyne Street, Invercargill.
Masonic Lodge, 80 Forth Street, Invercargill.
First Presbyterian Church, 155 Tay Street, Invercargill.

15. Bluff

Claimed to be the oldest town in New Zealand and once a thriving port town, Bluff today is distinctly down at heel. The famed Paua House has long gone and the lively old waterfront hotels have one by one closed, so today only The Eagle remains standing (it has an excellent menu). The town has seen it fortunes wax and wane over the years and it is what it is, an old port town – a bit rough around the edges, a bit windblown, but with a charm all its own in a battered sort of way. Most people stopping here either travel on to Stewart Island or just stand for the shortest time possible in the cold wind, take a quick snapshot of the famous signpost at Stirling Point before jumping in their cars and heading off (it is not even the most southerly point of the South Island, but it is the end of SH 1).

That said, Bluff has one of the best small museums in the country, with a strong emphasis on local maritime history. There are displays on whaling, the oyster industry and shipwrecks, an extensive collection of historical photographs, a working steam engine from the TST Awarua, the light from the Centre Island lighthouse and models of ships that have visited Bluff. Outside is a real oyster boat – the *Monica II* – which you can explore. While inside you can sit in the working Bofors gun from the *HMS Southland*, (www.bluff.co.nz/museum).

Rising to 265 m, Bluff Hill is a very old volcanic cone dating back to the Permian period well over 200 million years ago when New Zealand was part of the Gondwana supercontinent. The hill is the source of a hard volcanic stone, norite, locally known as Bluff granite. Facing the Southern Ocean, this is not the obvious place to take a stroll. On the coast starting from Stirling Point is a great walk, the Foveaux Walkway. Sure, it's a bit exposed, but a brisk walk in the fresh air will do you the world of good, so wrap up warm and off you go. This superb coastal walk on an excellent flat track winds around the rocky shore of Bluff Hill through tough, salt-resistant flax and hebes to a lookout point with views both far to the west and to the offshore islands.

From the Foveaux Walkway a track also leads up to the top of Bluff Hill, or you can return via the Glory Track, which is much more sheltered. This track takes its name from English ship *The Glory*, which was wrecked on the rocks below – ironically, while taking on board the local pilot. Containing many fine old trees including kamahi, kahikatea, rimu and rata, the track passes a substantial WWII gun emplacement and a low concrete lookout pit, both built in 1942.

Keeping the best to last Bluff is the home of an exceptional oyster (and not just 'world famous in New Zealand'). People are unequivocal about oysters: they either love them or hate them — no-one ever says oysters are just 'okay'. Those who eat them raw are in a group all of their own. For oyster fans, nothing beats the legendary Bluff oyster. So what makes these oysters so special? Born in the cold, clean waters of Foveaux Strait, these oysters mature slowly, resulting in a shellfish with a delicate and sublime taste. Plump and juicy, the Bluff oyster combines that velvety seafood texture with the wonderful salty taste of the sea like no other seafood can. While they can be frozen and cooked, the very best oysters are those eaten raw, fresh off the boat.

Now strictly controlled by quotas, the season begins in March and runs through to August (or when the quotas are full). Since 1991 an annual festival celebrating the oyster has seen thousands of seafood enthusiasts flocking to Bluff each year to celebrate the south's most famous delicacy (the one-day festival is ticketed and the tickets frequently sell out months ahead).

16. Riverton

Like nearby Bluff, Riverton is one of New Zealand's oldest European settlements but also always had a small Maori settlement known as Aparima, named after a high-born Waitaha woman, and today the river still retains this name.

Although pre-European Maori did not actively hunt whales, when European whalers moved into the area in the early nineteenth century the relationship between Maori and whalers was mutually cordial. Maori provided vegetables, fresh water and wood, while young Maori men were attracted to the adventure of whaling — American ships frequently recruited Maori. There is strong evidence that Queequeg in Herman Melville's famous whaling novel *Moby Dick* is based on a Maori whaler. Intermarriage was common between local Maori women and men from whaling ships.

Around 1836 Captain John Howell established a whaling station at the mouth of the Aparima and Pourakino rivers, and married Kohikohi, the daughter of Horomona Patu, a Ngati Mamoe chief. The house Howell built for his wife and family, known as Howell's Cottage or Te Whare Kohikohi, is the oldest European building in the South Island.

Hilltop is a small rocky outcrop that was once used to spot whales passing through the strait when Riverton was a whaling station. The view is grand with all the islands of the strait clearly visible, while to the west the view follows along the coast to the distant mountains of Fiordland. North lies the Takitimu Mountains, Eyre Mountains and the Hokonui Hills, and to the west the Jacobs River Estuary, Oreti Beach and Bluff Hill.

Spread along the broad river estuary and to the open sea at Riverton Rocks, the town was promoted as a seaside resort in the early twentieth century, 'The Riveria of the South'. No doubt the brisk Foveaux Strait climate put paid to that idea, but today Riverton has retained all the bucolic charms of a small coastal settlement. Along with a small fishing fleet (fresh blue cod is the local treat), Riverton also has an exceptional museum, Te Hikoi Southern Journey.

17. Cosy Nook/Mullet Bay

A nook but far from cosy, Mullet Bay – more popularly known as Cosy Nook – is a tiny rocky haven on this wild coastline. Once home to a small fishing fleet the numerous little huts, home-built out of cast-off materials, were occupied by the fishermen. While the fishing fleet and most of the old huts have gone, a handful of small cottages still cling to the rocky shore occupied by weekend fisherfolk: the 'Polyfilla Villa' is a classic.

 Signposted 5 km east of Orepuki and 5 km from SH 99, west of Riverton.

18. Otautau War Memorial

Otautau is an attractive small town on the banks of the Aparima River at the foot of the Longwood Range, and not being on the way to anywhere it doesn't attract a lot of visitors. The town, however, has an unusual war memorial: two World War I field guns, one Turkish and one German. Apparently, they were presented to the town in 1921, but how exactly they were acquired is open to speculation. Maybe a few of the local Otautau lads said, 'Hey, let's take a couple of these guns home', and somehow managed to sneak them on board a ship and haul them back to Godzone. Who knows, but imagine trying to slip a couple of field guns past customs these days! Strangely enough, the war memorial guns were in fact borrowed during the Second World War to train gunners, but were thankfully returned to their rightful place in Otautau where today they form the town's local war memorial.

 Main Street, Otautau.

19. Monkey Island/ Te Puka o Takitimu

In Maori legend this island is called Te Puka o Takitimu, the anchor stone of the waka *Takitimu* that journeyed from Hawaiki and was wrecked at the mouth of the Waiau River. Captained by Tamatea, the waka was struck by three huge waves so large that they drove the waka far inland, where a cross-wave finally overturned it. The upturned waka then became the Takitimu Mountains.

In 1864 this was a thriving port settlement of 3000 people suppling local settlers and gold miners working in the nearby Longwood Range, but all traces of the old town have vanished. Getting supplies ashore was difficult, and cargo was often hauled from ships using a winch known as a 'monkey' set on top of the island, hence the name Monkey Island.

The tiny island is accessible at low tide, and a short flight of steps leads up to the top with views across the wide expanse of Te Waewae Bay to the Humpback Ridge and the Princess Mountains well worth taking time to stop.

 1 km southeast of Tuatapere off SH 99.

20. Clifden Suspension Bridge

When built in 1899, this was the longest span of any bridge in New Zealand at 115 metres and replaced a punt across the Waiau River. Like most suspension bridges, Clifden has a grace that derives from a combination of good engineering and good design. The bridge remained in use until 1978 and is now open to pedestrians. Add to that an attractive limestone gorge, a pleasant picnic spot and a fast-flowing river, and the Clifden Suspension Bridge makes an attractive detour.

 12 km north of Tuatapere, Western Southland.

21. Lake Hauroko and the 1000-year-old Totara

Located in the southern part of the park, this lake attracts few visitors partly due to the location away from the tourist trail, and the fact that it's a 32-km drive into the lake, of which 20 km is rough gravel.

New Zealand has over 3800 lakes and Lake Hauroko in Fiordland at 462 metres is the deepest. You could drop Auckland's Sky Tower (328 metres) into it and it would completely disappear. The second deepest lake is also in Fiordland – Lake Manapouri at 444 metres.

In April 1967, local George Evans pulled his boat onto Mary Island in Lake Hauroko and decided to poke around the clefts in a rock face. To his great surprise, he found a skeleton held upright in a sitting position by manuka stakes and covered in a cloak. What George had found was a body of a woman of high rank dating back to the seventeenth century, and who was later identified as Te Maiairea Te Riri Wairua Puru of Ngati Mamoe.

What makes the burial particularly curious is that the lake and the island were very remote from major Maori settlements, and that those who buried this woman were taking exceptional care to protect the location of the burial site. Now known as the 'Maori Princess', the burial site is protected by a metal grille and is considered highly tapu. Stories soon circulated of a Maori curse on the lake that caused sudden squalls on the lake and is associated with the mysterious disappearance of three hunters in the 1960s – stories that local Maori dismiss as nonsense.

Mary Island is readily identifiable, as this is the only island in the lake. The best view of Hauroko and the island is from the Lake Hauroko Lookout. This track for the most part follows the lakeshore until the steep climb to the lookout, where you will be rewarded with spectacular views as far as Foveaux Strait. However, the track is a bit rough and steep towards the end. For the hardier the Dusky Track begins from the head of the lake and can be accessed by boat (prearranged) or by guided walk.

Just 5 km down the road to Lake Hauroko is the Lillburn–Monowai Road, an 18-km gravel no-exit road with a grove of truly majestic trees at the very end that includes an ancient totara. Worn and weary, massive and magnificent, the 1000-year-old Hall's totara looks every bit its age among the surrounding totara, rimu, beech and kahikatea. The trees are thickly hung with mosses, the ground is totally covered in lush crown ferns, and the forest is alive with the sound of the bellbird. The walk to the trees is easy and takes around twenty minutes, and while it's a long drive down a gravel road for such a short walk, the trees here are especially impressive.

 From Tuatapere, drive 13 km north to Clifden on SH 99 and then turn into the Lake Hauroko Road. Lake Hauroko is 32 km down this road, of which more than half is gravel.

22. Lake Monowai

Lake Monowai has had a bad rap. Usually used as an example of poor environmental planning, it is in reality a really lovely lake and there is a very good change you will have the place to yourself (plus sandflies of course). The lake's unfortunate reputation comes from the water level being raised two and a half metres in 1926 to increase the lake's capacity for hydroelectric power generation. The result was an ugly shoreline of dead trees that are still visible (though only in a minor way) over eighty years later.

The distinct U shape disguises the size of the lake, which is relatively large at over 30 square km, and its shape is reflected in the Maori name that means 'channel full of water'. Stretching deep into the mountains, Monowai was formed by glacial action with only one small river – the exotically named Electric River – flowing into the head of the lake. From the road end there are two good walking tracks to huts that both take around six hours return. One is to Rodger Inlet on Lake Monowai and the other crosses over the Mt Cuthbert Saddle to the Green Lake.

 The turnoff to Lake Monowai is 10 km off SH 99 near Blackmount School.

23. Mossburn

With a tiny population of just 210 people on the junction of SH 94 and SH 97, few visitors bother to stop here on their rush to get to Te Anau and Milford Sound. However, the miniscule township has two gems well worth hopping out of the car for: The Railway Hotel and Bracken Hall.

Once an important railhead for the transportation of stock, the original wooden hotel, built in 1885, burned down in 1923 and was replaced by the current brick building. Mossburn was not destined to prosper and eventually the railway closed and the town declined, and today the railway and the stockyards alongside the hotel are just a distant memory.

Good times were ahead, and tourism has boosted the fortunes of both the town and the hotel. Renovated in 1987 and again more recently, the lovely dining room evokes feelings of an earlier era and features historic photos on the wall, while the main bar opens on to garden bar centred on a beautiful old spreading elm. Notable New Zealand poet Bill Manhire was born in Mossburn – he was the son of the publican and grew up in the pub. He retains both fond memories and a strong connection to his childhood town and the pub has dedicated a wall to their most famous son. The hotel, located by the vanished railway line, is just a short two-minute drive off the main road.

In 1993 when five local women decided to establish a café and shop in the old community hall, locals (and their husbands) were intensely sceptical about the viability of a food outlet in such a rural location. But by focusing on good homemade Southland food, all made on the premises, not only did Bracken Hall succeed, it flourished.

The standout is their venison pie. Located in the heart of deer country, Bracken Hall uses the best quality wild venison from the Fiordland mountains. Distinctly flavoured, the venison is then marinated and cooked in Speights beer along with tomatoes and onions to create a superbly tasty pie. If you are at all uncertain about the flavour of venison, these pies are the ideal way to try out this flavoursome meat for the first time.

On the other hand, if venison pies are not for you, Bracken Hall has a good range of other excellent food including their legendary muffins, made all the more enjoyable by the relaxed atmosphere for both indoor and outdoor diners. Adjoining the café is a store stocked with carefully chosen gifts for locals and visitors alike.

 Railway Hotel, 16 York Street, Mossburn.
 03 248 6399.
 Bracken Hall, State highway 94, 33 Devon Street.
 03 248 6033.
 www.brackenhall.co.nz

Fiordland

Fiordland is a huge national park with an area in excess of 1,252,000 hectares, but much of its terrain is very wild and difficult to access unless you come well equipped for serious tramping. The road to Milford Sound, while no doubt spectacular, is now clogged with tour buses – one million visitors now take the trip every year. It's difficult but still possible to get away from the crowds, even in the middle of summer.

24. Gunn's Camp

In 1926 David Gunn purchased land in the Hollyford Valley, farming cattle and guiding tourists until his death in 1955. His son Murray returned, intending only to tidy up his father's affairs – a visit that continued for another fifty years until, at the age of eighty-one, Murray retired to Te Anau. A larger-than-life personality, it was Murray who created the camp that today is still one of a kind.

Located on the banks of a glacial stream, the camp has no cell-phone coverage, no electricity (generators provide power in the evening until 10 pm), and no phone lines, although they do now have a satellite internet connection. This is truly the place to get away from it all. In addition to camping and camper sites, there is accommodation in old 1930s Public Works huts, the larger of which originally housed families and comes complete with a range for cooking and heating.

A small museum (part of the store) houses Murray's collection of Hollyford memorabilia, though sadly an earlier museum burnt down. While you're at the store, don't miss checking out 'Murray's Fridge'. With no refrigeration on site, drinks are kept cool across the road in a stream, and when you buy a drink you take the warm bottle of drink across the road and swap it with the cold one already in the water. The store also has for sale the rare bowenite greenstone, a variation of pounamu only found in the Hollyford Valley. Gunn's Camp was badly damaged in floods in early 2020.

Gunn's Camp is located 5 km down the Lower Hollyford Road from the junction with the Milford Road.

gunnscamp@ruralinzone.net
www.gunnscamp.org.nz

25. Lake Marian and the Marian Falls

Just 1 km down the Hollyford Road from the junction with the Milford Road is a short walk that will take you through deep bush to a spectacular mountain basin above the snow line. The walk begins across a swing bridge (always a good start) and then follows a rushing mountain stream through lush beech forest steadily uphill. Only ten minutes into the walk are the Marian Falls, where a gantry above the stream looks down over the falls – which to be honest are more a cascade than your typical waterfall, but attractive nonetheless.

From there is a steady uphill climb to Lake Marian situated in a magnificent hanging valley at 695 metres above sea level and surrounded by the towering Darran Mountains, snow-capped even in the warmest months. Apart from the area around the Milford Tunnel, this walk is the easiest way for the casual visitor to experience the grandeur of a true alpine landscape away from the tour buses and bustling crowds.

 The track begins on the left, 1 km down the Lower Hollyford Valley Road from Marian Corner, the junction of the Milford and Hollyford Roads.

26. Hollyford Airstrip

If you're not keen on flying, this airstrip will send your head into a spin – so don't even go and look if you are scared of flying! At first glance it just looks like a narrow strip of road, and if there wasn't a sign indicating that this is a landing strip you would never know.

The ultimate bush airstrip, the 'runway' is narrow and very short with the bushes on each side trimmed back just enough to clear the wings. The strip is used to ferry trampers, mountaineers and hunters in and out of the valley, and if you want to see planes land and take off, check with the friendly people at Gunn's Camp store who might know when arrivals are due at this 'airport'.

 Hollyford Airstrip is located 6 km down the Lower Hollyford Road from the junction with the Milford Road.

27. Humboldt Falls

The total height of these falls is 275 metres (the Sky Tower in Auckland is 328 metres), though they fall in three stages, of which the tallest single drop is 134 metres. The walk is an easy thirty minutes return through bush, but the view of the falls is quite a distance across the Humboldt Creek and naturally they are more impressive after heavy rain.

 Humboldt Falls are located 8 km down the Lower Hollyford Road from the junction with the Milford Road.

Stewart Island

New Zealand's third-largest island is home to Rakiura National Park, created in 2002 and covering 85 per cent of the total island. The island has an exceptional unspoiled landscape of untouched bush, hidden bays, and rugged mountain ranges (the highest point is Mt Anglem at 980 m). With only 25 km of road and fewer than 400 people (most of those in the main settlement of Oban), the island has a gentle relaxed feel, but it does have a good range of accommodation, a great pub and a handful of good places to eat. The ferry is modern and fast, taking just an hour from Bluff to Oban, but be warned that Foveaux Strait has a reputation as a wild stretch of water. However, the ferry is small and is frequently booked out, especially in summer, so make sure you book ahead. While a day trip is worth the effort, especially if the weather is good, once on the island the place weaves its own magic that makes you just want to stay. There are also scheduled flights from Invercargill to Oban.

28. Cook's Globe, Rakiura Museum

When Captain James Cook sailed around the South Island early in 1770 mapping the coast as he went, he made one of his few rare mistakes and assumed that Stewart Island was a peninsula. The Rakiura Museum holds a most remarkable globe in that is only one of one two such globes in the world with a map of New Zealand showing Stewart Island as a peninsula linked to the mainland. The other mistake Cook made was exactly the opposite, in that he thought the Banks Peninsula was an island, and this too is shown on the globe.

The strait was, of course, well known to Maori, but the first European to discover the passage was an American sealer OF Smith, in 1804, who not surprisingly marked it on his chart as Smith's Strait. On his return to Sydney in 1806 he reported his discovery to the Governor of New South Wales. Eventually, and no one is quite sure how, the strait became known as Foveaux Strait, named after Major Joseph Foveaux, the Lieutenant-Governor of New South Wales, who never actually set foot in New Zealand.

- 9 Ayr Street, Oban.
- Open 10 am to 12 noon Monday to Saturday, 12 noon to 2 pm Sunday.
- Entrance fee.

29. Kiwi Watching

Most New Zealanders have never seen our national bird, the kiwi, in the wild though in certain places it is not hard to hear them at night in the bush. Here on Stewart Island the kiwi has developed strange and unusual habits. The island has a substantial brown kiwi population of around 20,000 birds (fifty times the human population), and while usually a solitary bird, on Stewart Island kiwi sometimes form family groups and are often active during the day as well as nocturnally.

At Mason Bay, kiwi come out of their usual bush habitat and scuttle down to the beach at night to feed on sand hoppers. While there is still no guarantee of seeing the bird *au naturel*, Stewart Island will probably be your best chance. There are several operators on the island who organise kiwi viewing trips.

 www.stewartisland.co.nz

Glossary

A&P Show: Agricultural and Pastoral Show

Bach: Small holiday house, usually by the sea or lake

Crib: Same as bach, but more widely used in the South Island

Dairy: Small general store

Domain: Public park usually with sports fields

Gumboots: Tall rubber boots

Hokey Pokey: Ice cream flavour of honeycomb toffee

Hui: Meeting, gathering

i-SITE: Information site

Iwi: Tribe

Jandals: Flipflops, thongs

Kia Ora: Hello, very good

Koha: Donation

Pa: Fortified Maori village

Pakeha: European New Zealander

Pounamu: Greenstone, jade

Rangatira: Chief

Tapu: Sacred, prohibited, forbidden, restricted

Togs: Swimsuit

Torch: Flashlight

Tramping: Hiking

Ute: Pickup truck

Waka: Maori canoe

Whitebait: young of six species of galaxiid fish, a New Zealand delicacy

First published in 2019 by New Holland Publishers

Sydney • Auckland

Level 1, 178 Fox Valley Road, Wahroonga 2076, Australia

5/39 Woodside Ave, Northcote, Auckland 0627, New Zealand

newhollandpublishers.com

Copyright © 2019 New Holland Publishers

Copyright © 2019 in text: Peter Janssen

Copyright © 2019 in images: Peter Janssen

All rights reserved. No part of this publication may be reproduced, stored in a retrieval system or transmitted, in any form or by any means, electronic, mechanical, photocopying, recording or otherwise, without the prior written permission of the publishers and copyright holders.

A catalogue record for this book is available from the National Library of New Zealand.

ISBN 9781869665371

Group Managing Director: Fiona Schultz

Publisher: Sarah Beresford

Project Editor: Elise James

Designer: Yolanda La Gorcé

Production Director: Arlene Gippert

Printed in China

10 9 8 7 6 5 4 3 2

Keep up with New Holland Publishers:

 NewHollandPublishers

 @newhollandpublishers